Performance Dashboards

Measuring, Monitoring, and Managing Your Business

Second Edition

WAYNE W. ECKERSON

John Wiley & Sons, Inc.

Library of Congress Cataloging-in-Publication Data:

Eckerson, Wayne W., 1958–
    Performance dashboards : measuring, monitoring, and managing your business /
Wayne W. Eckerson.—2nd ed.
        p. cm.
    Includes index.
        ISBN 978-0-470-58983-0 (hardback); 978-0-470-91841-8 (ebk); 978-0-470-91842-5
(ebk); 978-0-470-92040-4 (ebk)
        1. Management—Evaluation. 2. Organizational effectiveness—Evaluation. I. Title.
    HD31.E294 2010
    658.4'013—dc22   2010023270

Printed in the United States of America

10 9 8 7 6 5 4 3 2 1

To my wife, Christina, and my children, Henry and Olivia, who are the light of my life.

Contents

Foreword		vii
Preface to the Second Edition		ix
Preface to the First Edition		xiii

PART I	THE LANDSCAPE FOR PERFORMANCE DASHBOARDS	1
CHAPTER 1	What Are Performance Dashboards?	3
CHAPTER 2	The Context for Performance Dashboards	23
CHAPTER 3	Assessing Your Organizational Readiness	43
CHAPTER 4	Assessing Your Technical Readiness	57
CHAPTER 5	How to Align Business and IT	81
PART II	PERFORMANCE DASHBOARDS IN ACTION	99
CHAPTER 6	Types of Performance Dashboards	101
CHAPTER 7	Operational Dashboards in Action	123
CHAPTER 8	Tactical Dashboards in Action	139
CHAPTER 9	Strategic Dashboards in Action	157

PART III   CRITICAL SUCCESS FACTORS:
                 TIPS FROM THE TRENCHES   179

CHAPTER 10   How to Launch, Manage, and Sustain the Project   181

CHAPTER 11   How to Create Effective Performance Metrics   197

CHAPTER 12   How to Design Effective Dashboard Displays   223

CHAPTER 13   How to Architect a Performance Dashboard   251

CHAPTER 14   How to Deploy and Integrate Dashboards   273

CHAPTER 15   How to Ensure Adoption and Drive Positive Change 293

Index   309

Foreword

The Power of FOCUS... Over the past several decades we all have been trying to use information through technology to optimize our businesses and make our lives easier. So why have so many businesses failed and why do most organizations continue to struggle to find that "competitive advantage" that will take them to the next level? If you are interested in finding a sustainable solution that will help you look forward to where your business should be heading versus only looking backward at where you have been, you need to look through Wayne's "Organization Magnifying Glass" to help you focus on the future.

Whether you are just starting your career or have been in this industry for as long as I have, this book will take you on a thought-provoking journey and offer you many techniques that Wayne has gleaned for some of the best practitioners in the field on delivering real and sustainable value from your information. I have sold to, consulted with, and provided education to hundreds of organizations over the past 25 years and almost all of them struggled with putting all of the pieces of this puzzle together. As we move into the next decade and try to find our way in this new economy, we are quickly realizing that "business as usual" no longer applies. Businesses are facing a new global economic environment. If our businesses are to survive, we must figure it out quickly.

Wayne's approach and ideas to get the entire organization—both business and IT—to collaborate on a proven approach to performance management make this a must-have survival guide for your business.

- Corporate executives, business executives, and IT executives, you must at a minimum, read Chapter 1 and Chapter 5, proactively commit to being an "agent of organizational change," set a clear direction, and give a copy of this book to all of your team members.
- Department staff members, you should read this cover to cover, mark Chapters 1 and 5, ask your executive sponsors to read them, and work on developing a real partnership across your organization.

- If you are just getting out of college or starting your career, this book will serve you well as a best practice guide to designing and delivering actionable analytic solutions and will greatly increase your personal market value.

This book will help you put the pieces of the puzzle together with an organized and systematic strategy that will position you to take full advantage of whatever opportunities lie ahead.

Paul Kautza
Director of Education
The Data Warehousing Institute

Preface to the Second Edition

New and Different

A lot has changed since I wrote the original manuscript for this book in 2004. The book hit a sweet spot in a rapidly changing industry. Many organizations had discovered—independently of the products vendors were selling to them—that dashboards resonated with users and were a perfect way to deliver information to the masses. People snapped up the first edition and used it—much to my surprise—as a conceptual manual for how to implement a performance dashboard. Although I strove to add as much prescriptive advice as I could based on many conversations with practitioners in the field, I didn't have a methodology in mind when I wrote the book.

Given the book's success, my editor, Tim Burgard, needled me for several years to write a second edition or sequel. Work and personal commitments prevented me from acceding to his requests. But I finally relented in 2009. Only after I signed the contract and started outlining changes did I realize how much work I had taken on. So much had changed in the intervening five years that I realized I would basically have to rewrite large swaths of the book.

Thankfully, the framework that I outlined in Chapter 1 has stood the test of the time and remains basically intact. The only major change is that I have given the framework a name. It's now known as the MAD framework, which stands for Monitor, Analyze, and Drill to Detail. The name is a conglomeration of two of the "three threes," which describe the prominent characteristics of a bona fide performance dashboard.

However, almost everything else has changed or advanced. While I was a pioneer in discussing performance dashboards in 2004, I've been joined by a host of other folks, many more intelligent and informed than I am. I have leaned on them heavily, and sometimes shamelessly, to produce this second edition.

First, I've replaced the featured case studies in Part II with new ones. And instead of one case study per chapter and type of dashboard, I profiled two. There is so much variation among performance dashboards that I felt it important to cast as wide a net as possible when examining actual implementations. I've also created subtypes of dashboards. For example, I've defined "detect and respond" and "incent and motivate" operational dashboards. I also defined a new type of tactical dashboard that I call a "mashboard," which enables power users to create ad hoc dashboards from predefined report elements created with a vendor's business intelligence (BI) tool. I've also defined a new type of strategic dashboard that features many characteristics of a Balanced Scorecard but isn't one.

In Part I, I combined the chapters on business intelligence and performance management, since this is background information that most readers are familiar with. I rewrote much of the chapter on technical readiness, which delves in my BI Maturity Model. The new chapter offers a more comprehensive and logical handling of the subject. I also moved the chapter "How to Align Business and IT," which proved to be one of the most popular chapters in the book, to the anchor position in Part I.

I extensively rewrote all the chapters in Part III and added Chapter 13, "How to Architect a Performance Dashboard," which discusses how to engineer the front-end interface for optimal performance and examines the pros and cons of eight architectural options. The chapters "How to Create Effective Performance Metrics" and "How to Design Effective Dashboard Displays" are almost entirely new, and I'm confident they offer practical advice for newcomers and veterans alike.

Sections in the Book

The book is divided into three sections. Part I, "The Landscape for Performance Dashboards," provides the framework and context for understanding performance dashboards. Chapter 1 defines performance dashboards and describes their primary characteristics. Chapter 2 provides background on business performance management (BPM) and business intelligence and how they factor into the design and creation of performance dashboards. Chapter 3 provides an organizational readiness assessment for organizations preparing to implement a performance dashboard, and Chapter 4 offers a technical readiness assessment based on a BI Maturity Model that I developed in 2004 and which has been well received by BI professionals and their business counterparts. Chapter 5 tackles the thorny topic of how to establish an effective partnership between business and the information technology (IT) department, which is required to deliver a long-lasting, high-value dashboard system.

Part II, entitled "Performance Dashboards in Action," adds flesh to the conceptual framework defined in Part I by examining six case studies in depth, two for each type of performance dashboard. Chapter 6 compares the three types of performance dashboards and explains the major characteristics of each in detail. Chapter 7 examines operational dashboards at 1-800 CONTACTS and the Richmond Police Department. Chapter 8 looks at tactical dashboards at Rohm and Haas and Arizona State University. Chapter 9 examines strategic dashboards at Cisco and the Ministry of Works in the Kingdom of Bahrain.

Part III is titled "Critical Success Factors: Tips from the Trenches." This section synthesizes recommendations and guidance from dozens of performance dashboard projects that I've researched. Chapter 10 discusses how to launch and manage a performance dashboard project. Chapter 11 examines the anatomy of performance metrics and examines various methods for creating effective ones. Chapter 12 shows how to create powerful dashboard screens that communicate relevant facts quickly and concisely. Chapter 13 provides an overview of how to architect a performance dashboard, showing a variety of options available with today's technology. Chapter 14 describes where to start a performance dashboard initiative and how to integrate multiple dashboards. Chapter 15 provides advice on how to ensure end-user adoption and use a performance dashboard to drive positive organizational change.

Finally, I recognize that it is difficult to examine dashboard screenshots when they are printed in black and white. Thus, I've created a Web site where you can view the color versions of all the dashboard screenshots. The Web site is www.bileader.com. It also contains links to other reports, articles, and blogs that I have written, among other resources.

Acknowledgments

This second edition wouldn't be possible without the contributions of many people. I'd like to thank the many practitioners who offered their stories for inclusion in this edition, especially David Hsiao, Nanzin Shroff, and Jason Sidhu from Cisco, Mike Masciandaro of Rohm and Haas, John Rome of Arizona State University, Mark Ranford of the Kingdom of Bahrain, Jim Hill and John Williams of 1-800 CONTACTS, Stephen Hollifield of the Richmond Police Department, Dongyan Wang of NetApp, and Angela Chen at LiquidNet.

Industry experts who contributed to this edition include Stephen Few, whose books and conversations shaped the chapter of designing dashboard displays; Bill Barberg, who again provide incomparable perspective on strategy management and the Balanced Scorecard methodology; and Stephen Few, who painstakingly reviewed my chapter on design and whose ideas and books proved a major source of information. I'd also like to thank Doug Cogswell, Andreas Lipphardt, and David Parmenter, who contributed ideas or screenshots to the book.

I'd like to thank the following people who reviewed sections of the book and provided invaluable advice: Neal Williams, Mardell Cheney, Justin Manes, Douglas Chope, Mark LaRow, Brad Peters, Kevin Scott, Mark Brandau, Mark Gamble, Jeff Morris, and Nobby Akiha. I'm especially indebted to David Washo of Ingenium Consulting, who offered to review the book and was probably surprised when I took him up on the offer and sent him countless chapters, which he diligently read and provided welcome feedback.

Last but not least, I'd like to thank my wife and children, who once again patiently endured my long days, nights, and weekends hunched over my laptop writing about things they don't understand, nor want to!

Preface to the First Edition

A Path to Pursue

False Starts

Business Performance Management. The original focus of this book was business performance management (BPM). Tim Burgard, my editor at John Wiley & Sons, had read an in-depth report that I wrote on the topic in 2003 and asked whether I would be interested in turning it into a book geared to business professionals. Other than the normal reservations one might have about undertaking a book project in addition to a full-time job, I was not particularly thrilled about exploring BPM in greater depth.

My initial research showed that BPM meant different things to different people. It was a broad, catch-all category of applications and technologies, including everything from financial consolidation and reporting tools to planning, budgeting, and forecasting applications to dashboards and scorecards, among other things. BPM seemed to reflect whatever vendors had in their product portfolios at the time rather than representing a distinct and compelling discipline in itself.

Conceptually, however, most people seem to agree that the purpose of BPM is to focus organizations on things that really matter. Too many organizations spread their energies and resources far and wide and consequently never make much progress toward achieving their strategic objectives. The theory behind BPM is that organizations need to identify the key activities that contribute most to their success and make sure they do them well. In short, the purpose of BPM is to help organizations become more focused, aligned, and effective.

Dashboards and Scorecards. Thus, in the spirit of BPM, I decided to cast off BPM as a book topic and focus on something more tangible and concrete that organizations could use to implement the discipline of BPM. At the time, I did not know any companies that had implemented a BPM solution—whatever that might be—but I did notice that many companies were rolling out dashboards and scorecards. These applications seemed to resonate with workers up and down the organizational hierarchy, from boardrooms to shop floors and from customers and suppliers.

Better yet, dashboards and scorecards helped companies implement the principles of BPM better than any of the other so-called BPM applications or technologies that I saw in the marketplace. Now here was a topic worth exploring!

As I investigated dashboards and scorecards, I encountered much of the same definitional fuzziness as I did with BPM, albeit on a smaller scale. Every "dashboard" I saw looked and functioned differently and served different purposes. Some looked like reporting portals or electronic briefing books, while others contained mostly text and hand-entered data, and still others featured graphical dials and meters that flickered with real-time data.

The only clarity in the field came from the Balanced Scorecard community, which had a powerful and evolving methodology to help organizations create, display, and manage performance data. However, since there were already many excellent books about Balanced Scorecards that covered both theory and practice, I did not see how I could add much value to the topic.

Nevertheless, I knew that organizations were putting a great deal of energy into building dashboards and scorecards using business intelligence (BI) and data integration tools and technologies—two areas that I have been researching and speaking about for the past 15 years. I figured that I could add value by identifying the common threads among these initiatives, create a framework to clarify the discussion about their use, and synthesize best practices for designing, building, and growing these systems from organizations that have already done it. The result is this book.

The Puzzle of Performance Dashboards

Defining Performance Dashboards. It took many hours of thought, dozens of interviews, and thousands of words to piece together the puzzle of dashboards and scorecards in a way that provides a clear and complete picture without distorting current perceptions that people have about these systems. In highly abridged form, what I came up with is this: Dashboards and scorecards are part of a larger performance management system—which I call a performance dashboard—that enables organizations to measure, monitor, and manage business performance more effectively.

A performance dashboard is more than just a screen with fancy performance graphics on it: It is a full-fledged business information system that is built on a business intelligence and data integration infrastructure. A performance dashboard is very different from plain dashboards or scorecards. The latter are simply visual display mechanisms to deliver performance information in a user-friendly way whereas performance dashboards knit together the data, applications, and rules that drive what users see on their screens.

Three Applications. To flesh out this skeletal definition a tad more, I came to realize that a performance dashboard is actually three applications in one, woven together in a seamless fashion: (1) a monitoring application, (2) an analysis application, and (3) a management application.

The monitoring application conveys critical information at a glance using timely and relevant data, usually with graphical elements; the analysis application lets users analyze and explore performance data across multiple dimensions and at different levels of detail to get at the root cause of problems and issues; the management application fosters communication among executives, managers, and staff and gives executives continuous feedback across a range of critical activities, enabling them to "steer" their organizations in the right direction.

Three Layers. When I looked at the data that performance dashboards display, I discovered that it let users navigate through three layers or views of information: (1) a graphical metrics view, (2) a multidimensional view, and (3) a detailed or operational view. Users can access the performance dashboard at any of these layers, but most start at the graphical metrics view and drill down along fairly pre-defined pathways through the multi-dimensional and detailed views.

This layered approach meets the information and analysis needs of a majority of individuals in an organization who are not number crunchers by training and only want to use information as a tool to perform their jobs. Performance dashboards conform to the natural sequence in which these users want to interact with information. First, they want to monitor key metrics for exceptions; then, they want to explore and analyze information that sheds light on the exceptions and reveals hidden trends and issues; and finally, they want to examine detailed data and reports to identify root causes of problems and take action to remedy the situation.

New Face of BI. What I discovered in my journey is that performance dashboards are the new face of BI. They transform BI from a set of tools used primarily by business analysts and power users to a means of delivering actionable information to everyone in an enterprise. Thus, performance dashboards fulfill the promise of BI to help organizations leverage information to increase corporate agility, optimize performance, and achieve strategic objectives.

Three Types. The final thing I discovered about performance dashboards is that that there are three types—operational, tactical, and strategic—that are distinguished largely by the degree to which they use the three types of applications listed above (i.e., monitoring, analysis, and management).

Operational dashboards track core operational processes and emphasize monitoring more than analysis or management; tactical dashboards track departmental processes and projects and emphasize analysis more than monitoring or management; and strategic dashboards monitor the execution of strategic objectives and emphasize management more than monitoring or analysis. An organization can and should have multiple versions of each type of performance dashboard, but they should integrate them using consistent metric definitions, shared data, and a common infrastructure.

Success Factors. It is one thing to know what a performance dashboard is and another to implement one successfully. In the course of interviewing people at organizations that have deployed performance dashboards (regardless of what they call them), I discovered many critical success factors. On a macro level, the keys to success are: (1) get proper sponsorship and resources for the project, (2) create the right metrics and standardize their meaning, (3) design a compelling graphical user interface, and (4) plan ahead to ensure end-user adoption and drive organizational change.

Beyond these major success factors, I discovered dozens of tips and techniques that often spell the difference between a successful project and a mediocre one. This book does not pretend to provide a step-by-step methodology for implementing a performance dashboard or a comprehensive list of critical success factors; instead, like a good performance metric, it provides reasonable guidance for the road ahead.

Who Should Read This Book

This book is geared to business and technical managers who oversee performance management projects or who have been recently appointed to create or overhaul an organization's performance management system, including information systems and corporate policies and procedures. These managers generally have deep knowledge of their business and suitable experience managing information technology projects. Most are prime candidates to become Chief Performance Officers.

At the same time, business executives can benefit by reading this book. Although it covers the technical underpinnings of performance management and dives into project management and technical details at points, the book tries to convey all concepts in plain English. Conversely, technologists will find value in this book because it provides an overview of performance management concepts and a technical framework for implementing them. In addition, Balanced Scorecard professionals will find the book helps them understand how Balanced Scorecards relate to and can be integrated with other types of performance dashboards in their organizations.

Skim, Drill, and Examine. To help you get the most out of the next 250+ pages, let me tell you how I have approached writing the text. First,

I know that businesspeople are busy. If you are like me, you rarely get to read an article or report from beginning to end, let alone a book. You really just want the prescriptions, the key takeaways that you can apply at work tomorrow, next week, or next month.

To accommodate your needs, I have tried to make the book as easy as possible to skim while staying within the publisher's constraints. For example, I have made liberal use of headings, lead-ins, exhibits, captions, and sidebars so they serve as visual guideposts to the content. Glance at these markers as you flip through the pages, and if you spy something that catches your interest, drill down and read the text for a while. (Does this sound like a performance dashboard in book form? I hope so. That was my intent!)

Feedback Please! As someone who works for an educational organization, I know that the best learning occurs not in classrooms but in discussions with peers and colleagues. Once you finish reading (or skimming) this book, I hope that you take the time to send me your thoughts. Ideas do not stop evolving once they are put on paper. This book is not my final word on the subject; there is always more to learn! Undoubtedly, there are numerous perspectives I did not cover and nuances I overlooked. Please help me write the next edition; send your thoughts to weckerson@ tdwi.org. Happy reading!

The Landscape for Performance Dashboards

Part I provides context for understanding performance dashboards. Chapter 1 describes the MAD framework for designing performance dashboards, including the "three threes." Chapter 2 provides background on the disciplines of performance management and business intelligence, which intersect in the form of a performance dashboard. Chapters 3 and 4 help you evaluate the organizational and technical readiness of your organization to deploy performance dashboards. Chapter 4 in particular describes my BI Maturity Model, which shows how organizations evolve their BI environment, including performance dashboards. Chapter 5 zeroes in on the key to the success of any BI application, which is a strong partnership between business and the information technology (IT) department.

CHAPTER 1

What Are Performance Dashboards?

The Context for Performance Dashboards

The Power of Focus

Executives in Training. In the summer of 2004, I found my 11-year-old son, Henry, and his best pal, Jake, kneeling side by side in our driveway, peering intensely at the pavement. As I walked over to inspect this curious sight, I saw little puffs of smoke rising from their huddle. Each had a magnifying glass and was using it to set fire to clumps of dry grass as well as a few unfortunate ants that had wandered into their makeshift science experiment.

In this boyhood rite of passage, Henry and Jake learned an important lesson that escapes the attention of many organizations today: the power of focus. Light rays normally radiate harmlessly in all directions, bouncing off objects in the atmosphere and the earth's surface. The boys had discovered, however, that if they focused light rays onto a single point using a magnifying glass, they could generate enough energy to burn just about anything and keep themselves entertained for hours.

By the time Henry and Jake enter the business world (if they do), they will probably have forgotten this simple lesson. They will have become steeped in corporate cultures that excel at losing focus and dissipating energy far and wide. Most organizations have multiple business units, divisions, and departments, each with its own products, strategies, processes, applications, and systems to support it. A good portion of these activities are redundant at best and conflicting at worst. The organization as a whole spins off in multiple directions at once without a clear strategy. Changes in leadership, mergers, acquisitions, and reorganizations amplify the chaos.

Companies need an "organizational magnifying glass" that focuses the energies and activities of employees on a clear, unambiguous set of goals and objectives laid out in the corporate strategy.

EXHIBIT 1.1 Organizational Magnifying Glass

Organizational Magnifying Glass. To rectify this problem, companies need an "organizational magnifying glass"—something that focuses the work of employees so everyone moves in the same direction. (See Exhibit 1.1.) Strong leaders do this. However, even the voice of a charismatic executive sometimes is drowned out by organizational inertia.

Strong leaders need more than just the force of their personality and experience to focus an organization. They need an information system that helps them clearly and concisely communicate key strategies and goals to all employees on a personal basis every day. The system should focus workers on tasks and activities that best advance the organization's strategies and goals. It should measure performance, reward positive contributions, and align efforts so that workers in every group and level of the organization are marching together toward the same destination.

Performance Dashboard. In short, what organizations really need is a *performance dashboard* that translates the organization's strategy into objectives, metrics, initiatives, and tasks customized to each group and individual in the organization. It provides timely information and insights that enable business users to improve decisions, optimize processes and plans, and work proactively. A performance dashboard is really a performance management system. It communicates strategic objectives and enables businesspeople to measure, monitor, and manage the key activities and processes needed to achieve their goals.

To work this magic, a performance dashboard provides three main sets of functionality, which I will describe in more detail later. Briefly, a performance dashboard lets businesspeople:

1. **Monitor** critical business processes and activities using metrics that trigger alerts when performance falls below predefined targets.
2. **Analyze** the root cause of problems by exploring relevant and timely information from multiple perspectives at various levels of detail.
3. **Manage** people and processes to improve decisions, optimize performance, and steer the organization in the right direction.

Agent of Organizational Change

A performance dashboard is a powerful agent of organizational change. When deployed properly, it can transform an underperforming organization into a high-flier. Like a magnifying glass, a performance dashboard can focus people and teams on the key things they need to do to succeed. It provides executives, managers, and workers timely and relevant information so they can measure, monitor, and manage their progress toward achieving key strategic objectives.

One of the more popular types of performance dashboards today is the balanced scorecard, which adheres to a specific methodology for monitoring and managing the execution of business strategy. A balanced scorecard is a strategic application, but, as we shall soon see, there are other types of performance dashboards that optimize operational and tactical processes that drive organizations on a weekly, daily, or even hourly basis.

Historical Context. Although dashboards have long been a fixture in automobiles and other vehicles, business, government, and nonprofit organizations have only recently adopted the concept. The trend started among executives who became enamored with the idea of having an "executive dashboard" or "executive cockpit" with which to drive their companies from their boardroom perches. These executive information systems (EISs) actually date back to the 1980s, but they never gained much traction because the systems were geared to so few people in each company and were built on mainframes or minicomputers that made them costly to customize and maintain.

In the past 20 years, information technology has advanced at a rapid clip. Mainframes and minicomputers gave way in the 1990s to client/server systems, which in turn were supplanted by the Web this decade as the preferred platform for running applications and delivering information. Along the way, the economy turned global, squeezing revenues and profits and increasing competition for more demanding customers. Executives have responded by reengineering processes, improving quality, and cutting costs, but these efforts have provided only short-term relief, not lasting value.

Two Disciplines. During the 1990s, organizations began experimenting with ways to give business users direct and timely access to integrated information, an emerging field known as business intelligence (BI). At the same time, executives began turning to new techniques and methods to manage strategy and optimize performance, a discipline broadly defined as business performance management (BPM), or just performance management. (See Chapter 2 for background on BI and BPM.) Many organizations began using BI to provide the technical scaffolding to deliver information for performance management initiatives. Starting in 2000, it became clear that BI was converging with performance management to create the "performance dashboard."

This convergence created a flood of interest in performance dashboards. A study by The Data Warehousing Institute (TDWI) in 2004 showed that a majority of organizations (51 percent) were already using a dashboard or scorecard. The same study showed that almost one-third of organizations were using it as their *primary* application for reporting and analysis. The popularity of performance dashboards has continued to surge. In 2009, TDWI repeated the survey and found that almost three-quarters (72 percent) of organizations have deployed a performance dashboard. (See Exhibit 1.2.)

Benefits. The reason so many organizations are implementing performance dashboards is a practical one: They offer a panoply of benefits to everyone in an organization, from executives to managers to staff. Here is a condensed list of benefits:

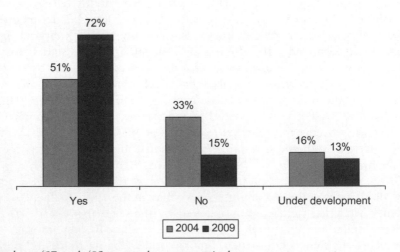

Based on 437 and 495 respondents respectively.

EXHIBIT 1.2 Has Your Organization Implemented a Performance Dashboard?
Source: TDWI Research.

- **Communicate strategy.** Performance dashboards translate corporate strategy into measures, targets, and initiatives that are customized to each group in an organization and sometimes to every individual. Each morning when businesspeople log into the performance dashboard, they get a clear picture of the organization's strategic objectives and what they need to do in their areas to achieve the goals.
- **Refine strategy.** Executives use performance dashboards like a steering wheel to fine-tune corporate strategy as they go along. Instead of veering drastically from one direction to another in response to internal issues or industry events, executives can use performance dashboards to make a series of minor course corrections along the way to their destination. (See Exhibit 1.3.)
- **Increase visibility.** Performance dashboards give executives and managers greater visibility into daily operations and future performance by collecting relevant data in a timely fashion and forecasting trends based on past activity. This helps companies avoid being surprised by unforeseen problems that might affect bottom-line results.
- **Increase coordination.** By publishing performance data broadly, performance dashboards encourage staff from different departments to work more closely together, and they foster dialogue between managers and staff about how to improve performance.
- **Increase motivation.** By publicizing performance measures and results, performance dashboards engender friendly competition among peer groups, improving motivation and productivity. Performance dashboards impel people to work harder out of pride and

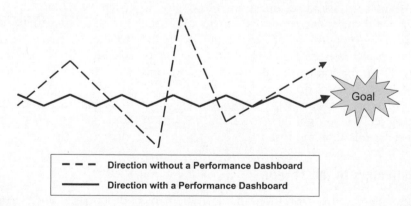

A performance dashboard enables executives to chart a steady course to their destination by making a series of fine-tuned course corrections instead of veering dramatically from one direction to another in response to internal or industry events.

EXHIBIT 1.3 Charting a Course

desire for extra pay when compensation is tied to performance results.

- **Consistent view of the business.** Performance dashboards consolidate and integrate corporate information using common definitions, rules, and metrics. This creates a single version of business information that everyone in the organization uses, avoiding conflicts among managers and analysts about whose version of the data is "right."
- **Reduce costs and redundancy.** By consolidating and standardizing information, performance dashboards eliminate the need for redundant silos of information that undermine a single version of business information. A single performance dashboard can help an organization shut down dozens, if not hundreds, of independent reporting systems, spreadmarts, data marts, and data warehouses.
- **Empower users.** Performance dashboards empower users by giving them self-service access to information and eliminating their reliance on the information technology (IT) department to create custom reports. Through layered delivery of information, structured navigation paths, and guided analysis, performance dashboards make it easy for average businesspeople to access, analyze, and act on information.
- **Deliver actionable information.** Performance dashboards provide actionable information—data delivered in a timely fashion that lets users take action to fix a problem, help a customer, or capitalize on a new opportunity before it is too late. A performance dashboard prevents users from wasting hours or days searching for the right information or report.

When we asked organizations the degree to which their performance dashboards have had a positive impact on business results, almost half (48 percent) responded either "very high" or "high." Another 42 percent said the impact has been "moderate" and only 11 percent said "low" or "very low." Thus, performance dashboards are not only pervasive; they are effective. (See Exhibit 1.4.)

In short, performance dashboards deliver the right information to the right users at the right time to optimize decisions, enhance efficiency, and accelerate bottom-line results.

Pretenders to the Throne

Although many organizations have implemented dashboards and scorecards, not all have succeeded. In most cases, organizations have been tantalized by glitzy graphical interfaces and have failed to build a solid foundation by applying sound performance management principles and implementing appropriate business intelligence and data integration tech-

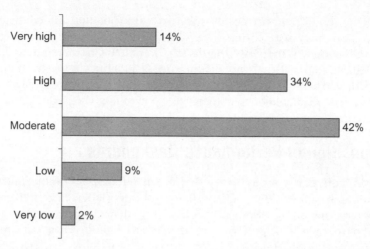

Based on 495 respondents, 2009.

EXHIBIT 1.4 To What Degree Has Your Dashboard Had a Positive Impact on Business Results?
Source: TDWI Research.

nologies and processes. Here are the common symptoms of less than successful solutions:

Too flat. Many organizations create performance management systems, especially tactical and strategic dashboards, using Microsoft Excel, Microsoft PowerPoint, and advanced charting packages. Although these applications often look fancy, they generally do not provide enough data or analytical capabilities to let users explore the root cause of problems highlighted in the graphical indicators.

Too manual. In addition, some organizations rely too heavily on manual methods to update performance dashboards that contain sizable amounts of information. Highly skilled business analysts spend several days a week collecting and massaging this information instead of analyzing it. The best performance dashboards automate the collection and delivery of information, ensuring a sustainable solution over the long term.

Too isolated. Some performance dashboards source data from a single system or appeal to a very small audience. As a result, they provide a narrow or parochial view of the business, not an enterprise view. In addition, these dashboards often contain data and metrics that do not align with the rest of the organization, leading to confusion and chaos.

In the end, performance dashboards are only as effective as the organizations they seek to measure. Organizations without central control or coordination will deploy a haphazard jumble of nonintegrated performance dashboards. However, organizations that have a clear strategy, a metrics-driven culture, and a strong information infrastructure can deliver performance management systems that make a dramatic impact on performance.

Composition of Performance Dashboards

Layered Delivery System. Every performance dashboard looks and functions differently. People use many different terms to describe performance dashboards, including portal, BI tool, and analytical application. Each of these contributes to a performance dashboard but is not a performance dashboard by itself. Here is my definition:

> *A performance dashboard is a layered information delivery system that parcels out information, insights, and alerts to users on demand so they can measure, monitor, and manage business performance more effectively.*

This definition conveys the idea that a performance dashboard is more than just a screen populated with fancy performance graphics; it is a full-fledged business information system designed to help organizations optimize performance and achieve strategic objectives. An equivalent, and perhaps better, term is *performance management system*, which conveys the idea that it is a system designed to manage business performance. Since the title of this book uses the term *performance dashboards*, I will stick with that term on most occasions, although I feel that the two are interchangeable.

Three Threes. One of the most salient features of performance dashboards are the "three threes": three applications, three layers, and three types. The "three threes" provide a convenient way to describe the major characteristics of performance dashboards and a litmus test to differentiate imposters from bona fide performance dashboards.

Three Applications

A performance dashboard weaves together three applications in a seamless fashion. These applications are (1) monitoring, (2) analysis, and (3) management. Each application provides a specific set of functionality. The applications are not necessarily distinct programs or code bases but sets of related functionality built on an information infrastructure designed to fulfill user requirements to monitor, analyze, and manage performance. (See Exhibit 1.5.)

EXHIBIT 1.5 Performance Dashboard Applications

	Monitoring	Analysis	Management
Purpose	Convey information at a glance	Analyze exception conditions and drill to detail	Improve alignment, coordination, and collaboration
Components	Dashboard Scorecard BI portal "Right time" data Alerts Agents	Multidimensional analysis Time-series analysis Reporting What-if modeling Statistical modeling	Strategy maps Initiative management Collaboration annotation Workflow Usage monitoring

1. **Monitoring.** A performance dashboard enables users to monitor performance against metrics aligned with corporate strategy. At an operational level, users monitor core processes that drive the business on a day-to-day basis, such as sales, shipping, or manufacturing. At a strategic level, users monitor their progress toward achieving short- and long-term goals.

   In general, organizations use *dashboards* to monitor operational processes and *scorecards* to monitor strategic goals. Dashboards and scorecards are visual display mechanisms within a performance management system that convey critical performance information at a glance. They are the lens through which users view and interact with performance data, but they are not the entire system in themselves. Although dashboards and scorecards share many features and people use the terms interchangeably, they have unique characteristics. (See Spotlight 1.1.)

Spotlight 1.1 Dashboards versus Scorecards

Dashboards and scorecards are visual display mechanisms in a performance management system that graphically communicate performance at a glance. The primary difference between the two is that dashboards monitor the performance of operational processes whereas scorecards chart progress toward achieving strategic goals. (See Exhibit 1.6.)

(Continued)

EXHIBIT 1.6 Dashboards versus Scorecards

	Dashboard	Scorecard
Purpose	Measures performance	Charts progress
Users	Supervisors, specialists	Executives, managers
Focus	Act	Review
Updates	Intraday/daily	Weekly/monthly/quarterly
Data	Details	Summaries
Display	Charts/tables	Charts/comments

Dashboards. Dashboards are more like automobile dashboards. They enable operational specialists and supervisors to monitor and act on events as they occur. Dashboards display detailed data in "right time" as users need to view them, usually on a daily or intraday frequency. Dashboards display performance visually, using charts or tables. Interestingly, people who monitor operational processes often find visual glitz or graphics distracting and prefer to view raw data as numbers or text, perhaps accompanied by visual graphs.

Scorecards. Scorecards, however, are performance charts—like school report cards—designed to help executives and managers track progress toward achieving goals and review performance with subordinates. Scorecards usually display weekly, monthly, quarterly, or annual snapshots of summary data. Like dashboards, scorecards also make use of charts and visual graphs but include textual commentary that interpret results, forecast the future, and record action items.

In the end, it does not really matter whether you use the term *dashboard* or *scorecard* as long as the tool helps focus users and organizations on what matters.

A monitoring application also delivers information to users in "right time"—within minutes or hours in an operational activity or within days, weeks, or months for a strategic one—so users can take steps to fix a problem or exploit an opportunity. We cover "right time" information delivery in Chapter 6.

Other key elements of a monitoring application are alerts, which notify users when events exceed predefined thresholds of performance, and agents, which automate the responses to well-known exception conditions, such as ordering new stock when inventory falls below predefined levels.

2. **Analysis.** The analysis application in a performance dashboard enables users to explore data across many dimensions and organizational hierarchies to ascertain the root cause of an exception condition highlighted in the monitoring layer. Performance dashboards leverage a variety of technologies to enable this analysis: online analytical processing (OLAP), parameterized reporting, ad hoc reporting, visual analysis using in-memory data, and predictive analytics. The analysis requires a data management infrastructure that creates clean, consistent, and integrated data, which is often modeled dimensionally and hierarchically. Chapter 3 describes various types of BI tools and data warehousing (DW) and data integration tools required to support a layered delivery system.

3. **Management.** Performance dashboards typically support a variety of features that foster collaboration and decision making. Many performance dashboards are tailored to support executive meetings that review strategy and/or operations and performance review meetings between a manager and subordinate. The tools let managers quickly create or navigate to a desired page and print the output, if desired. In addition, many performance dashboards let users annotate charts or pages, engaged in threaded discussions, or kick off workflows to follow through on action items. These features, for example, enable subordinates to explain performance discrepancies and list action steps and enable executives to review, comment, and approve the action plan. In addition, most dashboards enable IT administrators to track usage and trouble tickets. (See Chapter 15 for more on usage monitoring.)

Three Layers

Besides three applications, a performance dashboard consists of three layers of information. Just as a cook peels layers of an onion, a performance dashboard lets users peel back layers of information to get to the root cause of a problem. Each successive layer provides additional details, views, and perspectives that enable users to understand a problem better and identify the steps they need to take to address it.

Going MAD. This layered approach gives users self-service access to information and conforms to the natural sequence in which users want to handle that information: (1) monitor, (2) analyze, and (3) drill to detail, or MAD for short. That is, business users want to monitor key metrics for exceptions; then analyze information that sheds light on those exceptions; and, finally, drill into detailed reports before taking action. This layered approach helps users get to the root cause of issues quickly and intuitively. (See Exhibit 1.7.)

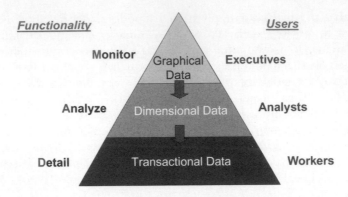

The MAD (monitor, analyze, drill to detail) framework shows how a performance dashboard parcels out information in layers.

EXHIBIT 1.7 MAD Framework

The MAD framework consists of a pyramid divided into three layers. The shape of the pyramid represents both the number of metrics and number of users at each level. Typically, there are about a dozen or so metrics displayed at the top layer, each of which explodes into 10 additional metrics in the middle layer (or dimensional views), each of which then expand into 10 more metrics (or views) at the bottom layer. So a dashboard of 10 to 12 metrics will deliver 1,000+ contextual views of those metrics at increasing levels of granularity.

Information Sandbox. Typically, performance dashboards consist of about 10 to 12 top-level metrics and 20 dimensions, creating a nice-size information sandbox for a specific role, subject area, or activity. This type of sandbox is big enough to provide casual users with 60 percent to 80 percent of the information they need to do their jobs on a regular basis, but not so large that they get lost in the data. Most performance dashboards provide structured navigation or drill paths that guide users from high-level views to more detailed analyses. Most also include "bread crumbs," or navigational clues, that show users exactly where they are in the dashboard and how to retrace their steps.

The three layers of information consist of:

1. **Graphical, metrics data.** The top layer provides a graphical view of performance metrics, usually in the form of charts and alerts. This layer is where users monitor information and is essentially a visual exception report. When performance exceeds a threshold, the dashboard alerts users via a colored icon (e.g., a "stoplight"), pop-up message, or animation, or sends a message via e-mail, pager, or another channel.

2. **Summarized, dimensional data.** The middle layer usually consists of dimensional data that lets users navigate the data by subject (e.g., customer, geography, or time) and hierarchy (e.g., country, region, or city). Dimensional analysis tools enable users to slice and dice, drill down or up, or pivot data to view exceptions and trends from any perspective they want. Some tools enable users to perform what-if analyses or apply various complex algorithms.

3. **Detailed, transactional data.** The bottom layer lets users view detailed data, such as invoices, shipments, or transactions, stored in data warehouses or operational systems. Users often need such data to understand the root cause of a problem, such as a decline in sales due to missing or incomplete orders or a salesperson who has been sick. Most data in this layer is delivered as reports or lists, which are usually displayed in a separate window.

Users. Users can enter the performance dashboard at any of the layers and drill up or down. Executives typically start at the top layer, analysts at the middle layer, and workers at the bottom layer. Ideally, the performance dashboard enables users to navigate seamlessly from one layer to the next without shifting application contexts or user interfaces. In the past, developers built performance dashboards by integrating three separate toolsets: portals at the top layer, OLAP in the middle, and reports at the bottom. This created a cumbersome experience for users who were forced to switch application and software contexts when moving from one layer to the next. Today, however, many vendors offer a more seamless navigational experience, although many stop short of supporting all three layers.

Evolution of BI. Interestingly, the MAD framework also shows the evolution of BI. In the 1980s, BI was simply the bottom layer or detailed, operational, or management reports. In the 1990s, vendors began offering ad hoc query and multidimensional analysis (i.e., OLAP) tools to provide interactive access to information. Then in the 2000s, vendors began offering monitoring tools (i.e., dashboards and scorecards) to visually manage exception conditions. A performance dashboard simply stitches together all three generations of BI technology in a seamless package.

User Mantra. This layered approach to delivering performance information meets the needs of most users in an organization. These so-called casual users simply want to monitor, analyze, and manage the key processes for which they are responsible and usually check information only a couple of times a week, depending on their role and responsibilities. (Chapter 2 discusses casual users in more depth.) As a result, performance dashboards do a great job of adhering to the casual user mantra.

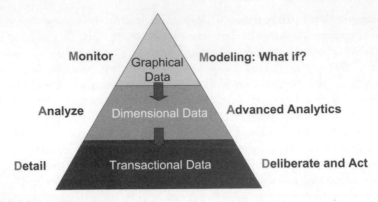

EXHIBIT 1.8 Double MAD

When you ask casual users what information they need, they typically repeat the mantra (more or less): "Give me all the data I want, but only what I need, and only when I really need it." In other words, casual users do not want to be overwhelmed with too much data on a regular basis— they only want to monitor summary data that is relevant to their jobs. But when a problem occurs, they want to access all data possible to understand its full scope so they can take appropriate action.

Double MAD. The functionality of performance dashboards is evolving rapidly. Next-generation performance dashboards are subsuming adjacent applications, such as planning, advanced analytics and visualization, and collaboration, to create what I call the "double MAD" framework. In this case, "M" stands for *modeling,* "A" stands for advanced *analytics, and "D"* stands for *deliberate and act. (See Exhibit 1.8.)*

In a double MAD performance dashboard, the graphical monitoring layer incorporates what-if modeling capabilities that enable executives and managers to change the value of one metric to see how it impacts performance of the rest of the metrics displayed in the dashboard. Since performance dashboards provide a snapshot of current performance, what-if modeling delivers a glimpse into future performance. This capability transforms performance dashboards from monitoring environments to planning environments. Most performance dashboards that support this feature today use Adobe Flash to present users with a visual slider to adjust variables, although HTML 5 appears poised to supplant Flash as the preferred method for delivering highly interactive Web-based applications. (See Chapter 13.)

Next-generation performance dashboards will also provide more advanced analytics in the analysis layer. Today, most offer some sort of drill-down or, in the best case, a full-featured slice-and-dice OLAP environment for analyzing dimensional data. But some performance dashboards now incorporate visual analysis capabilities (see Chapters 2 and 6 for more detail) that enable users to visually analyze information held in memory for superfast interactive analysis. Sometimes, these double MAD dashboards also incorporate regression and other statistical algorithms that enable users to forecast or categorize information. These predictive capabilities can help users segment customers, forecast revenues, and optimize processes.

At the bottom layer, double-MAD performance dashboards will add support for collaboration and action-oriented activities. In terms of collaboration, double-MAD dashboards enable users to annotate charts and tables, engage in collaborative dialogue via threaded discussions, and kick off workflow processes when multiple people need to review and/or approve certain actions. These collaboration features probably will be most evident in the graphical layer of the dashboard but should permeate all layers as well. Double-MAD dashboards will also be action-oriented, enabling users to define alerts that trigger actions when performance exceeds a specified threshold. Actions can range from alerts, to e-mail messages, to queries and database updates.

Three Types

The last thing you need to know about performance dashboards is that there are three types: operational, tactical, and strategic. Each type of performance dashboard emphasizes to different degrees the three layers and applications previously described. Here is a quick summary of the different types of performance dashboards. (See chapter 6 for more detail.)

1. **Operational dashboards** mirror the description of dashboards in Spotlight 1.1. They enable front-line workers to manage and control operational processes using detailed data that is refreshed frequently. Of the three applications, operational dashboards emphasize *monitoring* more than analysis or management. Chapter 7 profiles operational dashboards from 1-800 CONTACTS and the Richmond Police Department.
2. **Tactical dashboards** monitor and manage departmental processes and projects. Executives use tactical dashboards to review and benchmark the performance of peer groups across the company, while managers use them to monitor and optimize processes. Tactical dashboards tend to emphasis analysis more than monitoring or management. Chapter 8 profiles tactical dashboards at Rohm and Haas and the University of Arizona.

3. **Strategic dashboards** monitor the execution of strategic objectives and frequently are implemented using the balanced scorecard methodology. Executives use strategic dashboards to communicate strategy and review performance at monthly strategy or operational review meetings. Strategic dashboards tend to emphasis management more than monitoring or analysis. Chapter 9 profiles strategic dashboards at Cisco and the Ministry of Works in the Kingdom of Bahrain.

Integrating Performance Dashboards. Since each type of performance dashboard serves a different purpose, most organizations have multiple versions of each type. In fact, most departments have their own operational, tactical, and strategic dashboards. Ideally, all performance dashboards share a common set of metrics and rules and are populated with data from a shared BI and DW infrastructure. In reality, most performance dashboards are built independently and use unique metrics, rules, tools, and data. Although each performance dashboard provides local value, collectively they create information chaos. Chapter 14 discusses how to deploy and integrate disparate performance dashboards, a challenging endeavor for any organization.

Build or Buy

A common question that people ask is whether it is better to build or buy a performance dashboard. When I wrote the first edition of this book in 2004, all the companies that I profiled had built their own dashboards using custom code. However, during the past several years, many software vendors have shipped dashboard or scorecard solutions. As a result, more organizations are buying rather than building performance dashboards. Half of the companies profiled in this edition have built their own dashboards using custom code and half have extended a BI or dashboard tool.

Our 2009 survey shows that 45 percent of companies that have deployed a performance dashboard built it from scratch, 30 percent deployed a dashboard tool without customization, and 19 percent extended a dashboard tool with custom code. So there is a trend toward leveraging vendor products to deliver performance dashboards. (See Exhibit 1.9.)

Performance Management Architecture

A performance management system consists of a business architecture and a technical architecture. Exhibit 1.10 shows the components of these two architectures and how they relate.

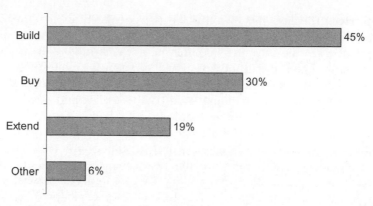

Build	45%
Buy	30%
Extend	19%
Other	6%

Based on 495 respondents. Build = Programmers code most of the solution by hand; Buy = Purchased a dashboard solution and deployed with minor configuration changes; Extend = Purchased a dashboard solution and deployed after lots of custom coding.

EXHIBIT 1.9 Build, Buy, or Extend
Source: TDWI Research, 2009.

Business Architecture

Stakeholders	Investors	Board	Workforce	Customers	Suppliers	Regulators
Strategy	Mission	Vision	Values	Goals	Plans	Objectives
Resources	People	Process	Technology	Initiatives	Projects	Knowledge
Semantics	Terms	Definitions	Rules		Metadata	Governance
Metrics	Outcome		Drivers		Diagnostic	

Technical Architecture

Displays	Dashboard		Portal		Scorecard	
Applications	Monitoring		Analysis		Management	
Data Stores	ODS	Memory cache	Data warehouse	Data marts	Reports	Documents
Integration	Custom API	EAI	EII	Direct queries	ETL	Manual
Data Sources	Legacy Systems	Packaged Apps	Web pages	Files	Surveys	Text

Performance Dashboard

Metrics are the linchpin that connects the business and technical architectures in a performance management system.

EXHIBIT 1.10 Performance Management Architecture

Metrics. The linchpin that ties the two architectures together is the metrics that define leading, lagging, and diagnostic measures of business performance. On the business side, the metrics embody the organization's strategy, represented by all the layers in the business architecture. On the technical side, the metrics contain rules that define how to design the performance dashboard, including what data to collect and how to aggregate, filter, calculate, and display metrics.

Performance metrics are the means by which organizations measure, monitor, and manage the effectiveness of their strategy and tactics to satisfy key stakeholders. They really are the heart and soul of a performance dashboard, and organizations must take great care in deciding what metrics to display and what targets to apply to each metric. Chapter 11 dissects performance metrics and examines how to design effective ones.

Business Architecture. The business architecture consists of stakeholders, strategy, resources, semantics, and metrics. To succeed, a performance dashboard must have a well-defined set of stakeholders or audience whose requirements dictate the strategy, resources, and metrics used. Semantics represent the corporate vocabulary, the words and meaning that enable stakeholders and others to communicate clearly and effectively. Semantics often prove to be the biggest stumbling block when launching a performance dashboard (or business intelligence) project. Chapters 3 and 10 provide tips and techniques for getting buy-in from stakeholders and establishing consistent semantics, among other things. Chapter 15 shows how to use the performance dashboard as an agent of organizational change and ensure adoption by stakeholders.

Technical Architecture. The technical architecture consists of the components that comprise the performance dashboard. The components in each layer represent a superset of functionality. Developers select one or more components (or buy a dashboard with the requisite combination of functionality) that best serves the needs of the stakeholders. Chapter 2 examines the core components of a BI and a DW infrastructure that often comprise a performance dashboard solution, and Chapter 4 shows how that infrastructure evolves over time. Chapter 13 describes how to architect a performance dashboard, and Chapter 12 examines how to design effective dashboard screens.

Although this book recommends building performance dashboards on a BI/DW infrastructure, this is not a hard-and-fast rule, especially with strategic dashboards, which often measure objectives for which there is no ready source of data to populate the metrics. In these cases, companies will need to manually count and enter data into a spreadsheet or other tool to populate the dashboard displays. (See Spotlight 1.2.) This is fine in the short term but is not usually a sustainable practice.

Spotlight 1.2 Small and Strategic

Although performance dashboards can store large volumes of data, this is not a prerequisite for success, especially with strategic dashboards. In fact, some successful strategic dashboards contain only a few gigabytes of data, less than you can store on a single thumb drive.

For instance, Brown & Root, a Halliburton subsidiary that provides marine oil rig construction and services, used a strategic dashboard with small volumes of information to execute a new business strategy that helped the company go from losing money to number one in its niche, with a net income increase of 30 percent. The strategy involved offering high-margin solutions that simultaneously lowered customer costs by integrating offerings from six operating companies in the newly merged firm.

To chart the effectiveness of the strategy, the company used several metrics, none of which required substantial amounts of data, according to Bill Barlberg, president of Insightformation, Inc., a strategy management consultancy and balanced scorecard provider. For example, the company tracked the number of contracts it won that contained integrated solutions involving two or more operating companies. Since the company does a limited number of huge projects each year, the data for these metrics were hand calculated and manually added to the strategic dashboard. Other key metrics included percent of revenue from integrated projects, number of integrated solutions created, and survey results of employee awareness and acceptance of new cultural values.

For strategic dashboards, the quality of information is the key, not the quantity. In some cases, they can deliver significant business value with just a few gigabytes of data, although this is not the norm. As long as a strategic dashboard focuses an organization on what is important, the volume of data is irrelevant.

Business–IT Partnership. To deliver a successful performance dashboard, the business must work closely with the IT department to create metrics that embody strategic objectives and compare performance to plans. Since strategy and plans are constantly changing, these two groups must work closely together to create a performance management system that delivers immediate and lasting value. Chapter 5 addresses the all-important issue of how to establish a strong partnership between the business and technical teams.

Summary

A performance dashboard sits at the intersection of two powerful disciplines: business intelligence and performance management. A performance dashboard is a layered information delivery system that parcels out information to users on demand so they can measure, monitor, and manage business processes and achieve strategic objectives.

A performance dashboard is composed of the "three threes." There are three types of applications (monitoring, analysis, and management), three layers of data (graphical, dimensional, and transactional), and three types of dashboards (operational, tactical, and strategic.) Different types of dashboards emphasize the three applications to different degrees. Bona fide dashboards support the three threes, but many vendor dashboards fall short of this ideal.

Ideally, a performance dashboard runs on a BI/DW infrastructure that provides a clean, integrated, and consistent set of data to populate dashboard metrics in a timely fashion. However, not all performance dashboards are automated or require large volumes of data, especially strategic dashboards, which often measure objectives for which there are no ready source of information.

The key to the success of any performance dashboard initiative is tight alignment between business and IT. The performance dashboard initiative must have strong sponsorship, engaged users, and managers who know how to use the dashboard metrics to drive change in a positive direction.

CHAPTER 2

The Context for Performance Dashboards

Chapter 1 showed that performance dashboards provide a visual way for organizations to measure, monitor, and manage critical business activity. However, to understand performance dashboards, we need to examine the business and technical context in which they operate.

This chapter examines the concepts and principles of business performance management that provide the business rationale for performance dashboards. It also explores business intelligence concepts and technologies, which power most (but not all) performance dashboards today.

Business Performance Management

Defining BPM

Business performance management (BPM) is a series of management disciplines, processes, and tools that enable organizations to optimize the way they execute business strategy. Performance dashboards play a pivotal role in BPM initiatives since they provide a window into business performance and a visual way to chart progress against goals.

Confusion. Unfortunately, there is still confusion about what BPM is—and is not. Much confusion stems from the fact that performance management involves multiple processes and applications that all organizations already implement to some degree. These include strategic planning processes, financial consolidation and reporting, planning and budgeting, forecasting and modeling, and dashboards and scorecards. When introduced to the concept of BPM, many managers rightfully exclaim, "We've been doing that for years!"

However, few organizations have integrated the disciplines in a concerted or cohesive way or implemented a common strategic and technical framework to drive all parts of the organization toward a common set of goals and objectives. Today, most organizations implement BPM applications in isolation, although this is changing as more companies understand the premise behind BPM and vendors offer more integrated BPM packages. For instance, an organization may deploy financial consolidation and reporting software to improve financial reporting but fail to automate planning and budgeting activities. Or they may kick off a budgeting initiative but neglect to integrate budgeting output with departmental and workgroup scorecards and dashboards.

The Vision of BPM. An integrated performance management system creates a nimble organization that adapts quickly to market changes without losing focus of its overall direction and goals. Because it continually monitors and measures key drivers of business performance through an integrated set of performance dashboards, the organization knows immediately how a new market condition will impact its ability to achieve targets. Every level of the organization quickly adjusts forecasts, plans, and budgets and launches new initiatives to respond to the change and shore up performance. If necessary, executives alter the strategy, moving the organization in a new direction that promises more favorable results. They communicate the new strategy in meetings and a series of integrated, cascading dashboards that align every part of the organization with the new objectives so everyone is marching in the same direction.

Confusion. Unfortunately, we have a long way to go to achieve the vision of BPM. Industry experts cannot even agree what to call it. Some prefer the term *business performance management* while others favor *corporate performance management* or *enterprise performance management*. To add to the confusion, most organizations have a performance management process that evaluates individual employees and determines incentive payouts. Finally, some vendors use the term *BPM* to stand for *business* process *management*, a related but distinct discipline. (See Spotlight 2.1.)

Spotlight 2.1 BPM versus BPM

Like the old Spy vs. Spy cartoons in *Mad Magazine*, business performance management (BPM) and business process management (BPM) are distinct but related disciplines. Both seek to optimize business processes, but one approaches the task from the top down and the other from the bottom up.

Business performance management is generally a top-down endeavor that focuses on executing strategy. Executives, managers, and staff use plans, budgets, reports, dashboards, and scorecards to communicate strategy and measure and monitor progress toward achieving strategic objectives at every level of the organization. The goal is to help the organization work more *effectively*.

Conversely, business process management is a bottom-up approach designed to automate, optimize, and integrate existing business processes. It uses modeling, workflow, and application integration tools to streamline processes and improve quality, responsiveness, and customer satisfaction. Its focus is on helping the organization work more *efficiently*.

Definition. Today, the industry seems to have settled on the generic term *performance management* to describe the combination of processes and technologies that help an organization measure, monitor, and manage its business to optimize performance and achieve goals. More succinctly, performance management is *a series of organizational processes and applications designed to optimize the execution of business strategy*.

Obstacles to BPM

The concepts behind managing a business are straightforward: Executives set strategy and goals, managers develop plans and budgets to achieve the goals, and staff executes the plans. Then everyone monitors progress toward meeting the goals using reports and analytical tools, making course corrections as needed to ensure they hit the targets. However, defining a good strategy and executing it are two different things.

Strategy Gap. The prospects for performance management are bright because the state of business management in most companies is so poor. The main problem is that there is a huge gap between strategy and execution. Executives spend days or weeks devising well-crafted strategies and then throw them over the wall to the rest of the company, hoping and praying that their vision will bear fruit. Usually, nothing much happens. The organization is deaf to the executives' guidance and direction. Inertia reigns supreme.

Broken Budgets. Another problem is that traditional planning and budgeting cycles—based on centuries-old bookkeeping practices—are no longer fast or flexible enough to meet the accelerated pace of business today. Most plans and budgets are simply irrelevant and out of date before they are completed. Most employees view the budget as a mindless hoop to jump through, a corporate rain dance, rather than a real aid to planning and management.

Nonaligned Reporting. Finally, reporting and analysis in most organizations is not aligned with strategic objectives. Most organizations have too many reports measuring too many things of too little importance. And most of the reports don't use consistent definitions for common entities, such as customer or supplier, or shared rules for calculating key metrics, such as sales or profits. Most reports are focused on operational or tactical processes and don't measure things that drive real value embodied in strategic objectives.

Benefits of BPM

Most people think that performance management is simply about improving performance in general, but it is not. Performance management is about improving performance *in the right direction*. It is possible for organizations to work efficiently but not effectively. Groups and teams may work long hours with great enthusiasm, but if they develop or refine the wrong processes, products, or services, then all their sweat, blood, and tears will not help the company achieve its strategic goals.

Performance management is designed to help organizations focus on the few things that really drive business value instead of many things that generate activity but do not contribute to the organization's long-term health or viability. Performance management bridges the gap between strategy and execution, resulting in three major benefits:

1. **Improved communication.** Executives can more effectively communicate strategy and expectations to managers and staff at all levels of the organization via dashboards and scorecards tailored to individual roles.
2. **Improved coordination.** Managers can more effectively exchange ideas and information between organizational levels and among business units, departments, and workgroups.
3. **Improved control.** Staff is better able to adjust plans and fix or improve operations in a timely manner using up-to-date information about market conditions and operational processes.

Research shows that most organizations implement performance management solutions to gain greater visibility into the business, execute strategy, improve process efficiency, react faster to business events, improve strategic planning, and deliver a more consistent view of business information. (See Exhibit 2.1.)

The desire among executives to gain greater visibility into the operations is fueled in part by the U.S. Sarbanes-Oxley Act of 2002, which established strict new standards for corporate governance and financial disclosure. In particular, section 409 of the act calls for organizations to

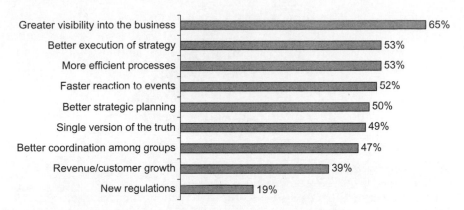

Note: Based on 635 respondents who have deployed a performance management system.

EXHIBIT 2.1 Why Implement Performance Management?
Source: TDWI Research, 2004.

provide real-time disclosure of material events that may affect performance. Combined with heightened competition and the accelerating pace of business, organizations feel a pressing need to know what is happening in their operations at all times.

Automating Management. From a technology perspective, performance management is merely the latest—and perhaps the last—business function that corporations are automating with packaged application software. Starting in the 1980s, organizations deployed software packages to integrate and automate back-office operations, such as manufacturing, finance, and human resources. In the 1990s, organizations deployed software packages to support and enhance front-office activities, such as sales, service, and marketing. In the late 1990s, organizations purchased software packages to optimize cross-functional processes, such as supply chains and customer relationships. (See Exhibit 2.2.)

Today, the last remaining business process to be automated or fully supported by packaged software is business management. This is the domain of performance management, and it might be the last great untapped market for business software. By virtue of its position at the top of the business pyramid, performance management software holds a commanding view of the rest of the organization. Whereas software at lower levels of the business pyramid focuses on increasing the efficiency of business processes, performance management serves as the brains or central nervous system of the entire organization. Performance management enables organizations to work more effectively, not just more efficiently, to achieve strategic objectives.

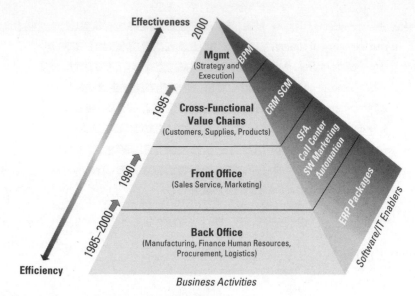

EXHIBIT 2.2 Evolution of Software Automation

A Framework for BPM

Four-Step Process. If performance management optimizes business management, what is the process by which it works? What are its components? What are the technologies required to support it?

Performance management consists of a four-step, closed-loop process that turns strategy into action as depicted in Exhibit 2.3. The steps are strategize, plan, monitor/analyze, and act/adjust. The four-step cycle revolves around integrated data and metrics, which provide a common vocabulary and means for measuring performance across all dimensions of the organization.

The top half of the circle in Exhibit 2.3 constitutes the "strategy" portion of performance management, while the bottom half of the circle represents "execution." Organizations define "strategy" by creating a vision and goals and devising plans for achieving them. They "execute" the strategy by monitoring and analyzing performance and adjusting plans and targets as needed.

When all steps in the BPM process are executed in a concerted manner, they enhance communication, control, and coordination among staff and groups in the organization. In many ways, performance management greases all the parts of the organizational engine to keep it moving in the right direction. Let's examine each step.

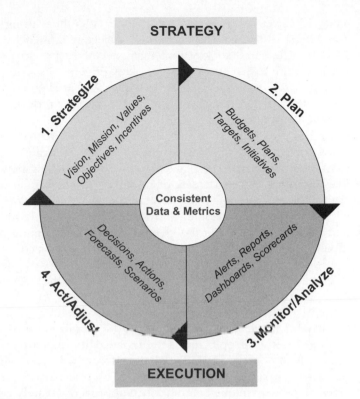

EXHIBIT 2.3 A Performance Management Framework

Step 1: Strategize. Here, executives define or refine the vision, mission, and values of the organization and set goals and objectives to achieve short- and long-term objectives. Every team, department, and business unit should develop strategies and plans that align with top-level strategies and plans. The best strategic plans define key *drivers* of business value and ways to measure them. Examples of drivers might be "high customer satisfaction" or "excellent product quality" and measures might be "customer satisfaction scores" and "number of defects per thousand." Measures of business drivers are called *key performance indicators* (KPIs). KPIs foster action that helps an organization achieve its strategic objectives. As we shall see in Chapter 11, it is not easy to create effective KPIs.

Some organizations use a *strategy map* to tell the story of their strategy. For example, the Ministry of Works in the Kingdom of Bahrain, profiled in Chapter 9, has 17 sets of strategy maps governing every aspect of the work it performs. A strategy map arranges strategic objectives on a single page and links them using cause-effect logic so that it's clear how each objective influences others. *Incentives* are another key tool that executives use to reinforce strategy and focus employees on key drivers of performance. Organizations, such as Cisco (see Chapter 9) that align compensation with strategic objectives can turbo-charge productivity and achieve corporate goals.

Step 2: Plan. Next, groups within the organization meet to develop plans to carry out the business strategy and allocate resources to execute the plans. The plans may involve launching new initiatives, projects, and processes, or refining and reaffirming existing ones. The primary planning tool is the *budget or plan*, which allocates resources—people, knowledge, technology, equipment, and money—to carry out the group's goals. The planning process involves breaking down high-level corporate objectives (e.g., "increase market share by 10 percent") into discrete targets and operating models for every group at each level in the organization. The groups then create projects and processes to meet those targets.

Experts agree that planning should be a collaborative process that ties together people across the organization rather than a corporate ritual that imparts little value. Unfortunately, the budgeting process is broken in most organizations. It projects last year's activities onto the coming year and, once approved, is rarely adjusted as circumstances change. In many organizations, the budget is already out of date by the time it is finalized and published.

Part of the problem is that most organizations use custom spreadsheets to disseminate and collect data, a process that is cumbersome, error prone, and time consuming. Another pitfall is that many companies do not have a standard planning process or shared definitions for calculating currency conversions or the fully loaded cost of hiring a new worker, for example. If each business unit has a separate planning system, it becomes virtually impossible to align the organization and deliver a consistent view of business activity.

New Web-based planning solutions promise to transform budgeting from a backward-looking, static, and labor-intensive process to one that is dynamic, forward-looking, and tied to strategic drivers and objectives. Leading-edge companies are moving away from grueling, bottom-up budgeting to continuous planning with rolling forecasts based on actual performance.

Step 3: Monitor/Analyze. Executing strategies requires people armed with good information and clear directions from the top. Therefore, a good performance management solution provides tools that enable users to monitor and analyze performance in a timely manner and take proactive steps to achieve goals—in other words, a performance dashboard.

Chapter 1 showed that a performance dashboard consists of business intelligence (BI) tools for reporting and analyzing information; a data integration infrastructure for collecting and integrating data from diverse sources; data storage systems, such as data warehouses and data marts; and monitoring and management tools. Collectively, these tools and components enable business users to access and analyze information and chart their progress toward achieving strategic objectives. (See the section "Business Intelligence.")

Step 4: Act and Adjust. The last part of the performance management process is the most critical. To execute strategy, workers must take action to fix broken processes before they spiral out of control and exploit new opportunities before they disappear.

Performance dashboards play a key part in the act/adjust phase because they alert users to potential problems and provide them with additional detail and guidance to help them make fast, high-quality decisions. "It's not enough to provide just metrics," says one information technology professional. "If the metrics show something is wrong, the first thing users want is more information." For certain well-known processes, organizations implement *intelligent alerts,* which automatically recommend action or execute tasks sometimes without human intervention. For example, one online travel site uses an operational dashboard to alert managers when surges in demand require the organization to expand its inventory of airline seats and hotel rooms.

Organizations also need to adjust plans and forecasts to reflect changing market conditions. With centralized, Web-based planning systems, staff can more easily adjust forecasts and planning models. Forward-thinking organizations are now moving to a continuous planning environment so they can adapt more quickly to market changes. For example, one equipment manufacturer now reforecasts sales eight times a quarter and financials once a quarter, creating plans 90 percent faster using half the staff.

Business Intelligence

If performance management defines the management principles and processes for executing strategy, business intelligence describes the underlying technical infrastructure needed to measure, monitor, and manage key processes that drive business performance.

Most of the companies profiled in this book built performance dashboards on top of a BI environment. Without BI, organizations cannot exploit the full potential of a performance dashboard to align people and processes with strategic objectives and make smart, timely decisions. In short, BI is the foundation upon which most performance dashboards grow and flourish.

Origins. BI emerged as a distinct discipline in the early 1990s as a way to provide end users with better access to information for decision making. The initial goal was to give users "self-service" access to information so they did not have to rely on the IT department to create custom reports. By the early 1990s, BI consisted of two data warehousing and query and reporting tools.

Companies began building data warehouses as a way to offload queries from operational systems. Data warehouses became "analytical playgrounds" that let users query all the data they wanted without bogging down the performance of operational systems. At the time, users needed to know SQL, a database query language, to query the data warehouse. Prescient vendors began shipping query and reporting tools that hid SQL behind a point-and-click Windows interface. Vendors converted these desktop query and reporting tools to the Web in the late 1990s and bundled them with other types of analytical tools to create BI suites or BI platforms.

Modern BI. Today, *BI* is an umbrella term that encompasses a raft of data warehousing and data integration technologies as well as query, reporting, and analysis tools that fulfill the promise of giving business users self-service access to information. Performance dashboards represent the latest incarnation of BI, building on years of innovation to deliver an interface that conforms to the way a majority of users want to consume information.

Conceptual Framework

BI is often used as a synonym for query, reporting, and analysis tools. However, the term *business intelligence* is broader than a set of software tools. Specifically, it is *the processes, tools, and technologies required to turn data into information and information into knowledge and plans that drive effective business activity.*

Given this definition, performance dashboards based on a BI infrastructure provide more than just a visual display of performance metrics. They are powerful tools for transforming companies into learning-based organizations that use fact-based decision making to achieve strategic objectives.

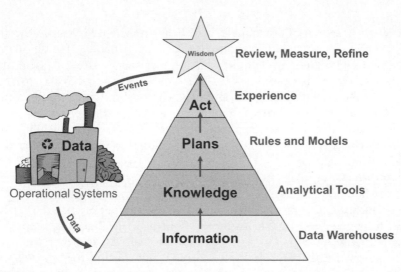

EXHIBIT 2.4 BI as a Data Refinery

One way to think about BI is as a data refinery. To understand this analogy, think of an oil refinery, which is designed to take a raw material—crude oil—and process it into a multiplicity of products, such as gasoline, jet fuel, kerosene, and lubricants. In the same way, BI takes another raw material—data—and processes it into a multiplicity of information products. (See Exhibit 2.4.)

Data. The cycle begins when operational systems that "run" the company—such as order entry, shipping, billing, and general ledger—capture business events and store them in databases. This detailed, transactional data is the raw material of BI.

Information. From there, a data warehouse captures data from multiple operational systems and harmonizes it as a granular level so the shared data have consistent meaning, attributes, and hierarchies. For example, a data warehouse might match and merge customer data from four operational systems—orders, service, sales, and shipments—turning data into a new product: *information.*

Knowledge. Then users equipped with query, reporting, and analysis tools examine the information and identify trends, patterns, and exceptions in the data. Analytical tools enable users to turn information into *knowledge.*

Plans. Armed with insights, users then create *rules* from the trends and patterns they discover. These rules can be simple— "Order 50 new units whenever inventory falls below 25" or "We expect to sell 1,000 widgets next month based on our past three months of sales and year-to-date comparisons." The rules can also be complex, generated by statistical algorithms or models. For example, statistically generated rules can dynamically configure prices in response to changing market conditions, or optimize freight-hauling schedules in a large carrier network, or determine the best cross-sell opportunities for use in a call center or Web site.

Users then create plans that implement the rules. For example, a marketing manager may create a marketing campaign that provides unique offers to customers in six market segments using a scientifically tested combination of direct mail and incentives tailored to each customer. Plans turn rules into *action*.

Action. Once plans are executed, they generate business events that are captured by operational systems, starting the process anew.

Wisdom. Each time an organization cycles through the process, executives, managers, and staff learn more about how the business works and what levers they can pull to achieve the desired effects. In effect, BI creates a continuous feedback loop and a learning organization that can respond flexibly and nimbly to new events in the marketplace.

Misconception. Some executives mistakenly think that there is no difference between BI systems and operational systems. They do not believe they need to spend hundreds of thousands or millions of dollars to create a BI system when their operational systems already generate reports and business analysts are adept at creating ad hoc analyses in Excel.

Eventually, these organizations become bogged down gathering and analyzing data, wasting hundreds of thousands of dollars in man-hours every year. Even worse, they make bad decisions based on incomplete, inconsistent, and inaccurate data, leading to a loss of sales or credibility.

Technical Framework

The diagram in Exhibit 2.5 depicts BI as two intersecting ovals. This is the technical framework for BI.

DATA INTEGRATION ENVIRONMENT

The left-hand oval is the data integration environment. This is where the technical team spends 60 to 80 percent of its time. Its job is to extract, clean, model, transform, transfer, and load transaction data from one or more operational systems (e.g., orders, shipping, and inventory) into the data warehouse. These tasks are not easy because operational data are rarely clean, consistent, or easy to integrate. Like archaeologists, the technical team needs to decipher the meaning and validity of thousands of data elements and values in multiple operational systems. It then needs to glue everything back together again into a single coherent model of the business, much like a paleontologist might reconstruct a life-size model of a dinosaur from an assortment of bones.

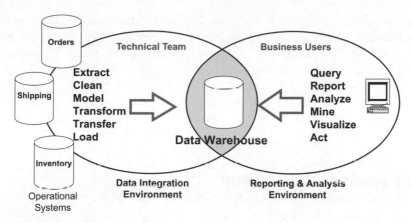

EXHIBIT 2.5 BI Environment

Needless to say, these tasks take a tremendous amount of time and effort. Just as it takes years for a paleontologist to piece together a dinosaur from its pieces, it can take months for a technical team to create an initial data warehouse or data mart. This is why most teams start small and incrementally build an enterprise view one subject area at a time. Also, just as paleontologists need expert knowledge of their domain, technical teams need a deep understanding of the business they are trying to model. To do this, most technical teams need to work closely with subject matter experts who are intimately familiar with the business and its data to assist them in gluing the business back together again.

Data Integration Tools. To build a data warehousing environment, technical teams must first analyze source systems to see what data they contain and also examine the condition of the data. Often, source systems contain incomplete, missing, or invalid data, which makes it challenging to build a data warehouse. Most teams now use *data profiling tools* to audit and assess the condition of source data and identify relationships among columns and tables. They use *data cleansing tools* to validate and fix known problems in source data as it is loaded into the data warehouse.

Once the team finishes analyzing the data in source systems, it creates a target *data model* for the data warehouse. The model, in effect, is a logical representation of how the business operates in a specific area, such as sales or service. Most technical teams create conceptual, logical, and physical data models using commercially available *data modeling software*, although some data modelers still work entirely by hand.

With a target model in hand and a good understanding of data in source systems, the team is now ready to map source data to the target data warehousing model. It does this by using *extraction, transformation, and loading (ETL) tools* or by coding transformation logic by hand. ETL programs are the heart and soul of a data warehousing environment because they contain all the rules for gluing data from multiple source systems into a single data store that provides an integrated picture of the business. ETL tools also contain engines that automate the process of extracting source data, transforming and mapping it to the target model, and moving and loading it into the data warehouse.

DATA WAREHOUSING ENVIRONMENT

Data Warehouses. Once the data archaeology is complete, the technical team loads the integrated data into a data warehouse, which is usually a relational database designed to handle large numbers of both simple and complex queries. A *simple query* might ask for the customer record for "John Doe," which was pieced together from multiple systems and stored in one row of the data warehouse database. A *complex query* might ask to see the top 10 customers for the previous 12 months who have outstanding credit but declining orders. Whereas simple queries take seconds to execute, complex queries may take many minutes or hours, depending on the complexity of the query and the volume of data in the data warehouse.

Data Marts. Rather than build an enterprise data warehouse that tries to meet everyone's needs at once, most technical teams minimize their risks and capital requirements by building a data warehouse one data mart at a time. A data mart is a subject-specific application designed for a department or group. It can be a set of tables within a data warehouse or a physically distinct system. Most teams can deliver a new data mart every three to six months, depending on scope and the cleanliness of source data. A typical dashboard project involves creating a data mart.

Hub and Spoke. Today, most companies use a hub-and-spoke architecture when building a data warehousing environment. Here, a central data warehouse feeds information to multiple logical or physical "dependent" data marts. (Stand-alone data marts are "independent" and generally undermine information consistency.) Most users and applications (i.e., a performance dashboard) query the data marts to ensure good performance. Only data-savvy business analysts are allowed to query the data warehouse directly.

Lightweight Infrastructure. Not all performance management systems require organizations to build data warehouses and deploy data integration middleware, which can be expensive. Some strategic dashboards succeed without them. However, just because an organization does not want to spend money creating a BI infrastructure does not mean it can succeed without it. (See Spotlight 2.2.)

Spotlight 2.2 Do We Really Need a BI Infrastructure?

Some executives balk at the cost and complexity of creating a BI infrastructure and question whether it is necessary to deliver performance dashboards.

If a manager simply wants to visualize an Excel spreadsheet, there is no need for a BI infrastructure. Of course, from an enterprise perspective, there is little value in a personalized dashboard, especially one created independently without standard data, definitions, and rules. In fact, such dashboards are no more than glorified spreadmarts, renegade systems that undermine information consistency.

However, most performance dashboards require a BI infrastructure of some sort to deliver clean, integrated, historical data, although there are some exceptions. Some operational dashboards may pull data directly from source systems to get the most current data possible. But many organizations are now operationalizing their data warehouses to do the same thing and preserve information consistency. (See the profile of 1-800 CONTACTS in Chapter 7 as an example.) Strategic dashboards are often populated manually from Excel spreadsheets because executives want to measure things or processes that aren't yet systematized.

Long-term Problems. Organizations that put off building a BI infrastructure when implementing performance management systems create problems for themselves in the long run. They usually hit a brick wall once they try to expand a performance dashboard beyond the initial department or target group of users. Successful projects are cursed with success, and the team must support three to four times more data and users than they anticipated. When this happens, the team often quickly slaps together a BI infrastructure that is not reliable, scalable, or aligned with corporate information standards. These makeshift BI infrastructures are costly to maintain and are prime candidates for consolidation into a more standard infrastructure.

Managing Costs. A robust BI infrastructure does not have to cost a fortune, and it does not have to be built all at once. Many companies profiled in this book bootstrapped their performance dashboards with little or no money and without making long-term technical compromises at the infrastructure level. Most built the BI infrastructure incrementally along with new applications and functionality requested by users. Some also leveraged existing data warehouses and data marts, accelerating development and avoiding duplication of resources. With a robust data BI infrastructure in place, the added costs to create a performance dashboard are minimal.

REPORTING AND ANALYSIS ENVIRONMENT

The right-hand oval in Exhibit 2.5 refers to the reporting and analysis environment, which is the domain of the business users. They use a variety of tools to query, report, analyze, mine, visualize, and, most important, act on the data in the data warehousing environment.

Standard Reporting Tools. Standard reporting tools allow power users or developers to craft custom queries and format the results in a standard report layout, such as a management report, master-detail report, pixel-perfect invoice, or even a performance dashboard. A decade or two ago, most standard reports were handwritten using a programming language, printed on paper, and distributed via snail mail. However, vendors now offer powerful Web-based reporting tools that enable users to interact with the reports in a variety of ways.

Ad Hoc Reporting. Ad hoc reporting tools enable users to query data marts or data warehouses directly. They usually provide users with predefined query objects (e.g., a semantic layer) that shield users from having to know SQL or master the complexity of back-end database structures. Users simply drag and drop the objects onto a "query panel" to formulate a query and view results, which they can manipulate further. These tools make it easy for users to explore data and create custom reports.

Analysis Tools. There are many types of analytical tools. In fact, one could make a case that interactive reports are analytical tools since they enable users to interact with data. Many business analysts use Microsoft Excel or Access to collect, massage, and present data, while others use online analytical processing (OLAP) tools that deliver dimensionalized views of data. The beauty of OLAP tools is that they let users query data the way they think about the business—dimensionally. For example, a typical OLAP query might be "Let me see net profits by product, by channel, by geography, and by time."

Visual analysis tools are the newest form of analytical tool. They let users interact with charts and tables at the speed of thought because they store data in memory. Leveraging advanced visualization, compression, and 64-bit operating systems, these tools are increasingly being used as a foundation for performance dashboards.

Search tools also aid in analysis. Increasingly, BI vendors offer keyword search as a way for users to find relevant reports and kick off ad hoc queries. BI search is a great way for casual users to explore data without having to know SQL or query tools.

Data Mining Tools. Data mining, also known as predictive analytics or knowledge discovery, enables statisticians and power users to discover patterns in large sets of structured data and generate statistical models. The models use historical patterns to predict the future. They are widely used in sales and marketing applications, but their range of potential uses is virtually unlimited. In addition, some vendors now sell *text mining tools* that discover patterns in call center comment fields, e-mail, social media, and other unstructured text-based files.

Performance Dashboards. As we know, performance dashboards provide a layered information service that combines monitoring, analysis, and reporting—and increasingly prediction and visualization—in a single integrated environment. By integrating the functionality of most BI tools, performance dashboards meet 60 percent to 80 percent of the information needs of most casual users.

BI Platforms. The six categories of BI tools described earlier—report design, end-user query and reporting, OLAP, data mining, and performance dashboards—deliver different types of functionality for different types of users. To meet user requirements, organizations must purchase multiple BI tools, something most executives are loath to do. For years, executives have made it abundantly clear that they want to purchase only one tool for all users to minimize upfront license fees and downstream maintenance, support, and training costs. The reality, however, is that one size does not fit all when it comes to BI tools.

Most companies purchase a different BI tool in each of the six categories, although increasingly these tools come from a single vendor. In the best-case scenario, the BI tools are simply functions or modules in a BI platform that leverage a common set of services (e.g., graphical controls, security, metadata, query, and rendering) and can exchange parameters when users shift from one module to another. These BI platforms provide a more seamless experience for users who want to switch from reporting to analysis and back again.

User Fitting

Exhibit 2.6 provides a simple framework for mapping users to BI tools. The framework divides all users into two categories: (1) *information producers*, who create reports and views for others, and (2) *information consumers*, who consume those reports and views. All information producers are also consumers, but certain consumers (i.e., executives, managers, customers, suppliers) are not producers.

Information Producers. Information producers are *power users* who create information building blocks for others to consume. They can be IT developers who create pixel-perfect reports, complex standard reports, and dashboards; superusers who create simple reports and dashboard for colleagues in their departments; business analysts who use a variety of analysis tools to explore issues; or statisticians and analysts who create predictive models.

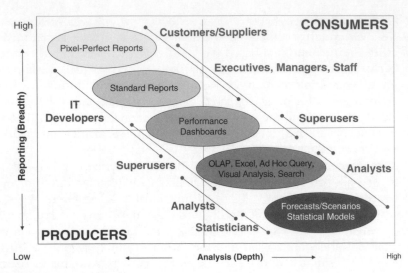

EXHIBIT 2.6 Mapping Users and BI Tools

Information Consumers. Most information consumers are *casual users* who regularly view reports but do not crunch numbers or perform detailed trend analysis on a daily basis. Casual users are executives, managers, staff, customers, and suppliers who primarily use performance dashboards and standard reports. Other consumers are superusers and analysts who primarily use exploratory tools, such as OLAP, Excel, visual analysis, and search, although some also use data-mining tools.

Historically, BI tools have been designed for power users, not casual users, and geared to exploration and analysis rather than monitoring and reporting, which are the bread and butter of casual users. As a result, the penetration of BI tools among casual users has been abysmally low, hovering around 20 percent, according to TDWI Research.

User Mantra. However, performance dashboards are beginning to reverse this trend, making BI pervasive among casual users. That's because performance dashboards conform to the way casual users want to consume information. Their needs are best summed up in the mantra "Give me all the data I want, but only the data I really need, and only when I really need it."

In other words, most casual users don't want to spend unnecessary time analyzing data unless there is an exception condition that demands their attention. When that happens, they want immediate access to all relevant information, but in a systematic and structured way so they don't get lost in the data.

Performance dashboards perfectly fulfill the requirements of the user mantra. They provide casual users all the information they need but dish it out on demand as they need it. They do not force users to search through hundreds of reports or remember how to use dozens of features, functions, and options. They are intuitive to use and tailored to the user's role. They highlight exception conditions and make it easy and fast for users to discover root causes.

In short, performance dashboards conform to the way users want to work instead of forcing them to conform to the way the tools work. As a result, performance dashboards and their underlying BI infrastructure are spreading like wildfire in organizations throughout the world.

Summary

The marriage of performance management and business intelligence has given rise to the performance dashboard. Performance dashboards leverage a business intelligence infrastructure to help organizations monitor their progress toward achieving strategic objectives as measured by key performance indicators. It's critical to understand the major elements of performance management and BI before launching a performance dashboard project.

CHAPTER 3

Assessing Your Organizational Readiness

Performance dashboards cannot take root in a hostile environment. The organization must be ready to accept and nurture a performance dashboard for it to succeed.

Paul Niven, author of *Balanced Scorecard Step by Step: Maximizing Performance and Maintaining Results*, defines seven criteria for evaluating an organization's readiness to implement a balanced scorecard. Although Niven created these criteria specifically for balanced scorecards (i.e., strategic dashboards), they are equally valid for any kind of performance dashboard.

Ten Criteria. I have adapted Niven's list and added three criteria to reflect the importance of a solid business intelligence (BI) infrastructure to support all types of performance dashboards, not just strategic ones. Although some strategic dashboards do not initially require an investment in BI and data integration software, most eventually do. Therefore, the next 10 criteria are good ways to evaluate an organization's readiness to deploy and sustain a performance management system for the long haul.

To evaluate readiness, ask whether your organization has:

1. A clearly defined strategy
2. Strong, committed sponsorship
3. A clear and urgent need
4. Support of mid-level managers
5. Appropriate scale and scope
6. A strong team and available resources
7. A culture of measurement
8. Alignment between business and information technology
9. Trustworthy and available data
10. A solid technical infrastructure

A Clearly Defined Strategy

A performance dashboard is a window into an organization's strategy and planning processes, especially a strategic dashboard. If the strategy and planning processes are unclear, unaligned, or uncoordinated, the performance dashboard will be ineffective and short lasting.

For example, Hewlett Packard Co.'s Technology Solutions Group (TSG) asks business sponsors a series of questions to ascertain whether their group or unit is ready for a balanced scorecard. (See Spotlight 3.1.)

Spotlight 3.1 Strategic Dashboard Readiness Assessment

In 2004, Hewlett Packard Co.'s TSG had a program office that created strategic dashboards (i.e., balanced scorecards) for its regional groups and other units. When working with a new group, the program office first met with the sponsoring executives to explain strategic dashboard concepts and discuss their concerns. To assess the group's readiness to use a strategic dashboard approach to manage performance, the program team asked executives to answer these six questions:

1. **Is the relationship between your strategy and measures clear and obvious?** This question communicates the need to translate strategy into a small number of carefully defined metrics with corresponding objectives, targets, and initiatives. Most companies have hundreds of metrics, most of which they rarely consult and few of which are truly relevant to their mission.
2. **Do you measure outcomes or causes?** This introduces executives to the concept of leading and lagging indicators and gets them to start thinking about measuring value drivers instead of historical activity.
3. **Is there consensus about the importance of the measurements and objectives?** Do all executives agree that existing metrics accurately define the strategy? If the strategy and vision are vague, the answer is usually no. Do employees agree that the metrics used to evaluate their performance are valid and produce the desired results? Without employee buy-in, a performance management system cannot work.
4. **If you select 10 managers at random, how many know whether they are helping to achieve the strategy?** Most managers and workers know what tasks they need to do each day, but

few know how their work contributes to the company's strategy. This step helps executives see that the strategic dashboard is a communications tool that lets employees literally see how their work contributes to the strategy and performance of the company.

5. **Is important information easy and readily available for the right people?** It is one thing to measure performance, but it is another thing to empower people with information so they can take action to improve performance. This step helps executives assess the state of their information delivery systems and determine whether they need to be overhauled.

6. **What do you do with the data you receive?** It's one thing to understand performance; it's another to improve it. When performance trends downward, who is supposed to take action? Do people know what to do, and are they empowered to make decisions to resolve the situation?

The organization must have a strategy that defines its mission, values, vision, goals, and objectives, as well as metrics for measuring progress toward reaching those objectives. It also needs a planning process that devises new initiatives, refines existing ones, and allocates resources to implement the strategy. The major components of a strategy are listed next.

- **Mission.** A mission statement communicates the purpose of an organization. It typically defines its target customers and competitive differentiators in about 50 words or less.
- **Values.** Values are principles that guide the way the company does business. Values, along with the mission, are very important in a crisis when a new situation confronts the organization, and it has no historical precedent to guide its decisions and actions.
- **Vision.** The vision statement describes what the organization wants to achieve in a given time frame. Ideally, it is an inspiring, if not daunting, call to action that requires employees to think and act in innovative ways.
- **Goals and objectives.** Goals and objectives define the path a business takes to achieve the vision. They state what the company is committed to doing and, more important, what it *will not* do. Goals are broad statements that define what the company wants to achieve in the coming year, while objectives are the steps needed to reach those goals.
- **Metrics and targets.** To monitor progress toward achieving goals and objectives, organizations use metrics and targets. Each goal and

objective has one or more metrics and each metric has one or more associated targets. Chapter 11 goes into detail about how to craft metrics and targets for performance dashboards.

- **Plans and initiatives.** Plans allocate resources to achieve goals and objectives, including short- and long-term initiatives designed to close the gap between current and future realities. Continuous planning revises plans monthly or quarterly instead of annually in a budget to better align resources with market changes.

Strong, Committed Sponsorship

It is almost an industry cliché to say that strong business leadership is critical to the success of any information management project, including performance dashboards. A committed and involved business sponsor evangelizes the system, secures and sustains funding, navigates political issues, effects cultural change, and helps prioritize projects. Research shows a high correlation between the commitment of a business sponsor and success rates of BI solutions, which include performance dashboards.

In fact, what is most interesting is that projects with a "very committed" sponsor are twice as likely to succeed as those with a "fairly committed" sponsor, while almost half of projects with "fairly committed" sponsors are struggling. So sponsors cannot be halfhearted or even three-quarters–hearted; they must give it 100 percent if they want a successful project.

The sponsor must also assign a trusted lieutenant to guide the project on a daily basis. These drivers or champions need to devote at least 50 percent of their time to the project. Like the sponsor, they must be well respected and connected in the organization, with a direct line to the executive suite. They need to lead interference for the project when it gets bogged down in politics, vendor negotiations, or budget planning. Often drivers are the people who initiate the idea for the project and sell it to the sponsor, whose influence and credibility are vital to the success of the project.

A Clear and Urgent Need

Urgency plays a pivotal role in whether a performance dashboard project succeeds or not. If the sponsoring group doesn't have a clear and urgent need, the performance management system will not take root. The best performance dashboards address a critical business pain that stems from lack of information. The greater the pain, the more likely a performance dashboard will flourish.

The next situations often create an urgent need for a new performance dashboard:

- **New top executive.** The company hires a new chief executive, chief financial, or chief information officer who is used to running a metrics-driven organization with performance dashboards.
- **New strategy or initiative.** Executives need a powerful way to communicate a new strategy or initiative, channel everyone's energy toward achieving the new objectives, and monitor progress along the way.
- **Merger or acquisition.** A company must align two incompatible sets of strategies, cultures, values, and goals and get everyone marching in the same direction quickly.
- **Business crisis.** Many events can put an organization into crisis mode: a new competitor or market-transforming technology, an economic downturn, a natural disaster, financial mismanagement, or criminal wrongdoing.
- **Organizational restructuring.** Executives who reorganize groups and divisions to improve productivity or competitiveness need to explain their rationale and monitor the effectiveness of the move.
- **Data fragmentation.** Executives can become exasperated by the lack of consistent data, which prevents them from getting a clear picture of the organization at any given moment.
- **Core systems overhaul.** An organization that replaces multiple legacy systems with a packaged business application needs to monitor the progress of the project and measure return on investment.
- **New regulations.** New regulations, such as the Sarbanes-Oxley Act or the Basel Accord, may force organizations to change their strategy or revamp core processes.
- **Ineffective metrics.** Many organizations have too many metrics but not the right ones to change behavior.

Support of Mid-level Managers

Successful performance dashboards need the support of mid-level managers to succeed. It is critical to win their support because they translate strategic goals and objectives into concrete plans and initiatives and manage day-to-day operations. Mid-level managers often know which metrics will work and which will not and what data are available to populate metrics. Moreover, their words and actions signal whether their staff should take executive edicts seriously or not. If they are unwilling partners—or worse, active saboteurs—the project will not succeed.

Mid-level managers "generally know the best sources of information, the biggest issues, and the best workarounds. We also use these mid-level managers as advocates, both up and down and across the organization, to educate people about the program, its benefits, and how it works," says Martin Summerhayes, former program manager at Hewlett Packard TSG.

Unfortunately, mid-level managers can also be the ones most threatened by a performance dashboard. They are adept at massaging and spinning numbers to present themselves and their group in the best possible light. But a performance dashboard undercuts their ability to do this. It broadcasts their performance to everyone through an unfiltered lens, leaving them feeling exposed and vulnerable. For the first time, they may have to scramble and compete for budget dollars, resources, and promotions.

It takes considerable effort and political savvy to win the hearts and minds of mid-level managers. Executives have to educate the managers about how the program benefits them personally as well as their group, and they have to quell all unfounded fears. Executives need to identify key individuals who can make or break a project and work with them early and often. If appropriate, executives should invite the most pivotal managers to sit on the steering committee that oversees the project. The managers may see this as an honor and view the project more favorably as a result; at the very least, it gives executives a good way to keep an eye on key managers and make sure they have a positive attitude toward the project.

Appropriate Scale and Scope

Most people assume a performance dashboard is always implemented on an enterprise scale starting with the executive suite, but this is not always true. Sometimes it is better to implement a performance dashboard in a business unit, region, or department that is highly receptive to it. If the initial project succeeds, it will spread quickly throughout the organization. However, if executives try to force-fit a performance management system into an organization or business unit that is not ready for it, the tool will not gain the momentum it needs to expand throughout the enterprise.

When deploying a strategic dashboard (i.e., balanced scorecard) in a business unit or group, Niven recommends selecting a unit that conducts business across an entire value chain of activities. In other words, the business unit should have a "strategy, defined customers, specific processes, operations, and administration." Selecting a unit with a narrow, functional focus will produce a strategic dashboard with narrow, functionally focused metrics that will not be readily transferable elsewhere in the organization.

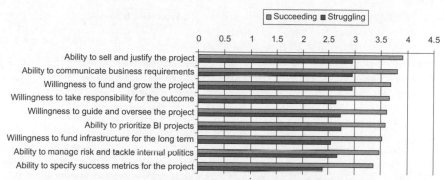

Chart based on a 5-point rating scale, with 1 being "poor" and 5 being "excellent."

EXHIBIT 3.1 Business Team Capabilities by Degree of BI Success
Source: Wayne Eckerson, "Smart Companies in the 21st Century: The Secrets of Creating Successful Business Intelligence Solutions," *TDWI Report Series*, 2003.

A Strong Team and Available Resources

To succeed, an organization needs business and technical people with the right skills who are willing and available to work on the project.

On the business side, the sponsor and driver must allocate enough time and attention to nurture the project through its entire life cycle. They also must stick around for the duration of the project or garner sufficient consensus and momentum so the project can continue without them. Successful projects have businesspeople who are skilled at selling, funding, prioritizing, and completing projects as well as communicating requirements, managing risk, and accepting responsibility for the outcomes (see Exhibit 3.1).

On the technical side, successful projects have technical teams with strong technical and project management skills. Successful technical teams score especially well on the soft issues, such as the ability to communicate technical issues clearly, respond to business requirements, and develop desired functionality (see Exhibit 3.2).

If the needed resources do not exist in-house, the organization must be willing to bring in outside consultants and contractors. However, it needs to put in place a plan to transfer consultants' knowledge and skills to in-house workers so the company is not dependent on the consultants. Organizations with successful solutions often rely heavily on management consultants to help formulate strategy and metrics, develop project plans, and implement change management programs; they use technical consultants largely to assist with application development, architectural design, product installation, requirements gathering, and application integration.

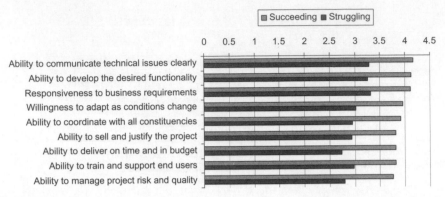

Chart based on a 5-point rating scale, with 1 being "poor" and 5 being "excellent."

EXHIBIT 3.2 Technical Team Capabilities by Degree of BI Success
Source: Wayne Eckerson, "Smart Companies in the 21st Century: The Secrets of Creating Successful Business Intelligence Solutions," *TDWI Report Series*, 2003.

A Culture of Measurement

Does the business already have a culture of managing through performance measures? If not, even the strongest desire may not be enough to overcome organizational inertia. At a bare minimum, does it compare performance with plan or forecasts? Does it hold individuals and groups accountable for performance? Does it conduct individual performance reviews using objective data? Similarly, the organization should have a history of using information and data to make decisions. If the organization relies primarily on intuition, it will struggle to succeed.

"Our company used to make decisions on gut feel," says a director of business information and analysis at a major U.S. manufacturer, "but now our executives believe strongly that fact-based decision making gives us a competitive advantage. Executives now ask, 'Where are the data to back up this decision?' and they expect sales people to use information to close deals, not just rely on the strength of their client relationships. And it's working!"

Performance dashboards work best in a corporate culture that encourages users to share information. They cannot flourish if executives tightly control information to insulate themselves from the rest of the company; or if managers use information as a political weapon to protect their turf; or if users are penalized for sharing information with colleagues. In contrast, organizations whose employees share information "very openly" are five times more likely to have a successful solution than those whose employees do not (17 percent to 3 percent). Organizations whose employees do not

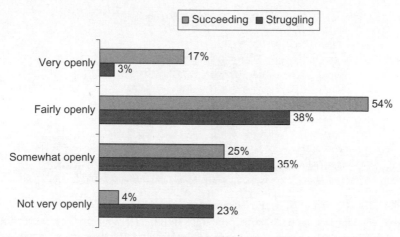

EXHIBIT 3.3 Level of Information Sharing by Degree of BI Success
Source: Wayne Eckerson, "Smart Companies in the 21st Century: The Secrets of Creating Successful Business Intelligence Solutions," *TDWI Report Series*, 2003.

share information openly are five times more likely to struggle (23 percent to 4 percent) (see Exhibit 3.3).

Alignment between Business and Information Technology

The degree of alignment between the business and the technical team also determines the readiness of an organization to adopt a performance dashboard. That is because performance dashboards are adaptive systems that continually change as the business changes. Performance dashboards require a great deal of ongoing interaction between the business user and the technical team to define new requirements, metrics, and targets and refine old ones. If the relationship between business and technical groups is tense and both groups eye one another with distrust and sarcasm, then the chances that a performance dashboard will succeed are minimal. Chapter 5 discusses strategies for aligning business and information technology in depth.

Like sponsorship, there is no middle ground with alignment. Teams that are "very aligned" are almost five times more likely to succeed, whereas teams that are only "fairly aligned" struggle a whopping 46 percent of the time. The key to guaranteeing success is to achieve total alignment between the business and technical sides of the team (see Exhibit 3.4).

What does a "very aligned" team look like? First of all, it has an actively involved business sponsor and business driver. Second, it is a team—not

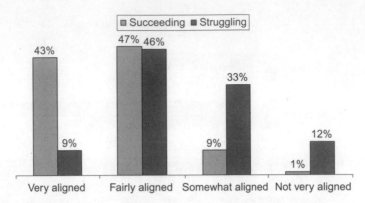

EXHIBIT 3.4 Alignment between Business and IT by Degree of BI Success
Source: Wayne Eckerson, "Smart Companies in the 21st Century: The Secrets of
Creating Successful Business Intelligence Solutions," *TDWI Report Series*, 2003.

two or more disparate groups with different leaders, objectives, and cultures. "We sit side by side with businesspeople and report into the same leadership," says a senior technology manager who helps run the BI team at a telecommunications firm. "The only difference is that we specialize in the data and they specialize in the business processes."

Trustworthy and Available Data

Does the organization have the right data to populate metrics in a performance dashboard? Although it is unlikely that data exist for all measures, a new initiative should supply data for most of the metrics under consideration. It is also critical that someone evaluate the condition of the data. Nothing can damage the credibility of a project faster than launching a performance dashboard with inaccurate and untrustworthy data.

Because data are at the heart of most performance management systems, organizations need to treat data as a vital corporate asset, as important as other assets, such as buildings, people, and cash. Companies whose executives view data as a corporate asset are six times more likely to be successful than those whose executives do not (31 percent versus 5 percent). Companies with executives who do not view data as an asset are between two and three times more likely to struggle with BI projects (see Exhibit 3.5).

A Solid Technical Infrastructure

To generate data for performance dashboard metrics, companies often must either overhaul operational systems and processes or establish a BI

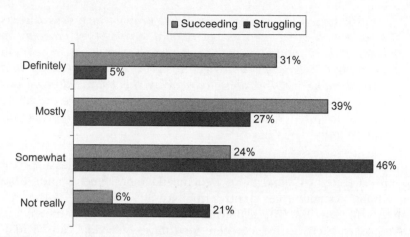

EXHIBIT 3.5 Executives' View of Data as a Corporate Asset by Degree of BI Success
Source: Wayne Eckerson, "Smart Companies in the 21st Century: The Secrets of Creating Successful Business Intelligence Solutions," *TDWI Report Series*, 2003.

infrastructure that delivers high-quality data, or both. However, not all performance dashboards require a robust technical infrastructure to initiate a project. Strategic dashboards, in particular, can often start by using manual processes to capture and disseminate key data elements (see Spotlight 3.2).

Spotlight 3.2 Growing into a BI Infrastructure

Balanced scorecard consultants argue that organizations should not delay a strategic dashboard project because they lack the requisite data or a robust BI infrastructure. Bill Barberg, president of Insightformation, Inc., describes a hypothetical scenario:

Suppose that the executives at a midsize manufacturing company that recently acquired several plants, each with its own IT systems, create a strategy to become a low-cost producer. One causal driver in this strategy involves driving scrap and rework to levels significantly below the industry average. Unfortunately, the company does not have good data to measure scrap and rework processes, and the data that exist are spread across many operational systems with different database fields and definitions. Few of the systems track why things are scrapped and do not reflect labor costs associated with the process. In addition, there are no industry benchmarks against which they can compare their performance.

(Continued)

The executives quickly realize that it might take several years to overhaul the company's operational systems and processes to capture the information they need and then create a BI solution to analyze, aggregate, and accurately track detailed scrap and rework information. Rather than delay the balanced scorecard project until they have a solid technical foundation, the executives decide to forge ahead and make do with less than perfect information.

Barberg says that even a set of rough monthly measures for scrap calculated by hand helps benchmark improvements and, more important, communicates a powerful message about the company's strategy for success. The scorecard motivates managers and staff to take positive steps to reduce scrap, and these behaviors can be reinforced through additional objectives and monthly scorecard review meetings.

Meanwhile, the company can work on a parallel track to upgrade its operational systems to capture data required for the balanced scorecard and implement an activity-based costing system to allocate labor cost to scrap. The company can also implement reporting and analysis tools that deliver a standardized view of scorecard metrics.

Although the company would have benefited from having integrated operational systems and a robust BI infrastructure to start, it can reap benefits without them. Eventually, its technical infrastructure will catch up with the scorecard initiative.

The BI infrastructure consists of the BI environment (data warehouses, data marts, and analytical tools), the technical platform (servers, storage, networks), and the people to feed and maintain the environment. Organizations that are very willing or fairly willing to fund a BI infrastructure are more likely to succeed than those that are not. We'll focus more on this issue in Chapter 4.

Summary

Not all companies are ready to implement a performance dashboard. Organizations need strong leadership, a receptive culture, and a robust technical environment. You can assess your organization's readiness to implement a performance dashboard by asking these questions:

- **Strategy.** Does your organization have a clear, coherent strategy with well-defined goals, objectives, and measures?
- **Sponsorship.** Is there a high-level executive who strongly believes in the project and is willing to spend time evangelizing and nurturing the project?
- **Urgent need.** Does the organization have a demonstrated need for the system? How much is it suffering from an inability to track and measure performance?
- **Buy-in.** How willing are mid-level managers to support the project? Will the open sharing of performance results threaten their positions and their hold on power?
- **Scope.** Does the group have sufficient scope so that the implementation can be adapted by other groups in the organization?
- **Team.** Does the group have business and technical people with proper skills and experience to deliver a successful project?
- **Culture.** Does the group already have a culture of measurement and make decisions by fact instead of intuition?
- **Alignment.** How aligned are the business and technical teams? Do they have a good working relationship and trust one another?
- **Data.** Do data exist to populate the measures? How clean, valid, and complete are the data?
- **Infrastructure.** Does the group have a solid technical infrastructure that generates the required data and delivers it to users in a format that is easy to monitor and analyze?

CHAPTER 4

Assessing Your Technical Readiness

Business Intelligence Maturity Model

In Chapter 3, we discussed 10 criteria for evaluating the readiness of an organization to implement a performance dashboard. This chapter focuses more specifically on evaluating an organization's technical readiness. Without a strong technical foundation—especially in business intelligence (BI)—most performance dashboards will not survive. They will be crushed by the weight of cumbersome and costly data-gathering processes, inaccurate and untrustworthy data, poor performance, and antiquated functionality.

Like organizational readiness, technical readiness does not happen overnight. It takes years to build a robust BI infrastructure and develop the internal skills and talent necessary to support an effective performance management system. During the past several years, many organizations that initiated performance dashboards became disillusioned when they could not automate the solution or populate its metrics with valid, accurate data.

I have created a BI Maturity Model to help organizations understand the maturity of their BI infrastructures and, by extension, their readiness to build and sustain a performance management system. The five-stage model shows the trajectory that most organizations follow when evolving their BI environments. Typically, the journey takes the BI program from a low-value, operational cost center to a high-value, strategic initiative that delivers a competitive advantage. The model provides organizations with a big-picture view of where their BI environment is today, where it needs to go, and how to get it there.

The model also shows that performance dashboards are best deployed once organizations reach Stage 3. At this level of maturity, organizations can quickly deploy performance dashboards without having to make significant investments to create a BI environment. In Stage 4, organizations are ready to cascade strategic dashboards throughout the enterprise and link them (logically at least) to operational and tactical dashboards. In short, it takes a reasonable amount of BI maturity for organizations to deploy a performance dashboard successfully on an enterprise scale.

Stages and Sticking Points

The BI Maturity Model consists of five stages: (1) Prenatal/Infant, (2) Child, (3) Teenager, (4) Adult, and (5) Sage, and two sticking points: the Gulf and Chasm. (See Exhibit 4.1.) As an organization moves through successive stages, business value increases, data become more consolidated, and business rules and definitions (i.e., semantics) become consistent. Architecturally, the BI environment evolves from operational reports and spreadmarts, to data marts and divisional data warehouses, to an enterprise data warehouse and finally BI services.

Bell Curve. The BI Maturity Model is shaped in a bell curve to indicate that most organizations today have reached Stages 2 and 3. Only a few are still stuck in the first stage (a combination of prenatal and infant), and only a few have made it to the advanced stages.[1] Because business intelligence emerged as a distinct discipline only in the 1990s, it is no surprise that after a decade or so, most organizations are stuck in "BI adolescence" and suffering the requisite growing pains. (See Spotlight 4.1.)

Characteristics. The BI Maturity Model defines each stage using a number of characteristics, such as scope, analytic structure, executive per-

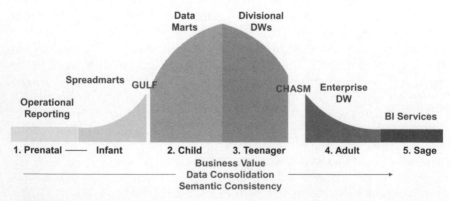

EXHIBIT 4.1 BI Maturity Model

Spotlight 4.1 Symptoms of BI Adolescence

Most organizations today are in the adolescent phase of business intelligence. If you remember correctly from your youth, adolescence is both an exciting and a painful time, full of change, transition, and surprises. The same is true for companies that reach adolescence in BI. Every step forward is tentative, and more setbacks are experienced than victories. The key to getting through this stressful period is to stay focused on the future and the value that awaits those who persevere while taking one step at a time in the present. Here are a few symptoms that signify that your organization is square in the middle of BI adolescence:

- The BI team moves perpetually from one crisis to the next.
- The BI program manager has to explain continually why the BI budget should not be cut.
- Usage of the BI environment peaked several months after deployment and continues to decline.
- The BI manager has to evangelize continuously the value of the BI environment to executives and business users.
- The number of spreadmarts, independent data marts, and other data warehouses with redundant data keeps increasing instead of decreasing.
- Users keep asking the information technology (IT) department to create custom reports even though the organization recently purchased a "self-service" BI tool.
- Executives still believe BI is a tool, not a strategic information resource to drive the organization in the right direction.

Managing a BI environment in its adolescence is painful. Perhaps the only comforting thought is that most companies are also experiencing the same growing pains. Like your organization, they spend more time reacting to problems than proactively solving them and put more effort into putting out fires than delivering lasting business value. The good news is that with persistence and some luck, you will eventually cross the chasm into adulthood.

ceptions, types of analytics, stewardship, funding, technology platform, change management, and administration. This book focuses on only a few of these characteristics.

Skipping Stages. Organizations evolve at different rates through the five stages and may exhibit characteristics of multiple stages at a given time. Thus, organizations should not expect to move cleanly and precisely from one stage to the next. Although it is possible to skip stages, it is unlikely. Organizations must learn critical lessons at each stage before they can move to the next. Organizations that feel compelled to catch up and skip stages will encounter problems that eventually bog down the project.

However, it is possible for organizations to move rapidly through each stage if they have strong sponsorship, adequate funding, and veteran BI experts equipped with a battle-tested methodology to guide the project. A solid methodology creates a logical road map for the BI environment that consists of a set of prioritized analytical applications and an information infrastructure to support them. The methodology will implement just enough infrastructure at each stage of development to support the new application and ensure a seamless evolution to an enterprise environment.

In essence, an accelerated BI program "thinks global, but acts local." It creates a full-fledged, enterprise DW environment one data mart at a time. Each new application extends the existing logical data model with new subject areas, brings new data into the data warehouse, and equips users with new reports and analytical functionality. By following a logical road map, an organization can usually accelerate through development stages without hitting architectural dead ends.

Even so, BI is not something that can be rushed because ultimately it is an exercise in change management. BI asks the business and users to alter the way they consume information and make decisions. Such changes don't happen overnight. And these days, business sponsors typically are willing to fund only short, tactical projects with a rapid return on investment (ROI), not large infrastructure projects that cost millions of dollars and take years to complete.

Regressing Stages. Rather than skipping stages, it's more likely that an organization will regress stages and slip backward in the evolutionary cycle. Often the cause is beyond the project team's control: a merger, acquisition, new executive leadership, changing economic or competitive circumstances, or new regulations. Here, BI projects and plans are shunted aside to address new concerns and issues in the most expedient (i.e., architecturally nonstandard) way possible. This makes many BI professionals feel like Sisyphus, the ancient Greek hero who was condemned forever to roll a huge stone up a hill only to see it roll down upon reaching the top.

Sticking Points. Almost every organization gets stuck at two points in the life cycle, represented by the "Gulf" and the "Chasm." The Gulf represents the obstacles that afflict early-stage BI deployments, including lack of sufficient sponsorship, funding, scope management, data quality, and spreadmarts. The Chasm represents challenges that afflict most later-stage BI deployments, including the transition from departmental- to enterprise-scale BI deployments, the lack of consistent definitions and rules, unrelenting business volatility, report chaos, and lack of awareness of the strategic value of BI.

As you can see from the challenges on this list, the Chasm is deeper and wider than the Gulf, and many organizations never cross it. We'll delve into the Gulf and Chasm in the next section.

Five Stages

Stage 1: Prenatal/Infant

The Prenatal and Infant stages are depicted separately in the model, but I treat them as a single stage since they are flip sides of the same coin. The lack of accessible, interactive reporting in the Prenatal stage spawns the creation of spreadmarts, which are the hallmark of the Infant stage.

Production Reporting. Most established organizations have production reporting systems that generate standard reports that are distributed to large numbers of employees on a regular basis, usually weekly, monthly, or quarterly. Because programmers hand-code the reports, it can take several days or weeks to produce a new report or custom version of an existing report. This creates a backlog of requests that the IT department can never fulfill in a timely manner, as well as many frustrated users who cannot obtain critical information to do their jobs.

Spreadmarts. Consequently, many users take matters into their own hands, especially business analysts who know their way around corporate information systems and whose job is to crunch numbers on behalf of executives and managers. These individuals circumvent the IT department by extracting data directly from source systems and loading the information into spreadsheets or desktop databases.

Spreadmarts are spreadsheets on steroids. They are shadow data systems, renegade data marts, if you will. Each spreadmart contains a unique set of data, metrics, and rules that do not align with other analytical systems in the organization. An organization afflicted with spreadmarts has no consistent view of the business and no single version of truth from which every employee can work.

Spreadmarts ultimately wreak havoc on organizations. They bleed organizations dry, often without the organizations knowing it. Users spend inordinate amounts of time collecting and integrating data, becoming, in effect, human data warehouses. Executive meetings dissolve into chaos as managers argue about whose data are right rather than making effective decisions, a phenomenon known as dueling spreadmarts.

Spreadmarts are difficult to eradicate—because they are ubiquitous, cheap, and easy to use. Many users, especially business analysts and financial managers, cannot function without spreadsheets, which give them a high degree of local control at extremely low cost. As a result, spreadmarts proliferate like weeds—organizations have dozens, if not hundreds or thousands, of these pernicious analytical structures. Unfortunately, the ubiquity of spreadsheets (or any low-cost analytical tool) undermines an organization's ability to obtain a consistent view of business activity. Running a business on spreadmarts is like having a thousand points of light but no clear direction in which to head.

The Gulf

To move from the Prenatal/Infant stage to the Child stage, organizations must cross the Gulf. As mentioned earlier, the Gulf represents the challenges that organizations face when trying to launch a BI program. Ironically, many companies in their rush to implement a BI solution don't fully address these early-stage challenges—especially those pertaining to spreadmarts. So, while they may appear to cross the Gulf by deploying a new data mart or reporting system, their fledgling BI program won't bear real fruit until they address the challenges posed by the Gulf.

Sponsorship. The first and most difficult challenge is obtaining suitable sponsorship. As mentioned in Chapter 3, sponsorship is critical to success of any BI or IT endeavor. With BI, sponsors come in two flavors: (1) enlightened executives who understand the value of running the business by the numbers and view BI as a no-brainer and (2) traditional executives who won't endorse a program until they see tangible benefits and a favorable ROI. The first set of executives make excellent sponsors as they stay put long enough to see the initial project through to completion. They may require a formal cost justification as part of the planning process but not as a litmus test for approval.

Chicken and Egg. The traditional executives, however, get caught in the chicken-and-egg syndrome. They won't allocate funds until you prove returns, but you can't demonstrate value until you deploy a solution. Essentially, traditional sponsors force you to bootstrap a BI solution and get creative in cost justifying the project. At this stage, you need to show tactical cost savings from implementing BI. This can include savings from shutting down legacy reporting systems, reducing training costs, and consolidating staff. You might be able to get away with some softer tangibles, such as time saved by analysts who no longer have to spend days gathering and preparing reports.

Of course, as mentioned in Chapter 3, the more pain a traditional executive feels from lack of adequate information to make decisions and monitor operations, the more he or she is likely to embrace a BI project. So, improve your chances of success by hunting first for enlightened executives and then for traditional executives who are suffering from information pain. If none of these executives exists, then bide your time and wait. It's likely that your organization won't be attaining its objectives and the board will bring in a new slate of executives who might be more enlightened when it comes to BI. Or if patience isn't your strong suit, look for another job.

Project Scope and Data Quality. Most early-stage BI initiatives founder on the shoals of ambitious project plans. In an effort to gain sponsorship and funding, BI managers often oversell the project. They promise to deliver too much data from too many sources and offer too much functionality in the initial deliverable. What looks great on paper often fails miserably in practice. This is primarily because a huge wildcard is the quality and condition of source data.

Typically, data that are sufficient to run operational systems are woefully inadequate when merged and aggregated for use in analytical systems. Source data often contain many errors, especially if portions are entered by hand, such as from a Web site. The data may be formatted and represented differently in each system, and they may not be consistently defined, creating a semantic reconciliation nightmare. And administrators may have added, deleted, or changed fields in a system without proper documentation, making it difficult to sort out what is valid data and what isn't.

The ideal scope for an initial BI project is to source data from one or two well-known data sources. This limits the surprises that you'll encounter once you open the data stores and peer inside. Although sponsors may not get the full application they seek in the first deliverable, they will obtain enough benefits (it is hoped) in a short enough period of time to continue funding the initiative.

Spreadmarts. Spreadmarts can ultimately strangle any BI initiative. Although you may succeed in finding a sponsor, obtaining funding, and building an initial solution, if users cling to their spreadmarts, your BI solution will die on the vine. Although spreadmarts are difficult to eradicate, there are remedies for curing this "disease" before it poisons the BI program. (See Spotlight 4.2.) Ultimately, the best remedy is a successful enterprise BI program that delivers the right data to the right users at the right time.

Spotlight 4.2 Strategies for Eradicating Spreadmarts

Spreadmarts are renegade spreadsheets and desktop databases that contain vital pieces of corporate data needed to run the business. However, because they are created by individuals at different times using different data sources and rules for defining metrics, they create a fractured view of the enterprise. Without centrally defined metrics and a single version of corporate information, organizations cannot compete effectively.

Today, spreadmarts are the bane of workers in IT departments, who cannot control their proliferation, and the nemesis of chief executives, who cannot gain an accurate view of the enterprise because of them. Although it is impossible to completely eradicate spreadmarts (and probably not wise to until BI tools offer comparable analytical flexibility as spreadsheets), here are five strategies—the five Cs—for minimizing the proliferation of spreadmarts:

1. **Coerce.** Have the CEO mandate the proper use of spreadsheets and desktop databases. By itself, this strategy rarely works because it is difficult to enforce. In fact, coercion usually makes the problem worse. Users go underground, managing their divisions and departments with clandestine spreadmarts that run parallel to official systems. However, without a strong executive mandate, users won't change their analytical habits. So, it's best to use this tactic in conjunction with one or more of the next approaches.

2. **Convert.** This strategy involves selling the benefits of the organization's standard BI environment. The key is to make sure the BI environment provides at least 150 percent the value of spreadmarts (which is sometimes difficult!). The BI environment should provide:

   a. All the data users need to monitor processes and conduct ad hoc analyses.
   b. Better-quality data defined consistently across all subject areas.
   c. Deeper insights that come from delivering cross-functional views of information.
   d. Comparable functionality to what users already have, including flexible "what-if" modeling and custom analysis (e.g., custom groups, calculations, ranking).
   e. New functionality that goes beyond what they have, such as collaboration, publishing, what-if modeling, and offline usage.
   f. Central support services.

3. **Corral.** The previous convert tactic should be enough to convert most casual information users (e.g., executives, managers, and

front-line staff) but not power users, who conduct ad hoc analyses using data from a variety of sources. For them, you'll need to create an analytical sandbox inside the data warehouse that enables them to combine their own local data with data in the warehouse. This gives them the best of all worlds: unfettered access to enterprise data, a robust server environment to conduct their analyses, and the ability to add unique data to the mix. Of course, such sandboxes require that administrators understand how to create partitions and use mixed workload utilities. Another option is to create an outboard analytical sandbox using a data warehousing appliance that holds a replica of data in the warehouse.

4. **Coexist.** This strategy turns Excel into a full-fledged client to a BI server. Rather than force users to switch tools, let them use Excel to access reports on a BI server or data in a multidimensional database. This gives them all the spreadsheet features they know and love and lets the organization manage data in standard way. This is perhaps the best option when used in conjunction with the Convert strategy (number 2).

5. **Co-opt.** This strategy takes the approach: If you can't beat them, join them. This strategy automates spreadmarts by running them on a central server. IT does not change the data access methods, processes, or rules set up by spreadmart users, it just maintains the spreadmarts on their behalf, freeing them to spend more time analyzing data and less time collecting and massaging it. Gradually, over time, the IT department can transfer the spreadmarts to a more standard environment.

Stage 2: Child

In the Child stage, departments recognize the need to empower knowledge workers with timely information and insight, not just business analysts and executives, who are the primary beneficiaries of spreadmarts. Departmental leaders fund the development of data marts, assign project managers to oversee the initiatives, and purchase BI tools so users can access and analyze data in the marts.

A data mart is a shared, analytic structure that generally supports a single business process or department, such as sales, marketing, or finance. The departmental team gathers information requirements and tailors the data mart to meet the needs of the members in its group. A data mart requires members of a department to consolidate or replace multiple spreadmarts and negotiate data definitions and rules to ensure data consistency throughout the department.

Unfortunately, data marts often fall prey to the same problems that afflict spreadmarts. Each data mart supports unique definitions and rules and extracts data directly from source systems. Although these so-called independent data marts do a great job of supporting local needs, their data cannot be aggregated to support cross-departmental analysis. What is needed is a mechanism to integrate data marts without jeopardizing local autonomy. This is the hallmark of the Teenager stage.

Also, most companies purchase more BI licenses than they need. They do not realize that many BI tools are geared to power users who are technically literate and conversant with the company's databases and access methods, not casual users who prefer to examine canned reports and dashboards. Since power users comprise fewer than 20 percent of all knowledge workers, BI in the Child stage serves only a small minority of users. In essence, while BI has established a beachhead in the organization, it is by no means pervasive.

Stage 3: Teenager

Proliferation of Data Marts. In BI, success breeds demand for more BI. When one group in a business unit successfully deploys a data mart, every other group wants one too. Soon the business unit has a proliferation of data marts, each developed independently for a different group with unique requirements.

Before long, a business unit executive recognizes that these so-called independent data marts cost a considerable sum of money to maintain and undermine a single view of the business. Typically, the executive initiates a project to consolidate existing independent data marts onto a single data warehousing platform. This consolidation is usually triggered by a business event or strategic initiative that requires clean, consolidated, and integrated data, such as a new customer loyalty initiative or an acquisition, merger, or reorganization.

Architectural Consolidation. Meanwhile, BI architects have recognized that the proliferation of data marts is overloading source systems with multiple, redundant extract programs. To streamline processing and ease administration, they backfill the data marts with a staging area that consolidates all data in one place and simplifies extract processing. This staging area then feeds data marts on a regular basis. Typically, the architects establish an update schedule for each data element based on user requirements. In most organizations, a majority of data elements will be updated once a day.

Next, architects recognize that many data marts share common dimensions, hierarchies, and metrics even though each data mart defines them differently, which creates problems for executive decision makers. Architects decide to create a new set of tables inside the staging area that represent shared dimensions, hierarchies, and metrics across all data marts. These tables are modeled in a dimensional format, called a star schema or snowflake schema, and become the standard reference data for all data marts. The data marts can query them directly or create a replica for use in their own databases.

Divisional Data Warehouse. At the same time, executives seek greater data unification and consolidation, BI architects are ready to deliver a data warehouse with conformed dimensions and metrics that is updated in right time according to user requirements. This divisional data warehouse is a hallmark of the Teenager stage.

BI Program. Not surprisingly, the divisional data warehouse brings along the sponsors and users of each data mart, each of whom has different expectations and requirements for the shared resource. At this stage, the BI initiative is no longer a series of projects carried out independently by one or more teams of developers with no particular BI expertise; it's a BI program managed by a director of BI who must work with business sponsors to prioritize projects and align them with strategic objectives. Ideally, the BI director creates a BI road map that spells out the short- and long-term direction of the program.

To execute the program, the BI director hires a team of BI specialists to build solutions. These include BI project managers, data acquisition and transformation specialists, data modelers, business requirements analysts, BI architects, BI developers and report writers, technical writers and trainers, data administrators, quality assurance specialists, and data warehousing administrators. Individuals may handle multiple roles, and some roles may be outsourced to contractors or offshore developers.

Performance Dashboards. Whereas power users reap most of the benefits in the Child stage, general casual users enjoy most of the benefits in the Teenager stage. Once the BI team has ostensibly met the BI needs of its most demanding users, it is ready to make BI more pervasive by putting tools in the hands of casual users that conform to the way they want to consume and act on information. These tools are performance dashboards.

As mentioned in Chapter 1, performance dashboards are layered information delivery systems that enable business users to visually monitor business processes and drill into successive layers of information to discern the root cause of a problem or issue. The best performance dashboards display key performance indicators (KPIs) in a graphical manner, so users can glance at the dashboard to see whether performance is on track to meet predefined targets. If not, they can drill down to analyze dimensionalized data or access transactional details, if needed. The best performance dashboards tailor the display to each user, delivering the right information at the right time to take action while there is still time to affect outcomes.

The Chasm

Unfortunately, many BI teams never advance beyond the Teenager stage. They do not capitalize on their momentum and fall headfirst into the Chasm, which represents challenges that later-stage BI teams face when migrating from departmental and divisional views of information to an enterprise view with a single, integrated set of information and analytical tools for everyone.

What Is an Enterprise? Some people question whether every organization needs an enterprise data warehouse. The answer depends on their definition of enterprise. Certainly, a multinational conglomerate with many distinct business units, each with its own products and customers, doesn't need an enterprise data warehouse. Yet each of its divisions—which function as profit/loss centers—certainly do.

Cross-functional Views. The value of enterprise information—no matter what the scope of the enterprise—comes from viewing information across functional boundaries. Most organizations of any size quickly fragment into a variety of departments, such as finance, sales, marketing, research, development, and so on. The people in each department carry out a specific set of related tasks and report to a single department head. After a while, everyone in the department focuses more on departmental requirements than enterprise ones.

These physical and mental silos are why it's so hard to build an enterprise data warehouse and yet why it's so important to do so. Unlike single-subject data marts, enterprise data warehouses encourage deeper levels of analysis. This is because users can now submit queries across functional boundaries, such as finance and operations, and gain new insights not possible when data were confined to departmental subjects.

Ironically, even when a new data warehouse provides access to cross-departmental data, most users never move beyond their mental silos, which are still departmental in scope. BI managers must spend a great deal of time educating users about highly profitable insights that they can obtain by examining the full value chain of information and processes.

Semantic Integration. One of the challenges in building an enterprise data warehouse is getting users in each department to agree on the definitions of commonly used terms, such as *sale*, *customer*, or *return*. For example, the finance department might say that a sale occurs when a customer payment clears the bank, while the sales department says it occurs when the customer submits a purchase order, while the marketing department says it occurs when the customer enters into negotiations to purchase.

Obviously, when calculating "sales," each department will come up with completely different numbers, which drives executives crazy. Getting each department to relinquish its definition is challenging, if not impossible. But standardizing terms and definitions is critical for obtaining a consistent view of enterprise activity. Since gaining consensus is a political, not a technical, issue, the only way it occurs is when the CEO locks the heads of each department in a room and doesn't let them leave until they achieve consensus.

Typically, what happens is that the department heads agree to disagree: They keep their metrics where reasonable but agree to give them distinct names so people aren't comparing apples to oranges. However, if there are 20 definitions of *customer*, department heads need to narrow it down to a handful of definitions. They often also need to identify one definition that will serve as the enterprise metric and know how to translate their local metrics into the global one.

Corporate Volatility. Another equally vexing problem is dealing with the vicissitudes of corporate life. A Greek philosopher once wrote, "The only constant is change." Anyone who has spent five years in an organization knows that just as you or your department starts hitting its stride, something happens and you have to adjust. Mergers, acquisitions, reorganizations, new executives, new competitors, new technologies, or new regulations happen on a disturbingly regular schedule to upend the best-laid plans of any BI or IT department.

Each change causes executives and managers to ask a new set of questions that your data doesn't support. Yet they need the answers immediately since the survival of the organization is at stake—or at least their ability to meet strategic objectives or budget goals. But these questions often require a major rework of the BI infrastructure to answer. The BI team must gather new requirements, revise data models, recode extract, transform, and load (ETL) programs, rewrite reports, and update metadata. None of these things is easy to do and none was designed to be changed on a regular basis.

Adaptable System? How do BI teams create an adaptable system? How do BI teams meet business demands for new solutions in a timely manner? How do they stay ahead of the project backlog? There are no straightforward answers here, but most BI teams are looking for ways to become more nimble and agile.

Slowly, there is emerging a set of best practices that enable the BI team to go as fast as the business wants. BI practitioners are coming up with new ways to gather requirements; developers are embracing agile development methodologies; modelers are abstracting more of logical model to make revisions easier; BI teams are cross-training staffers and creating small, interdisciplinary teams; and vendors are offering a slew of innovative technologies that promise to accelerate time to value while lowering costs, including open source BI products, specialized analytic databases, cloud-based BI implementations, and in-memory analytics, to name a few.

Report Chaos. By the time BI teams reach the Chasm, power users have taken the self-service BI tools and created hundreds if not thousands of reports, most of which are variations on the same theme. With so many reports, casual users can't find the right ones to use and fall back on IT to create their reports for them, which re-creates the report backlog that initiated the BI project to start. In addition, many of the reports embed custom calculations and metrics that don't sync up with other reports. The result of all this activity is report chaos, and it can torpedo the BI program, sending it back to Stage 1.

BI teams need to know the difference between self-service BI and self-serving BI. BI teams love the notion of self-service BI because it seemingly kills two birds with one stone: self-service BI gives users what they want (direct access to data) while eliminating the report project backlog at the same time. But BI teams can't abdicate responsibility for reporting. While self-service BI tools work for a while, they ultimate wreak havoc on the BI program unless the BI team creates standard reports for each department and establishes a governance program for managing ad hoc reports.

Strategic Value. Finally, BI programs stuck in the Chasm still have to fight for every budget dollar while it's getting harder and harder to justify BI on tactical, cost savings. At this point, BI teams need to sell their services based on the strategic value to the organization. This is impossible to do unless the company has enlightened executives (see the earlier discussion on "The Gulf") or the BI team has become indispensable to users. Sometimes the only way to determine the value of the BI system is to turn it off and see what the reaction is. If users scream immediately and loudly, then the data warehouse is delivering significant value.

Of course, I don't recommend disabling the data warehouse, but understanding users' dependency on the BI system is the first step in defending its value and budget dollars. It is hoped that you can also point to one application that generated outsized ROI or was instrumental in holding on to a major client. You need these quick wins and anecdotes to build a positive storyline that becomes associated with the BI brand. It's also important to begin building more value-added applications that the business can't live without. Certainly, a performance dashboard is one of those, as is a balanced scorecard and deep analytics on big data.

Stage 4: Adult

In the Adult stage, an organization overcomes the challenges posed in the Chasm and delivers an enterprise-wide information resource for insights and decision making. It has established standard definitions for commonly used terms and consolidated various divisional data warehouses and independent data marts into a single, integrated architectural environment. It has embraced agile development methodologies and other techniques in all disciplines of BI to become more adaptable to changing business requirements and demands. The BI program is viewed as a strategic asset.

A BI program in the Adult stage exhibits these attributes and characteristics:

- **Strong BI governance.** In the Adult stage, the BI team no longer drives the BI program, the business does. The business decides the direction of the BI program through various governance committees, and the BI team implements their wishes. A steering committee comprised of sponsors from the major business units and departments prioritizes projects, approves the road map, and secures funding. A working committee comprised of power users from each department refines the BI road map, discusses application enhancements, selects products, and addresses problems.
- **BI Center of Excellence.** At the same time, the BI team has formed a BI Center of Excellence. This new moniker simply means that the team has defined and documented best practices for implementing BI solutions. This includes processes and procedures for gathering requirements, managing BI projects (versus transaction processing projects), developing BI software, administering data warehousing systems and processes, selecting new products, and training and supporting users. The BI Center of Excellence also has defined architectural and technology standards that align with the organization's overall IT standards.

  Until now the BI team has developed most of the BI solutions, but now it provides consultative services with fledgling BI groups in the rest of the company. It is viewed as a corporate resource for sharing knowledge and skills—not a body shop—and plays a critical role in ramping up BI expertise throughout the organization.
- **Marketing machine.** A hallmark of an Adult stage program is that it knows how to market itself. To ensure the organization gets full value from its BI investments, the BI team works hard to evangelize the BI solution to executives and users. To win hearts and minds, it creates a marketing plan that tailors messages to each constituency through a variety of channels, including a Web site, a newsletter, and presentations at internal meetings and forums. The team has branded the BI program with a catchy name and has developed posters, advertisements, and other marketing material to increase market awareness.
- **Sales savvy.** An Adult stage program recruits technically savvy business users from each department to serve on its team. These business-oriented people help solidify alignment between business teams and the BI program, serving as strategic advisors to the business

units from which they came. They help the business understand how the BI resource can help them address current issues while gathering new requirements to bring back to the BI team. The people who straddle the worlds of business and IT are known as purple people because they are neither business (blue) or IT (red), but a blend of the two (purple).

- **Performance driven.** The BI team has moved beyond simple dashboards and developed performance management systems that cascade strategy from the executive suite to every employee. Organizations now have a complete set of operational, tactical, and strategic dashboards and top-level objectives, KPIs, and targets that are translated uniquely at every level.
- **Analytics driven.** At the same time, the BI team has helped the organization move beyond simple reports to sophisticated analytics. The BI team has empowered business analysts and statisticians with new tools, specialized databases, and analytical sandboxes so they can explore large volumes of data and create sophisticated predictive models that optimize various departmental processes.
- **Intraday updates.** To support embedded modeling and user demands for fresher data, the BI team has rearchitected the data warehouse to deliver near-real-time data using trickle feed, change data capture, and/or replication technologies. A right-time-enabled data warehouse combined with predictive analytics enables the organization to deliver valuable new customer-facing applications, such as cross-sell engines, fraud detection systems, and targeted marketing campaigns.
- **Master data management.** Finally, the BI team extends its expertise to data in the operational system and helps steer a master data management initiative. The BI team has developed technical and political skills needed to standardize reference data for the data warehouse and understands how standardized operational data can benefit the organization and simplify data warehousing operations.

Stage 5: Sage

Once BI becomes a strategic enterprise resource that drives mission-critical operations, you may think the job is done. But the real challenge and opportunity is just beginning!

Commercial Services. The Sage stage turns the BI resource inside out and makes it available to customers and suppliers. By providing secure access to their account data, the BI team can help customers and suppliers better manage their business operations and work smarter and more efficiently. This improves customer service and loyalty. In some cases, these extranet applications enable customers and suppliers to compare their performance against peers to benchmark their standing in the industry. If the company charges for such access or embeds the cost in a broader service offering, the data warehouse changes from a back-office cost center to a front-office revenue generator.

Application Services. At the same time, a Sage stage BI team embeds BI deeper into the business processes that drive the company, turning BI from a reporting tool into an analytical service that any person or application can tap to obtain information and insights. With such services, users no longer have to shift from an operational application to an analytical application to analyze data. The data, information, and insights they need to do their jobs will be embedded in the core applications they use on a daily basis. For example, customer service representatives can view cross-sell recommendations generated in real time from the data warehouse while working within their customer management software.

Decision Engines. These BI services also make it possible for companies to capitalize fully on their investments in statistical analysis and analytical modeling. They turn statistical models into decision engines embedded in internal and external applications. Workers or applications feed information into these engines and receive recommendations instantaneously. For instance, a fraud detection system reviews your credit card transactions, compares them to a statistical model of your past purchasing behavior, and spits out a score that indicates the degree to which a given purchase may be fraudulent. Other examples of decision engines are Web recommendation engines and automated loan approval applications.

Bottleneck. Although there are great opportunities in the Sage stage, there are significant challenges. Ironically, the biggest challenge is the hardest to see because it is the BI team itself.

As the BI team has grown and assumed more control over the delivery of information, it has become a bottleneck for getting things done. We see the bottleneck, of course, but we think the answer is more staff, faster machines, and better software. We don't see that *we* are the bottleneck and that the only way to reduce or eliminate the project backlog is to do something that is both counterintuitive and terrifying: We must let go. That is, we must empower departments and business units to build their own data warehousing and BI solutions.

This is the Zen of BI: We must embrace the very thing that we have resisted for years. Entrusting departments to build their own analytical systems is a terrifying prospect for most BI veterans. We fear that the departments will create islands of analytical information and undermine data consistency that we have worked so hard to achieve. Rather than let go, we grip the proverbial BI steering wheel tighter and tighter. But asserting control at this stage usually backfires.

Trust in Standards. BI veterans need to heed the advice of Yoda in the movie *Star Wars* who counsels his Jedi warriors in training: "Let go and trust the force." But, in this case, rather than the "force," we must trust the BI standards that we've developed in the BI Center of Excellence, such as standards for ETL scheduling and error management, BI semantics, project planning, and BI tool selection. It's now time to educate the rest of the business about these standards.

BI veterans who have gone down this path add the caveat: "Trust but verify." Educating and training departmental BI staff about proper BI development is critical, but it's also important to create validation routines where possible to ensure they conform to standards.

Fox in the Henhouse. The cagiest BI veterans recognize that the key to making distributed BI development work is to recruit key analysts in each department to serve on a BI working committee. The working committee drives the BI effort on a weekly or monthly basis and reports its recommendations to the BI steering committee. The working committee addresses problems, prioritizes enhancements, selects new tools, helps design subject areas, and creates the road map. This tactic ensures buy-in and compliance from business analysts who are most apt to undermine corporate BI standards and architectural integrity.

Hybrid Approach. With an extended BI Center of Excellence in place, a Sage stage team can then manage a hybrid BI environment in which the corporate BI group manages the data warehouse and conformed dimensions (or BI semantic layer) and allows distributed teams, if they desire, to build and manage their own data marts and reports using the central resources and standard practices. Business units that don't have or want the requisite BI skills in house will continue to rely on the BI Center of Excellence to build local capabilities. In other words, the BI Center of Excellence provides a flexible set of development and support services that business units can exploit as much or as little as they want without undermining the consistency of enterprise information.

Maturity Dynamics

So far, we have examined each stage in the BI Maturity Model as well as the Gulf and the Chasm. Now it's time to step back and examine how key characteristics of a BI program evolve over time.

Autonomy and Control

Exhibit 4.2 depicts the five stages at the top of the table along five other characteristics defined in text: (1) scope, (2) funding, (3) team, (4) sponsorship, and (5) architecture. The two curved lines represent a sixth characteristic: the dynamic interplay between autonomy and control that evolves over the life of a BI program.

Scope. But first, let's quickly review the first five characteristics, most of which should be obvious from our description of the five stages. Ignoring the Prenatal substage for now, the scope of a BI program evolves from an individual (i.e., spreadmarts) to department, business unit, enterprise, and finally interenterprise level, when the organization makes the data warehouse available to customers and suppliers.

Funding and Sponsorship. Funding and sponsorship follow a similar trajectory with a few twists: Funding at the Sage stage comes from direct or indirect revenues generated by the data warehouse; and sponsorship in the last two stages becomes formalized in a BI governance program, described earlier. Team composition evolves from an individual analyst, to a project team, to a BI program, and finally to a BI Center of Excellence in the Adult stage and a hybrid team in the Sage stage, where responsibilities are divided between central and distributed groups.

Autonomy and Control. The straight line represents local control, or the autonomy of departments and business units to create and manage their own information and reporting and analysis environment. The dotted line represents enterprise standards, or the ability of the BI team to set standards governing the definition and management of information. As you can see in Exhibit 4.2, there is a big gap between local control and enterprise standards in the Infant stage. This gap explains why spreadmarts are so prevalent. The mantra of business analysts is "Think local, resist global." They have the upper hand at this stage and create information structures that suit their parochial needs.

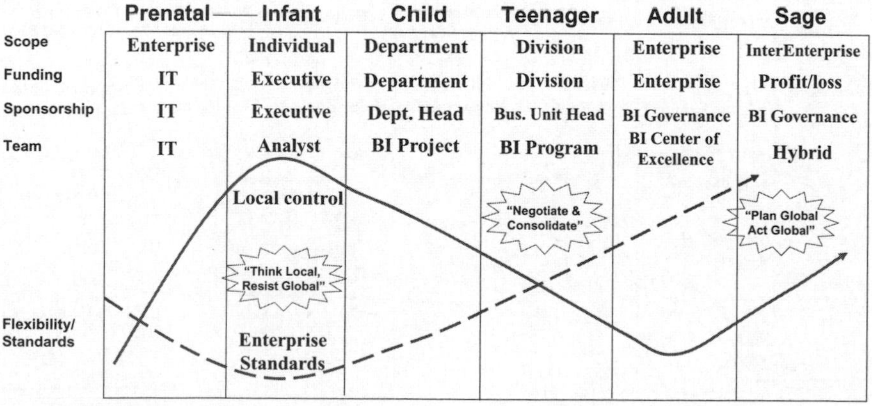

	Prenatal	Infant	Child	Teenager	Adult	Sage
Scope	Enterprise	Individual	Department	Division	Enterprise	InterEnterprise
Funding	IT	Executive	Department	Division	Enterprise	Profit/loss
Sponsorship	IT	Executive	Dept. Head	Bus. Unit Head	BI Governance	BI Governance
Team	IT	Analyst	BI Project	BI Program	BI Center of Excellence	Hybrid

Local control

"Think Local, Resist Global"

"Negotiate & Consolidate"

"Plan Global Act Global"

Flexibility/ Standards

Enterprise Standards

EXHIBIT 4.2 Autonomy versus Control

As a BI program evolves local control ebbs while the ability of the BI team to enforce standards increases to the point where the balance of power shifts in the Teenager stage. Here, the mantra of the two groups (i.e., business and IT) is "Negotiate and consolidate." Unfortunately, in most cases, the dynamics keep moving in the same direction. By the Adult stage, the BI team or BI Center of Excellence has most of the power, and local groups are starting to feel shortchanged as the BI project backlog builds.

Unless the BI team can figure out ways to respond more quickly to the needs of local groups, the line representing "local control" will continue to plummet and local groups will abandon the BI effort altogether and start creating spreadmarts, repeating the cycle all over again. The bottom inflection of this curve represents the chasm and the need for BI teams to embrace agile techniques. It also reflects what BI teams must do in the Sage stage, which is push more development effort back to the business units without sacrificing architectural standards and integrity.

Users and Usage

Exhibit 4.3 depicts three more characteristics in the BI Maturity Model: types of users, types of tools, and applications. In the Prenatal substage, everyone in the company uses largely static operational and management reports, which means they are not tailored to anyone in particular. This creates an IT backlog as users request custom reports. While most casual users glance

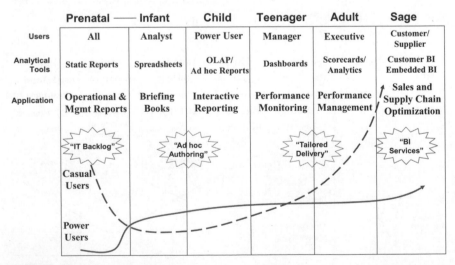

EXHIBIT 4.3 Users and Usage

at them, most power users ignore them entirely, which is why BI usage among power users (straight line) is zero during this stage.

In the Infant substage, analysts armed with spreadsheets and desktop databases conduct custom analyses for executives, creating a briefing book from what they discover. During this substage, almost all power users are engaged in conducting analyses, although none is using standard BI tools. In the Child stage, the company rolls out standard BI tools, which brings on the remaining power users (e.g., mainly technically savvy business users) and some casual users. These early BI adopters largely use reporting and OLAP tools to create ad hoc reports.

In the Teenager stage, organizations roll out dashboards to managers who need to monitor the performance of business processes. Here, usage among casual users starts to climb since dashboards conform to the way they want to consume information. In the Adult stage, companies roll out performance management systems via scorecards and move beyond reporting to analytics. In both stages, BI applications are tailored to individual users and groups and BI becomes pervasive.

Finally, in the Sage stage, the organization offers BI to its customers and suppliers to optimize sales and improve supply chain efficiency and embeds it in core processes. The result is that BI becomes ubiquitous and usage grows exponentially. In this stage, people are using BI without really knowing it.

Business Value and ROI

Exhibit 4.4 depicts three more characteristics of BI maturity: type of system, executive perception, and ROI.

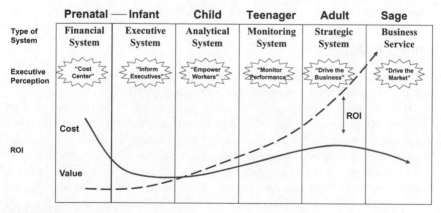

EXHIBIT 4.4 Business Value and ROI

In the Prenatal substage, BI is largely a back-office financial reporting system that is viewed by executives as a necessary cost of doing business, or cost center. Costs are high and perceived value is low, creating a negative ROI. In the Infant substage, BI is largely an executive support system in which individual analysts using spreadsheets prepare custom reports for executives. Here, the cost is low (except for the salaries of the business analysts) and the value from an organizational perspective is low, although each individual executive derives significant value from having his or her own "human data warehouse."

In the Child stage, power users armed with ad hoc reporting tools are empowered to explore data and deliver insights on a departmental basis. Value increases as does cost. In the Teenager stage, BI becomes a monitoring system to improve performance on a departmental level. This generates significant value and adds to costs only incrementally, especially if existing BI tools and data marts and divisional data warehouses are used to build the dashboards.

In the Adult stage, BI becomes strategic to the organization. Executives and managers use dashboards and scorecards to manage core processes, continually improve performance, and monitor progress toward achieving strategic objectives. Analysts apply deep analytics to big data to deliver valuable insights. At this point, BI is a mission-critical resource that drives the business. In the final stage, BI becomes a revenue-generating business service and embedded application service that gives the company a competitive advantage. Overall costs actually start to decline as the data warehouse is fully populated with detailed data from all subject areas. Consequently, ROI grows exponentially.

Exhibit 4.4 is a valuable chart to show to sponsors because it shows that ROI doesn't start accumulating until a BI program reaches its final stages of maturity. The message is that sponsors need to be patient and invest continuously in BI to achieve its full promise.

Insights to Action

Exhibit 4.5 depicts several more characteristics of BI programs, including BI focus, BI output, data capture, and business purpose.

The focus of BI exploration evolves significantly over the life of a BI program. At first, users use monthly static operational or management reports to find out "what happened." Then business analysts use spreadsheet models based on historical data and business assumptions to create scenarios about what can happen based on different variables and market tendencies. When organizations deploy BI tools, users create ad hoc reports or use parameterized reports to explore why things happened or the root cause of various trends or market anomalies.

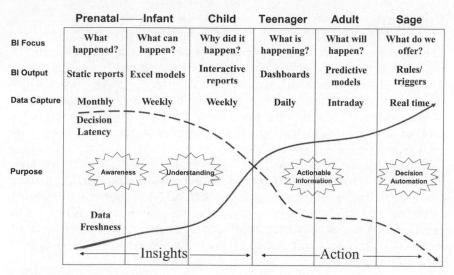

	Prenatal——Infant		Child	Teenager	Adult	Sage
BI Focus	What happened?	What can happen?	Why did it happen?	What is happening?	What will happen?	What do we offer?
BI Output	Static reports	Excel models	Interactive reports	Dashboards	Predictive models	Rules/ triggers
Data Capture	Monthly	Weekly	Weekly	Daily	Intraday	Real time

Decision Latency

| **Purpose** | Awareness | Understanding | | Actionable Information | | Decision Automation |

Data Freshness

← Insights → ← Action →

EXHIBIT 4.5 Insight to Action

In the Teenager stage, we use operational dashboards refreshed daily to find out what is happening right now. In the Adult stage, we use predictive models and intraday data to forecast what will happen by the end of the transaction or end of the day or week. And finally in the Sage stage, we use simple and complex rules and database triggers and other automation engines to make real-time offers to customers and anticipate events before they happen.

Decision Latency and Data Freshness. The dotted line in Exhibit 4.5 refers to decision latency, which is the time between when an event happens and business user needs to decide what to do about it. The straight line refers to data freshness, or how current the data is when it's delivered to business users. In the early stages of a BI maturity, data are fairly old, and there is a big delay between events and decisions. Consequently, the focus of early-stage BI programs is building awareness and understanding of what's happened in the past in order to optimize processes and develop future plans.

Decision latency and data freshness flip-flop dramatically in the Teenager stage, when companies deploy dashboards to monitor current performance. Here, the focus is acting on information to affect outcomes before it's too late. The Sage stage takes this notion to the extreme by automating certain processes using decision engines, as described earlier. The radical inversion of the lines in Exhibit 4.5 underscores the impact that performance dashboards can have on the business in general and the BI program specifically. Here, BI becomes a power agent of organizational change and improvement.

Summary

The BI Maturity Model is a good way to assess an organization's technical readiness to deploy a performance management system. The model shows that performance dashboards typically are deployed in Stage 3 when organizations have implemented BI tools and one or more data marts and are in the process of consolidating them into a divisional data warehouse. This level of infrastructure makes it possible to deploy performance dashboards without a lot of additional investment.

Many people who have heard presentations about the BI Maturity Model say it is therapeutic. They find comfort in knowing that others have encountered the same growing pains they have. Many view the BI Maturity Model as a tool to help them envision the future and the steps needed to get there. They also view it as a perfect way to explain the potential of BI to business sponsors and the investments they need to make to deliver long-term value.

Note

1. Since the first edition was published in 2005, overall BI maturity has advanced. Our latest research shows that the bell curve has shifted to the right. The majority of companies (60 percent) are now in the Teenager stage, on the precipice of adulthood; 29 percent are in the Child stage; and 10 percent in the Adult stage. I still prefer to draw the bell curve as depicted, however, for simplicity.

CHAPTER 5

How to Align Business and IT

Pitched Battles

Lack of Trust

Tension Abounds. There has always been distrust between the business and the technical sides of an organization, but performance dashboard projects seem to heighten the tension to extreme levels. I have been in the technology industry for 20 years, and frankly, I'm shocked by the intensity of the distrust that I have witnessed between these two groups while researching this book.

Although there is much talk about the need to align business and information technology (IT) departments, little progress has been made. Part of the problem is systemic to IT departments and technical people, but another part involves the willingness of business executives and managers to engage with IT constructively on a long-term basis.

A performance dashboard project exacerbates the tension between business and IT because the two groups need to work closely together to deliver an effective solution. Unlike operational systems that are designed once and run for long periods of time without major modification, performance dashboards must continually adapt to the changing needs of the business. Consider this comment from a business manager who spearheads a performance dashboard project:

> We're supposed to submit a project plan to IT that spells out what we are going to do every month and quarter and budget accordingly. But we can't operate that way. We know there will be a reorganization, new processes, and a major acquisition that forces the company to change strategy and move in a different direction. We have a project roadmap, but we have to remain flexible so we can adapt to the business.

In many cases, the pitched battle between business and IT occurs because a business group has developed a performance dashboard outside IT's purview but, due to its own success, can no longer keep up with demand. It needs IT's support and expertise to scale the application and expand it to the rest of the company.

Ceding Control to IT. The business is terrified about ceding control over the design, architecture, and budget of its pet project to a central IT group, which it views as slow, incompetent, and uncompromising. The business cites numerous examples of IT ineptitude to reinforce notions that the IT department will suck the lifeblood out of the project and cause it to die a slow, inexorable death.

Here are a few comments from a business manager who used a small team of developers and rapid development techniques to build a performance dashboard in three months for an operations department.

> *We need things today, not tomorrow, or else we go out of business. That's not how the IT world sees things; their business acumen is not the same and they lack a sense of urgency. For instance, we asked IT for a data extract and they said it would take four months. We couldn't wait that long so we leveraged GUI [graphical user interface]–based technology and in one weekend created a temporary fix that worked well. But when IT finally delivered the extract, it had errors and required rework. Then, after we launched the dashboard, it was so successful that it began consuming more disk space than they anticipated. Rather than working with us to come up with a satisfactory solution, they threatened to randomly delete our data unless we offloaded the data ourselves.*

Shortsighted and Uncooperative. Of course, the IT group sees these types of business managers as spoiled children who are too impatient and shortsighted to wait for IT to lay the necessary foundation to ensure the long-term success of their own system. IT is bitter that the business expects it to deliver an ever-increasing number of high-priority projects in shorter and shorter time frames while dealing with reduced costs, shrinking staff, and the constant threat of outsourcing and offshoring.

One IT director recently lamented:

> *We work hard to meet the needs of our business customers but they are constantly adding and changing requirements, and they do not have the discipline to adhere to their own priorities. This makes it difficult for us to plan and impossible to succeed. It's a no-win situation.*

Stalemate. The result is a tense standoff in which each group fulfills the other's worst predictions of each other. If the business has the upper hand, it will maintain control of the technical aspects of the project, creating another nonintegrated system that will be costly to maintain in the long run. If IT gains control, it will halt development of new end user functionality until it brings the infrastructure into conformance with its architectural standards and nothing of value will get accomplished.

What can be done to slice through this Gordian Knot? What will it take for both sides to enter into a relationship of mutual respect? Like a marriage on the rocks, business and IT need some serious counseling before they can work together effectively. Part of the counseling involves taking a number of baby steps that improve communication and overcome mutual distrust by helping each side better understand the other's challenges and dilemmas.

General Counseling

Counseling for IT. During the past 10 years, IT has come to recognize that its job is not to deliver technology for technology's sake but to provide exquisite service to its customer: the business. Like an alcoholic who publicly admits the problem, this is a step in the right direction. However, this is only the first step. Verbal acknowledgment alone does not translate into remedial action.

To take the next step, IT must translate goodwill into action. The next questions can help an IT team determine whether it is paying lip service to meeting business needs or actually doing it. If the IT department can respond positively to most of the following questions, it is on the right path.

Does the IT team:

- Sit side by side with the businesspeople it serves?
- Read the same trade magazines as its business counterparts?
- Attend the same conferences?
- Go to lunch regularly with business clients?
- Read the company's annual report?
- Read and understand the short- and long-term strategic plans for the company?
- Know the entire business process that drives the application it is developing and maintaining?
- Have an average of 10 years of experience in the company's industry?
- Have degrees in database administration and business administration?

IT Subculture. What better way to align with the business than to eat, sleep, and breathe like a businessperson? Unfortunately, the IT department often functions as a subculture within the organization—it has its own jargon, dress code, and working hours. And as a separate department, it has its own reporting structure, incentives, and career paths that are different from those of the business groups it serves.

In contrast, technical teams embedded in departments or lines of business often enjoy a much healthier relationship with their business counterparts than corporate IT. Why? Rather than exist as a technical subculture, embedded IT staff members sit side by side with the businesspeople and function as a single team, with the same goals, bosses, and incentives.

Counseling for Business. Although IT groups generally get the lion's share of the blame for misalignment between business and IT, it takes two to tango, as they say. The business shares equal responsibility for the tension between the two groups—perhaps more so, since it does not always recognize how its actions and behavior contribute to the problem.

The business needs to understand that it often moves too fast for IT to keep up. It harbors a short-term bias toward action and rarely takes a long-term view toward building sustainable value. This is especially true in U.S. companies, whose Wild West heritage makes them notorious for acting first and asking questions later. Businesses need to slow down sometimes and ask whether change is really needed or if they are reacting in knee-jerk fashion to the latest event or issue of the day. They need to prioritize their needs and evaluate what is required now and what can wait. By working incrementally, the business discovers that it gets what it needs faster than by trying to build a solution all at once.

Decentralized organizations magnify this Wild West behavior, parceling out authority to divisions and departments to make decisions faster and in the context of local markets. Although there are advantages to decentralization, considerable downsides contribute to the perpetual misalignment of the business and IT. The scores of analytical and operational silos, including the hundreds and thousands of pernicious spreadmarts that hamstring corporate productivity, testify to the businesses' fixation on speed and decentralized decision making.

Lack of Self-Discipline. Finally, the business has the upper hand in its relationship with IT, and it often leverages its position in a high-handed and capricious manner. In many organizations, executives threaten to outsource or offshore IT when it does not deliver sufficient value, ignoring the possibility that their own actions and decisions may have crippled IT's ability to function effectively. The business also lacks a reasonable degree of restraint and self-discipline when it comes to IT projects. One IT manager said his company's annual technology planning process is a sham because the business cannot discipline itself to live within its limits. Says the beleaguered IT manager:

Prior to the beginning of every calendar year, the business prioritizes IT projects for the next 12 months. Out of 90 projects, they identify 60 of them as "high priority" and we create a schedule to deliver them. . . . But even before January 1 arrives, the business adds 20 more "high-priority" projects to our list and adds another 20 projects before April. And then they tell us in March that we are already two months behind schedule!

The IT manager said that he had negotiated a new project prioritization process with the business that required it to operate in a zero-sum environment. If projects were added after the budget was finalized, others had to be cut. Although the IT manager was hopeful the new policy would succeed, he also half-jokingly commented that if he tells the business to abide by its new guidelines, he may lose his job.

Alignment Tactics

Although it is not the sole source of the stalemate, the IT department needs to take the first step toward reconciliation. It needs to show that it wants to be an equal partner in the business, not an auxiliary that is more interested in technology than the bottom line. It can do this by becoming more responsive to business needs by improving the way it gathers business requirements, adopting rapid development techniques, and creating and selling a portfolio of analytical applications. To do these things, some organizations are creating an information management (IM) group that sits between the IT department and the business and is responsible for the timely delivery of information-centric applications and resources, such as data warehousing, business intelligence (BI), analytical modeling, spatial and text analysis, master data management, and customer relationship management.

Business Requirements

According to Jill Dyche, a founding partner at Baseline Consulting, business requirements are the most "elegant bridge between IT and the business because each organization shares accountability for communicating and representing an understanding of what the business needs." However, many requirements-gathering sessions lead to less than stellar results. Part of the problem is that business users do not know what they want in a report or dashboard screen until they see it. Just asking what data users want to see invariably leads to the answer "All of it," which helps neither side bridge the gulf.

Some organizations recruit business requirements analysts to interview users and translate their requirements into technical specifications for developers. Other organizations start with open-ended survey questions and then follow up with one-on-one interviews. Other techniques to gather requirements include joint-application design sessions, use-case modeling, process modeling, and application storyboarding, among others. (See Chapter 11 for more specifics on requirements-gathering techniques.)

Incremental Delivery

Once requirements are gathered, the technical team needs to step up and deliver value to the business much faster than it does today. Most IT managers understand that the days of five-year multimillion-dollar projects are over; they know they need to deliver projects much faster with fewer dollars and a guaranteed return on investment.

However, most IT managers have not yet figured out how to deliver value fast without compromising architectural standards that are in the best interests of the company in the long run. Because of the adaptive nature of BI systems, project managers have learned how to develop the architecture and infrastructure incrementally as they go along. (See Exhibit 5.1.)

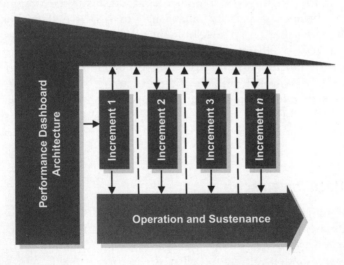

Organizations build the BI architecture and infrastructure incrementally as it adds applications. Each increment, which is typically three months in length, delivers new application functionality while extending the existing architecture and infrastructure.

EXHIBIT 5.1 Incremental Development of BI Architecture

Any IT manager knows that the hardest part about building applications is not what's on the surface that users can see but what lies beneath. Supporting each application is an architecture that consists of data models, data transformation programs, metadata, security mechanisms, administrative utilities, and a computing infrastructure (e.g., hardware and software). Instead of spending months or even years creating this architecture, BI managers create it as they go along, one subject area at a time, usually in three-month increments.

During this three-month period, the technical team:

- Gathers requirements for the new subject area (i.e., customer profitability).
- Extends the data model to support the subject area.
- Identifies what data to use among operational systems and elsewhere.
- Analyzes and maps the data to the target model.
- Documents these mappings or transformations.
- Develops reports and application screens.
- Tests and debugs the application.
- Pilot tests the application with users.
- Launches the application.
- Trains users.

"We roll out our KBI portal in incremental releases, and we treat each release as a production application. It doesn't launch until users sign off on it and we've gone through all the design and testing. This makes sure you have the numbers right," says Jim Rappé, an IT manager at International Truck and Engine Corporation.

However, three months is still too long for most business managers to wait for applications or enhancements. Many business users want instant turnaround. The good news is that technical teams can meet these requirements if the data exist in a usable form. "If users ask for a new metric and the data are already in the data warehouse or an OLAP cube, we can do it in a few days," says Rappé.

Data Federation. If the data is not already in a data warehousing repository and users don't want to wait, in certain situations a technical team can populate dashboard metrics by querying source systems directly using data federation tools. Many commercial dashboard products use this technique to deliver dashboards quickly. The setup is fairly straightforward and primarily involves mapping data in source systems to dashboard metrics. While this approach works well in a pinch, often the tools don't support large volumes of data or numbers of concurrent users and cannot apply complex transformations. (See Chapter 13 for more detailed discussion of data federation and other dashboard architectures.)

Agile Development. On the front end, BI teams are learning to apply agile development techniques to developing dashboards and other BI solutions. Agile development techniques create small, self-organizing cross-functional teams, which include a customer representative, to deliver working features in short iterations of one to two weeks. During each iteration, the team works through the complete software development cycle—planning, analysis, design, coding, and testing—and presents the output for users to review and accept. After each iteration, users can reshuffle their requirements, ensuring that the final solution meets ever-changing business requirements.

Agile development techniques were designed for building transaction processing applications, not BI solutions. While agile works great for building front-end solutions, like dashboards, BI practitioners are adapting the methodology to handle data management tasks, which typically require longer increments and don't deliver a visual output that users can evaluate (or appreciate). Also, testing BI solutions before data infrastructure has been built is challenging.

Most BI programs have embraced agile or rapid development techniques to accelerate the delivery of BI solutions. According to TDWI Research, 29 percent of BI programs are using agile development techniques, 20 percent are using traditional methods (e.g., waterfall development), and 51 percent are using a hybrid of the two.

Portfolio Planning

BI Road Maps. One problem with the incremental development is that business users do not want their application delivered "piecemeal." They want it all at once or not at all. They do not see the usefulness of having a portion of the functionality they want or need and then waiting months or years for the rest. To curb the restless appetite of the business, it is helpful to unveil the bigger picture of where the project is going and how it will get there. You can do this by developing a BI portfolio that shows how IT can deliver a series of related applications built on a common infrastructure over a period of time, such as 18 to 24 months.

Exhibit 5.2 depicts a BI portfolio road map plots proposed applications on a visual timeline so executives can see what the team will deliver in each three-month increment. During phase 1, the team begins work on the "Product Sales Analysis" application, which takes two-and-a-half increments to deliver. During the second increment, they begin work on the "Customer Behavior Analysis" application, which takes two increments. During the third increment, they complete the first two applications. In the fourth increment, they kick off work on "Sales Analysis/Contact Management" application, and so forth.

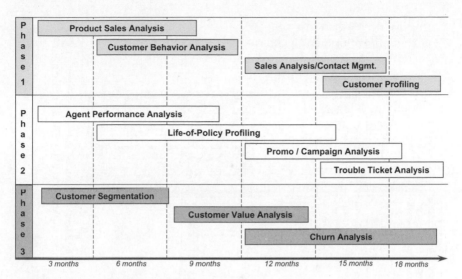

EXHIBIT 5.2 BI Portfolio Road Map
Source: Copyright © 2005, Baseline Consulting. Reprinted with permission.

The road map depicts three phases with the applications developed during each phase by increment. By overlaying all three phases on the same visual timeline, executives can see how they might accelerate development by funding two or three parallel development teams. Otherwise, each phase is handled sequentially and all applications are delivered over the course of three 18-month periods, or 4.5 years. The road map shifts responsibility for rapid development from the BI team to the business. It shields the BI team from accusations that it works too slowly, leaving decisions about speed and cost to the business.

Exhibit 5.3 shows the infrastructure that supports the portfolio of applications in Exhibit 5.2. The data model consists of multiple subject areas, such as customer, product, provider, and contact. Each subject area is populated with data from one or more data sources and merged together in the subject area model. For example, many source systems contain customer data, and each typically models "customer" differently. A subject area in a logical model creates one standard representation of "customer" to which all source data is mapped.

Subject Areas. Each BI application draws data from one or more subject areas. And some subject areas, such as "customer" and "product," are shared by many applications. Once a BI team models one subject area and populates it with data, it can be reused many times. So, rather than starting from scratch each time, a BI team can leverage existing subject areas in a data warehouse to greatly accelerate development. Each new

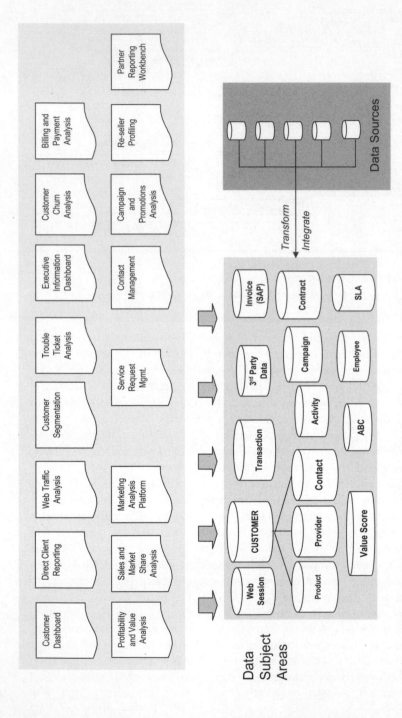

EXHIBIT 5.3 Mapping Applications to Subject Areas

Source: Copyright © 2005, Baseline Consulting. Reprinted with permission.

With a BI infrastructure, there is no longer a one-to-one ratio between applications and data structures. Each new subject area, which is populated with data from various data sources, multiplies the number of new applications that a BI infrastructure can support.

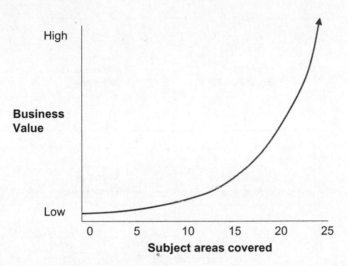

The value of a BI increases exponentially as more subject areas are added. Each new subject area enables the organization to build many new applications on top of integrated data.

EXHIBIT 5.4 Exponential Value of Adding Subject Areas

subject area enables the BI team to build many new applications or at least parts of applications. Thus, the value of a data warehouse expands exponentially as more subject areas are added. (See Exhibit 5.4.)

Standardization Wars

One big stumbling block for the business is the IT department's insistence on adhering to technical standards. Standardization enables the IT group to respond more quickly to user needs because the group can reuse skills, code, and products rather than start from scratch each time. However, IT's zealous adherence to standards drives businesspeople crazy. Says one performance manager:

> *The head of information systems and architecture wants to restructure existing applications to run on a single set of ETL [extraction, transformation, and loading] and BI tools. But one size doesn't fit all, and what's it going to cost to harmonize everything into the new architecture? We spent a half million dollars on our scorecard—it's served hundreds of people for two years and it's stable—but it will cost $2 to $3 million to rebuild the application using the new standards. Meanwhile new work is backed up in the queue so where's the business value?*

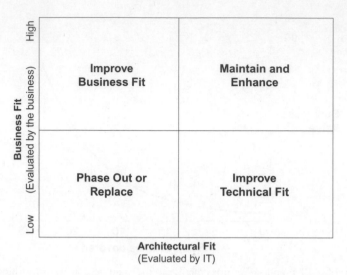

EXHIBIT 5.5 Business-driven Architecture

The quadrant chart above can be used to evaluate existing or potential applications in a company's portfolio. It is an excellent tool to help business and IT begin to communicate their needs and requirements in a more proactive, positive manner.

Business-driven Architecture. An IT manager at a health insurance company developed a strategic plan to foster a more collaborative partnership between corporate IT and the business. One of the more innovative elements in the plan was a way to create a standard application architecture that had buy-in from both the business and IT. The process of creating the standard architecture required both business and IT to evaluate current and proposed business applications, including performance dashboards. The plan calls for the business to evaluate the "business fit" of the applications and the IT department to evaluate the "architectural fit." By plotting the results on a quadrant chart, the teams can begin to view the existing application portfolio and all proposed applications through a common lens. (See Exhibit 5.5.)

Applications in the lower left quadrant are candidates for elimination or consolidation, while applications in the upper right quadrant represent an optimal fit from both a business and technical perspective and should be preserved. Applications in the remaining two quadrants—lower right and upper left—need to be modified, and business and IT leaders need to develop a strategy to bring each into compliance.

The process of evaluating applications in this manner is one way for the business and IT to communicate their requirements to each other and overcome the mutual distrust that has darkened relations for years.

Business–IT Communications

Business Requirements Analysts. Another way to minimize the inherent conflict between business and IT is to use an intermediary to communicate between them. For example, many companies hire business requirements analysts to interview users and translate their requirements into technical specifications for developers.

However, these types of intermediaries have had mixed success. A business sponsor at a large insurance company said his firm hired specialists to "bridge the chasm" between the worlds of business and IT. "The results have been poor," he said. An IT manager was even more vocal: "Business requirements analysts are a big mistake because users never really know what they want when you ask them."

It's important to train business requirements analysts not to ask "What data do you need?" but to ask "What are you trying to accomplish?" By focusing on goals and outcomes, a requirements analyst can elevate the conversation and better understand business needs even if users don't know what data they need to conduct their jobs. Requirements analysts should also take the time to understand the business processes that the person manages and how information can help optimize those processes. They should also find out the person's incentive plan because that will indicate what he or she cares most deeply about doing.

BI Governance Committees. Most companies use steering committees to align business and IT and govern enterprise IT initiatives, including performance dashboards. Most companies have both a steering committee and a working committee. (See Chapter 4 for a description of BI governance committees.)

Some companies have multiple layers of committees to guide an enterprise-scale project. A major insurance company, for example, has these committees guide its enterprise data warehousing and BI effort:

- **Data Warehousing Advocacy Team.** Represents the executive steering committee, which sets the strategic direction for the data warehouse. Serves as a liaison to the Business Advisory Team.
- **Business Advisory Team.** Owns the data warehousing strategy and prioritizes projects. Is comprised of business representatives from all functional areas and meets every three weeks.
- **Data Governance Team.** Defines definitions and rules for data elements and enforces policies about data ownership, changes to data, and user training. Is comprised of 20 end users representing every functional area.
- **BI Solutions Team.** The technical team that translates the decisions of the Business Advisory and Data Governance team into the system. Trains users.

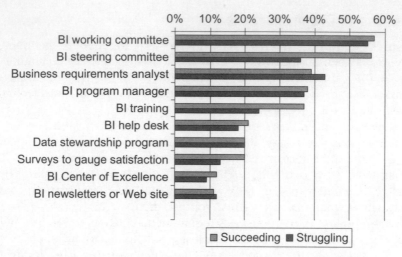

Companies use a variety of strategies to align business and IT and keep BI projects on track.

EXHIBIT 5.6 Alignment Strategies
Source: Wayne Eckerson, "Smart Companies in the 21st Century: The Secrets of Creating Successful Business Intelligence Solutions," *TDWI Report Series*, 2003.

TDWI Research shows that companies with successful BI solutions are more likely to employ BI working and steering committees than other alignment strategies. (See Exhibit 5.6.)

Information Management Groups. One of the best ways to align business and IT is to create a separate business unit that sits between the two groups and is charged with meeting business requirements in a timely fashion. These groups go by many names—Information Center, Information Management, or BI Center of Excellence—and are still a relatively new phenomenon. (Most BI teams are still embedded in the IT department or finance department.) Those who run such organizations feel they deliver significant value. (See Spotlight 5.1.)

Spotlight 5.1 Information Management at Absa Bank

Absa Bank Ltd. in South Africa, now a division of Barclays Bank, established an information management (IM) group in 2001, originally spinning components out of IT and marketing (i.e., customer information management) so it could focus on managing customer information, which corporate executives deemed "essential to the future success of the organization," according to Dave Donkin, group executive of IM at the time. Today, the IM group's charter is to (1) allow information- and knowledge-based strategy formulation and decision making, and (2) leverage information to improve business performance.

Absa's IM group is a shared service unit that sits between corporate IT and the strategic business units. Corporate IT is responsible for operating the bank's 400-plus operational applications, hardware, servers, and databases, and establishing its technology and applications architecture. The IM Group is responsible for all business-facing, information-centric capabilities: data warehousing, business intelligence, reporting, data mining, geographic information systems, data governance, and end user tools. The IM Group also develops the bank's information strategy that defines how the bank stores and manipulates information in a cost-efficient and effective manner.

Although this division of responsibility seems clear-cut—corporate IT handles operational systems and IM manages analytical systems—there are many areas in which the two groups need to work closely together, such as defining the overall enterprise architecture for the bank. Also, whereas the IM Group designs the data warehouse and analytical systems, corporate IT manages data warehousing operations (including extracting data from source systems) and builds and maintains the systems that run the IM Group's analytical applications.

When the IM group was formed four years ago, Absa's data warehouse was "suboptimized: not customer centric, operationally unstable, and not business directed," according to Donkin. Today, Absa's 20-plus-terabyte data warehouse is more stable (99 percent uptime) and more responsive to changing business needs. Also, it offers a slew of relevant business applications, such as scorecards, fraud detection, risk management, and customer analytics, which drive cross-sell, up-sell, retention, customer segmentation, and lifetime value scores.

One way that the IM Group stays in touch with the information requirements of the business units is to assign a "business development manager" to each unit. These business development managers, who are business managers with substantial information and technology experience, meet regularly with their counterparts in the business units to discuss ways the units can better leverage information to meet their strategic objectives and address business problems.

The business development managers have been so effective in delivering value back to the business units that the IM Group has added eight business development representatives in the past two years. "The best part is that the business units are so eager to get business development managers that some of them have transferred staff over to the IM division to enable establishment of the role," says Donkin.

Deutsche Börse. For example, Deutsche Börse, one of the leading international stock exchange organizations, established the Information Center, a technical group that is charged with turning data into information products requested by the business. To make this happen, the Information Center is responsible for data warehousing, ETL, data marts, reporting and analysis tools, data quality, job scheduling, and metadata management. The group is supported by corporate IT, which provides server support, database administration, and custom programming using Java, C, and other languages for components not available as commercial tools. This division of responsibility enables IT to focus solely on managing technology instead of trying to empower the business with information, which is not its strong suit, according to Dr. Klaus Detemple, director of information operations at the stock exchange.

Information management groups take the pressure off the IT department from having to play a role it is not comfortable playing. The information management group enables technologists to focus on technology instead of the business. It gives them a separate career track and an organizational structure designed to maximize their capabilities. It is a win-win situation for both the business and IT.

Purple People. A key to the success of IM groups is having individuals who combine a knowledge of the business and IT and are equally comfortable operating in either environment. Although rare today, these types of individuals are the future of IT. They know how to communicate with the business because they come from the business, but they also have a strong technical background or experience managing IT projects. I call these people purple people because they are a perfect blend of business (blue) and IT (red).

BI requires "purple people" to succeed because BI is not like most IT disciplines; it requires a thorough and ongoing understanding of business issues, processes, tactics, and strategy to succeed. BI is about delivering information that answers business questions. And since those questions change from day to day and week to week and are often shaped by the larger market landscape, BI solutions can't succeed unless they continuously adapt.

The only way to create "adaptable systems"—intrinsically a contradiction in terms—is to find people who are comfortable straddling the worlds of business and technology. These "purple people" can speak the language of business and translate that into terms that IT people can understand. Conversely, they can help businesspeople understand how to exploit the organization's information repository and analytical tools to solve pressing business problems. Purple people are key intermediaries who can reconcile business and IT and forge a strong and lasting partnership that delivers real value to the organization.

Summary

For years, business and IT have been locked in a battle of mutual antagonism: The business doesn't trust the IT department to place its interests above technical requirements, and the IT department doesn't trust the business to stick to its priorities and provide adequate resources to meet technical requirements.

This cold war can begin to thaw if both sides take steps to understand each other's predicament and find new ways of working together. The IT department must learn the business and to think and talk in business terms. It also needs to develop infrastructure incrementally and create a BI portfolio that shows the business how it will generate valuable analytical applications over an extended period. It needs to establish an IM group that sits between IT and the business and uses purple people who combine both business and technical expertise to establish harmonious relations between the two groups.

At the same time, the business needs to understand that Rome was not built in a day. It needs to give IT time to develop a standard infrastructure that, once built, can accelerate development while reducing costs. And, while business units may be tempted to build their own applications, they need to work with IT to transfer these early successes into valuable enterprise resources built on a common technology platform.

The good news is that during the past decade, both sides have acknowledged the problem and seem earnest to address the issues that divide them. While this is a good first step, there is still much work to do to align business and IT.

Performance Dashboards in Action

Part II provides examples of performance dashboards that various organizations have deployed. Chapter 6 describes in detail the similarities and differences among three types of performance dashboards: operational, tactical, and strategic. Chapter 7 shows examples of operational dashboards from 1-800 CONTACTS and the City of Richmond Police Department. Chapter 8 describes tactical dashboards from Rohm and Haas and from Arizona State University; and Chapter 9 describes strategic dashboards deployed by Cisco and Bahrain's Ministry.

CHAPTER 6

Types of Performance Dashboards

Overview

Three Types

When you examine performance dashboards in organizations today, you find a bewildering array of displays and functionality used for an endless variety of purposes. There does not seem to be a common thread among the systems.

But after a while, your eyes focus, and you start to recognize common patterns and features, and slowly these patterns fuse into a general classification that brings order to the chaos. At least that was my experience. While not perfect, the framework I've devised provides a reasonable model to explain the similarities and differences among performance dashboards and, most important, to help organizations articulate the type of performance management system that best suits their needs.

In Chapter 1, I laid out three types of performance dashboards:

1. **Operational dashboards** monitor operational processes, events, and activities as they occur (every minute, hour, or day).
2. **Tactical dashboards** measure and analyze the performance of departmental activities, processes, and goals.
3. **Strategic dashboards** track progress toward achieving strategic objectives in a top-down fashion (e.g., a "Balanced Scorecard").

All Together Now. Interestingly, these dashboard options aren't exclusive: A majority of organizations have all three. In fact, as we'll see, the three dashboards are complementary: Each serves a unique purpose, and no organization is truly effective without all three.

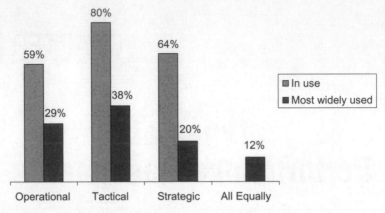

EXHIBIT 6.1 Dashboard Usage

My research shows that 59 percent of organizations have operational dashboards, 80 percent have tactical dashboards, and 64 percent have strategic dashboards. Thus, almost two-thirds have all three types of dashboards with tactical dashboards being the most popular, followed by strategic dashboards in second and operational dashboards not far behind. (See Exhibit 6.1.)

The results are much the same when survey respondents were asked to identify the type of dashboard that is *most widely used* in their organization. Tactical dashboards still dominate with 38 percent of respondents, but operational dashboards (29 percent) surge past strategic dashboards (20 percent) to grab second place. A small percentage of organizations say they use all three dashboards equally (12 percent). Thus, although strategic dashboards are pervasive, they aren't used as intensively as the other two types.

One key reason that tactical dashboards are more common and widely used than the other two is that they support departmental initiatives, which is the primary channel through which most new information technology (IT) applications are deployed in organizations. Also, there are many more mid-level managers in organizations than either executives or operational staff, who are the primary users of the other two types of dashboards, respectively.

Also, strategic dashboards often run into political issues that bog down projects, especially when they are deployed top down on an enterprise, as many are. In addition, many strategic dashboards never make the transition from Excel or PowerPoint to a more robust data infrastructure that is needed to deliver clean, timely, integrated data on an ongoing basis with minimal manual effort.

Users. Exhibit 6.2 maps types of users to types of dashboards. Executives primarily use strategic dashboards, although they view tactical dashboards (and sometimes operational ones) to better understand what is happening in the trenches. Mid-level managers primarily use tactical dashboards to monitor departmental processes, but they also use both strategic and operational dashboards when they need to manage "up" or "down" the organizational hierarchy. Workers primarily use operational dashboards to monitor key processes, and they check tactical dashboards when they need to view departmental data.

Metrics. Exhibit 6.3 shows that all three types of dashboards have about the same number of top-level metrics, total metrics, and users. On average, strategic dashboards display 14 metrics on the opening screen compared to 12 on tactical dashboards and 11 on operational dashboards. Strategic dashboards also have more total metrics (183) than either operational (141) or tactical dashboards (110). But, despite the higher number of metrics, strategic dashboards have fewer average users (180) than tactical (236) or operational (230) dashboards.

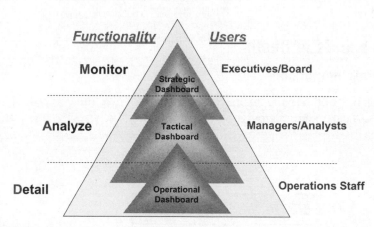

EXHIBIT 6.2 Mapping Users to Dashboards

EXHIBIT 6.3 Dashboards at a Glance

	Operational	Tactical	Strategic
Number of top-level metrics	11	12	14
Total number of metrics	141	110	183
Total number users	230	236	180

Build, Buy, Extend. There are three primary ways to deploy a performance dashboard:

1. You can build them from scratch using programmers and development frameworks, such as .NET and Java or office products, such as Excel or PowerPoint.
2. You can buy a dashboard product that you deploy with minor configuration.
3. You can buy a dashboard product and customize it with code to create new functionality, don a new look and feel, or integrate it with applications or portals in your environment.

My research shows that about half of organizations build dashboards from scratch using programmers, one-third buy a software package without modification, and about one-quarter customize the package with custom code. (See Exhibit 6.4.) Five years ago, when I wrote the first edition to this book, nearly all dashboards were custom built; obviously, vendor dashboard products have improved. In another five years, I expect the majority of organizations to buy or buy and extend dashboard products.

Dashboards in Depth

General Comparison

Exhibit 6.5 outlines the main characteristics of the three types of dashboards. A clear pattern emerges when examining the types by their purpose,

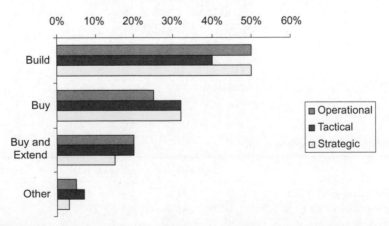

EXHIBIT 6.4 Did You Build, Buy, or Extend Your Dashboard Solution?

EXHIBIT 6.5 Main Characteristics of Performance Dashboards.

	Operational	Tactical	Strategic
Purpose	Control operations	Optimize processes	Manage strategy
Scope	Operational	Departmental	Enterprise
Users	Staff+	Managers+	Executives+
Primary activity	Act	Analyze	Review
Focus	Current	Past	Future
Data refresh	Daily/Intraday	Daily/Weekly	Monthly/Quarterly
Information	Detailed	Detailed/Summary	Summary
Architecture	Core systems	Data warehouse	Excel or data mart
Metrics	Drivers	Drivers/Outcomes	Outcomes
"Looks like a ..."	Dashboard	Metrics Portal	Scorecard

scope, function, and graphical interface as well as the types of users, metrics, data, and sources they support.

As mentioned, operational dashboards are used primarily by front-line staff to control operations using the most current data possible; tactical dashboards are used primarily by managers to optimize departmental processes using detailed historical data; and strategic dashboards are used primarily by top executives to manage strategy using summarized historical data drawn from a variety of sources as well as manually captured data.

Architecturally, operational dashboards often run directly against source systems, while tactical dashboards are built using a traditional business intelligence and data warehousing environment. Strategic dashboards, however, often use Excel to both store and display data, although more advanced deployments are supported by relational data marts.

In terms of appearance, operational dashboards tend to look more like automobile dashboards with alerts, dials, and gauges that are continuously updated and whose metrics are forward indicators (i.e., drivers) of behavior or activity, while strategic dashboards tend to look more like school report cards that track a student's performance each term. Tactical dashboards fall somewhere in the fuzzy expanse between the two: They tend to look like customizable portals that enable departmental users to track a multiplicity of processes and data in one place.

Conceptually, while operational and tactical dashboards monitor performance of business processes, strategic dashboards monitor progress toward achieving strategy. Operational and tactical dashboards alert users when a process exceeds a specified threshold of performance, whereas strategic dashboards monitor whether requisite actions to improve new or existing processes have been taken and are working as theorized. In short, operational and tactical dashboards measure processes, while strategic dashboards measure process improvement aligned with strategy.

Of course, there are no hard-and-fast rules. Every organization operates in a unique way. The key is to understand the characteristics of the three types of dashboards and create a solution that best fits the needs of your organization. For example, you may decide to add a strong analytical element to your operational dashboard, just as the Richmond Police Department did. (See Chapter 7.) Or you may want to create an enterprise view for executives within your tactical dashboard, just as Rohm and Haas did. (See Chapter 8.) And you may want to update your strategic dashboards daily instead of monthly or quarterly, using it as much as a dashboard as a strategic management tool.

Ultimately, the distinction between types of dashboards is flexible. Use this framework as a general guide to help you understand the contours of performance dashboards in action.

Spotlight 6.1 What Is Considered Enterprise?

I've used the terms *departmental* and *enterprise* to describe the scope of tactical and strategic dashboards respectively. But these terms are not always clear.

The term *department* is fairly straightforward, referring to functional units—such as sales, marketing, service, and procurement—that manage a set of related processes, people, and tasks. However, the scale of a department varies widely—a sales department could be local, regional, national, or global.

In contrast, the term *enterprise* could refer to any number of organizational structures: a global sales department; a business unit or subsidiary with its own profit/loss responsibility; multiple related business units with shared customers; or the entire global organization. An organization could justifiably classify a dashboard or data warehouse that supports each of these entities as an enterprise system.

For the purposes of this book, *enterprise* means a business entity with profit/loss responsibility and self-contained functional departments that support its mission and operations. In this definition, strategy and metrics roll down from the executive level to departments and data rolls up.

Operational Dashboards

Overview. Operational dashboards are used to control operational activity and make sure processes stay within prescribed limits for productivity, quality, and efficiency. Typically, front-line personnel use operational dashboards to monitor business events as they occur (every minute, hour, or day) by examining transaction data from core systems and acting immediately to address exception conditions. The focus of operational dashboards is to display what is happening now.

For example, store managers need to monitor inventory to avoid stock outs; dispatchers need to monitor the location, destination, and cargo of trucks to optimize carrying capacity and profits; plant supervisors need to monitor manufacturing quality and yields to meet shipment schedules and quality requirements; and call center managers need to monitor call volumes, call lengths, customer wait times, and resolution outcomes to ensure there are enough agents with the right skills to meet call demand.

Subtypes. There are two major subtypes of operational dashboards: *detect-and-respond* dashboards and *incent-and-motivate* dashboards. Each fulfills different purposes. (See Spotlight 6.2.)

Staff. The primary users of operational dashboards are operations workers. However, I've seen many top executives who want to check key operational activity every few hours. These hands-on executives want to keep their fingers on the pulse of the company and don't like surprises. In the next chapter, we'll see how 1-800 CONTACTS built a sales dashboard for top executives that is updated every 15 minutes.

Action Oriented. Operational dashboards are more action oriented than the other two types of performance dashboards. They enable workers to address issues before they escalate into serious problems or exploit opportunities before they evaporate. Thus, it's imperative that operational dashboards deliver timely information in a form that is easy to understand.

But sometimes "real-time" information doesn't arrive fast enough. Consequently, many operational dashboards apply statistical models to forecast future activity. For example, the Richmond Police Department (Chapter 7) updates crime statistics continuously and predictive models every four hours to anticipate where violent crime might intensify during the next shift so duty sergeants can position patrols in the right neighborhoods. And 1-800 CONTACTS forecasts closing sales every 15 minutes so executives and managers can take actions to achieve sales targets for the day.

Alerts. Operational dashboards also make heavy use of alerts to notify users about exception conditions as they happen. For instance, an alert might notify a dispatcher that a truck is leaving later than scheduled or

Spotlight 6.2 Subtypes of Operational Dashboards

A *detect-and-respond* dashboard dedicates staff to monitor an activity either to optimize a process or avert problems. Most detect and respond dashboards optimize a business process, such as call center, logistics operations, or Web site traffic. Others are designed to avert problems or minimize risk, such as those that monitor real-time activity on highways, computer networks, trading systems, rail lines, pipelines, computer systems, and point-of-sale terminals (i.e., fraud detection). Many of these are built using a complex event processing architecture and and are refreshed in near real time. These are used in a war room environment where large-screens display real-time activity in a simulated display (e.g., trains moving along a track.)

In contrast, *incent-and-motivate* dashboards are designed primarily to increase employee productivity by displaying individual and team performance against goals. These dashboards are either displayed on large monitors in a call center or on an individual's desk. Most are refreshed every 15 minutes or every hour. They often display the top 10 performers across various categories, engendering friendly competition among individuals 'and teams. Employees use the dashboards to check how their performance translates into merit pay, and managers use them to identify workers who need extra coaching to achieve sales goals.

send an e-mail message to a store manager when inventory for a particular product has dropped below target. Alerts can show up on a dashboard via an icon next to the relevant metric or be sent directly to one or more people via e-mail, mobile phone, or pager. The alert should contain a high-level summary of the condition and a link to view details.

Some alerts go a step further and automate actions based on complex rules applied to multiple variables. For instance, an alert might detect that the number of inbound service calls for three of the past four hours has increased by 20 percent over expected levels while the number of orders increased only an average of 5 percent during the same time. In this situation, it appears that excessive call volume is bogging down order processing. The rules engine triggers an intelligent alert that identifies the proper person to notify and sends an automated message with a recommendation to add customer service representatives.

These types of intelligent alerts are typical of complex event processing (CEP) systems, which are an emerging class of performance management system used to support *detect-and-respond* types of operational dashboards. (See Chapter 11 for a description of CEP systems.)

Metrics. Most operational dashboards measure the output of low-level processes, such as shop floor machines, Web or network traffic, sales transactions, or call center activity. Although most of these metrics may have only operational significance, some have broader implications and may contain "driver" metrics that directly influence "outcome" metrics displayed in higher-level dashboards.

For example, Cisco (profiled in Chapter 9) has identified numerous functional metrics, such as mean time between failure in the manufacturing department, which directly correlate with, or "drive," customer experience and satisfaction measures that, in turn, drive customer loyalty and revenues. Thus, Cisco draws a statistical line between low-level functional metrics captured in an operational dashboard and the health of the company as measured by customer satisfaction, loyalty, and revenues.

Information. Operational dashboards contain detailed or lightly summarized data that is pulled either directly from operational systems or from a data warehouse or data mart populated with current data. Some operational dashboards display only one level of data, while others provide several levels of drill down, sometimes into a core operational system or device. For example, at Arizona State University, admissions officers and college deans can drill from a geographic view of admitted students to a student's record in a PeopleSoft human resources application within a few clicks.

Dashboards that query operational systems always contain the most current data. Data warehouses and data marts can also contain current data if they are architected to support near-real-time updates. Typically, this is done by loading data into a data warehouse using change data capture techniques that update data that has changed since the last update. For example, most call center dashboards refresh every 15 minutes, coinciding with the update interval of the underlying data mart.

But data warehouses can also be updated by "trickle feeding" transactions from the source system using either a data replication utility or messaging backbone that streams events to the dashboard. Many organizations are now moving to capture and analyze operational information in "right time" to respond faster to changing market conditions and opportunities as well as improve data throughput as nightly processing windows shrink. (See Spotlight 6.3.)

Dashboard Refresh Rates. Dashboards can refresh at the same or different rate as their source system(s), whether a data warehouse or core operational system. Some operational dashboards "twinkle," that is, their displays are dynamically refreshed as events occur. Here, the dashboard display is programmatically linked to the source system so updates in the

---

Spotlight 6.3 From Real Time to Right Time

Businesspeople use the term *real time* to mean something that happens quickly. But how fast is real time to them: Is it a second? A minute? An hour? In the end, the definition of real time varies from person to person. For example, airline executives interpret real time as anything that happens within 14 minutes. That's because the airline industry defines "on time" as 14 minutes or less from an aircraft's scheduled arrival or departure time.

Right Time. Perhaps a better term to describe the timely delivery of information to decision makers is *right time*. Ultimately, business executives don't care about the degree of latency in a performance management system. They simply want the system to deliver the right information to the right people at the right time so they can make optimal business decisions. *Right time* puts the emphasis on the business value of information, not its latency.

---

source are automatically displayed in the dashboard. Most dashboards, however, are refreshed periodically. Most require users to hit a "refresh" button or reopen the dashboard display to get the latest information. Some dashboards poll (i.e., query) the source system on a regular interval.

Data Quality. Interestingly, the near-real-time nature of most operational dashboards actually improves data quality. The dashboards expose source data with all its warts and defects, which doesn't usually happen in a traditional data warehousing environment because administrators fix data errors before users see them. But when top executives see errors in an operational dashboard and the data are important to them, they often issue directives to fix the problem, usually at the source system where most problems originate since that is the least expensive approach in the long run.

Tactical Dashboards

Overview. Although tactical dashboards are the most pervasive of the three types of dashboards, they are the least well understood. Tactical dashboards are used primarily to optimize business processes in each department, such as finance, sales, marketing, and human resources, although some tactical dashboards may provide an enterprise view as well. Managers use tactical dashboards primarily to analyze performance against goals using a combination of detailed and summary data. A distinguishing feature of tactical dashboards is that they run against a data warehouse, data mart, or BI reporting server and rely on standard reporting and analysis tools to display data.

The top level of a tactical dashboard typically displays a dozen or so key performance indicators (KPIs) and provides links to other tactical dashboards and reports. Tactical dashboards often look like a metrics portal or mashup, consisting of a panel display of analytical and functional charts and tables. In general, the focus of tactical dashboards is to display what happened in the past and help users explore how to improve it.

Portal Based. Many tactical dashboards are embedded within a corporate portal, whose access controls ensure that individuals see only those dashboards that are pertinent to their jobs. (And access controls within the dashboard ensure that users see only the dashboard data they have permission to see.) A portal's single sign-on services mean users don't have to log into a separate dashboard tool to view data and its collaboration and personalization capabilities enhance the dashboard experience.

BI Platform. Most tactical dashboards leverage a BI platform—an integrated set of reporting and analysis modules—to generate the metrics, charts, and encodings in a tactical dashboard. Some BI platforms rely more on reporting capabilities to generate dashboards, while others rely on online analytical processing (OLAP) or portal capabilities, and some have developed dashboard specific capabilities. As a result, tactical dashboards assume many shapes and forms. The best BI platforms offer dashboard-specific functionality that leverages reporting, OLAP, and portal elements to deliver a seamless navigation experience through all layers of the monitor, analyze, and drill to detail (MAD) framework.

Types. There are three types of tactical dashboards: *enterprise dashboards, mashboards*, and *analytical dashboards*. (See Spotlight 6.4.)

Analysis. A major emphasis of tactical dashboards is analysis. This doesn't mean that they don't support monitoring or reporting but, comparatively, there is more analysis conducted in tactical dashboards than the other two types. Most of the analysis is based on time series or categorical comparisons with various options to drill up and down hierarchies and across dimensions and attributes.

For example, Arizona State University (profiled in Chapter 8) has a research dashboard that displays trends in proposals, grants, and expenditures for the previous month, 12 months, 36 months, and fiscal year to date using a variety of charts and tables. The operations department at BNSF Railway uses heat maps and geographic maps to compare the performance of dozens of operating groups using 45 metrics and various yardsticks.

In most tactical dashboards, the analysis layer is comprised of an OLAP client running against an OLAP server (i.e., multidimensional database) or

Spotlight 6.4 Three Types of Tactical Dashboards

An *enterprise dashboard* provides line-of-sight visibility into the performance of all business units, departments, and groups. (For an example, read the profile of Rohm and Haas in Chapter 8.) An enterprise dashboard is built on an integrated BI platform and enterprise data warehouse that support a range of integrated dashboards, starting with an executive dashboard at the top and multiple departmental dashboards below. Users see only the dashboards and metrics they have permission to view. The dashboards use stoplights to encode performance against goals—typically budget, prior period, and forecast—and let users view detailed data in the form of charts, tables, reports, and lists. Users can generally filter, sort, and calculate data and navigate to related views by drilling or clicking on the dashboard objects or controls (e.g., tabs, radio buttons, checkboxes).

A *mashboard* is a personal or workgroup dashboard that serves as a container for charts and tables derived from existing reports as well

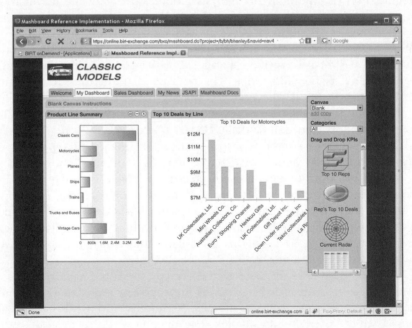

A mashboard enables users to drag and drop predefined reports, report parts, and external URLs onto a dashboard canvass to create custom dashboards.

EXHIBIT 6.6 Mashboard

Source: Copyright © 2010, Actuate Corporation. Reprinted with permission.

as external Web pages accessible via a URL. A mashboard is the dashboard equivalent of an ad hoc report: It enables power users to quickly "mash" together existing report elements and Web pages within a dashboard framework. Mashboards don't require a data warehouse or data mart, just a BI tool that can source data from anywhere via reports. Power users then select report parts and drag and drop them onto a dashboard canvas using a desktop publishing paradigm. (See Exhibit 6.6.) Each mashboard object can pull data from a different source and be updated at different intervals. The objects can query a BI server cache or a remote database via the report definition stored on the BI server. (See Chapter 13 for a description of the mashboard architecture.)

An _analytical dashboard_ is designed for business analysts (e.g., financial, marketing, and sales analysts) who need to explore data sets to identify trends and anomalies and deliver recommendations. These dashboards expose rich navigational features that let users explore data at the speed of thought and usually incorporate some form of statistical or predictive analytics. OLAP-based dashboards let users navigate dimensional hierarchies with ease and support dimensional calculations not possible with standard SQL, while visual analysis tools enable analysts to interact with data visually, making it easy to spot trends and outliers. (See "Visual Analysis" section.)

star schema data mart. This enables users to slice-and-dice data dimensionally to examine relationships, trends, and exceptions. But the analysis layer can also consist of parameterized reports that let users filter a predefined data set by selecting variables from a pick list.

Visual Analysis. Increasingly, analysis is being done with visual analysis tools that enable analysts to visually interact with charts and tables at the speed of thought and quickly spot outliers. The tools compress and store data in memory, providing subsecond response times for any action taken against the data (e.g., filtering, drilling, calculating, sorting, and ranking). Visually, analysts point and click to interact with charts, apply filters, and change views. For instance, analysts can use their mouse to lasso data points in a scatter plot to create a new group. This action also automatically filters other charts on the page so users can quickly ascertain the characteristics of the new group. (See Exhibit 6.7.)

Compared to OLAP tools, visual analysis tools don't require an IT person to design a dimensional data model. The tools use a load-and-go approach in which analysts load raw data from multiple sources and simply link tables along common keys to get a unified view of the data set. As a

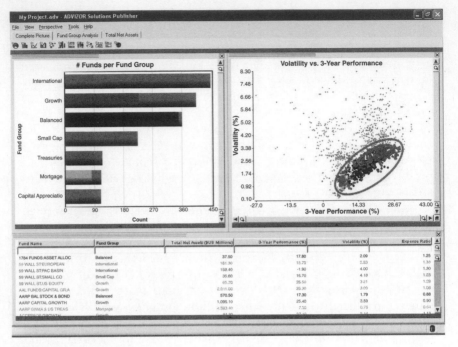

EXHIBIT 6.7 Visual Analysis

Source: Copyright © 2010, ADVIZOR Solutions. Reprinted with permission.

result, most visual analysis tools can be deployed in a few hours or days, depending on the complexity and cleanliness of source data.

Analysts or developers often use visual analysis tools to create and publish interactive, departmental dashboards for casual users. They often create the dashboards on desktop machines and then publish them to a departmental server for general consumption. When doing so, the developers generally strip out some analytical functionality and options that might overwhelm casual users.

Data. The data in tactical dashboards usually come from an enterprise data warehouse, which stores data dimensionally and at a detailed, granular level. Data warehouses typically store five to seven years of detailed data, enabling tactical dashboards to display extensive time-series data. The analytical layer in tactical dashboards can store data in multidimensional databases, which generally preaggregate data in a dimensional format to speed queries and analytical calculations.

Tactical dashboards are typically refreshed daily or weekly, although certain data elements may be updated more frequently based on user requirements. Dashboards query the data in response to user requests so dashboards always display the most current data that exists in the data warehouse.

Metrics. Tactical dashboards contain a mix of driver and outcome metrics, which befits their position sandwiched between strategic and operational dashboards. The outcome metrics represent departmental goals and objectives, while the driver metrics often represent operational metrics in subordinate dashboards.

Strategic Dashboards

Strategic dashboards typically are deployed in a top-down fashion to manage the execution of strategy on an enterprise scale. Executives use strategic dashboards to review progress toward achieving strategic objectives in monthly or quarterly review meetings with business unit and departmental managers. The scorecards generally contain summary-level data updated monthly or quarterly from operational systems or individuals who compile data in spreadsheets. They also enable users to add comments to metrics, such as explaining why a target has not been met and action steps to remedy the situation. The focus of strategic dashboards is the future (i.e., strategic objectives and goals) and how to achieve it.

Strategy. Another name for a strategic dashboard is a scorecard. Scorecards enable executives to manage strategy more effectively. Strategy defines the direction a company wants to go and how it plans to get there. Strategy is embodied in an organization's mission, vision, and values and then explicitly defined in a series of annual objectives with associated metrics and targets.

Traditionally, executives spend a few days or weeks every year crafting and documenting the organization's strategy. Then they pass it over the wall to employees and expect them to implement it. Typically, nothing much happens: The strategy gathers dust on a bookshelf, and business continues as usual. A scorecard, which is a manifestation of a strategic management system, changes this. It gives executives and managers a vehicle to communicate strategy to employees and measure their progress toward achieving strategic objectives on a monthly basis. And as strategy changes in response to new circumstances, whether internal or external, strategic dashboards reflect this by disseminating new metrics and targets to focus individuals and groups on what's important.

Types. There are two types of strategic dashboards: *balanced scorecards* and *management scorecards*. Balanced scorecards conform to the methodology defined by Robert Kaplan and David Norton, while management scorecards apply many of the concepts and principles of the balanced scorecard methodology but without rigid attention to all of its tenets. (See Spotlight 6.5.)

Cause-Effect Linkages. One of the unique things about a scorecard is that it correlates metrics in a cause-and-effect chain. The purpose is to identify

Spotlight 6.5 Types of Strategic Dashboards

A *balanced scorecard* is a strategy management system that originally was designed to help organizations define a balanced set of measures across four perspectives (financial, customer, internal, and learning/ growth) so they could focus efforts on activities that ensure long-term value creation and growth. Today, the methodology focuses more on strategy than measurement and requires organizations to map objectives in a cause-effect diagram called a strategy map. A scorecard displays strategic objectives and associated metrics, uses stoplights to show performance against goals, and contains links to strategic initiatives. Executives use balanced scorecards to conduct monthly or quarterly review meetings and gauge the organization's progress toward achieving strategic objectives.

Similarly, a *management scorecard* measures progress toward achieving strategic objectives but generally doesn't adhere to any formal methodology. A management scorecard borrows elements from the balanced scorecard methodology, such as perspectives, but discards others, such as strategy maps, which require more time and commitment than some executives want to invest. Management scorecards are quicker to implement than balanced scorecards, but since measures aren't explicitly aligned with objectives, they tend to accumulate measures over time that eventually may reduce the effectiveness of the scorecard.

lower-level activities that drive desired outcomes. In some scorecards, metrics are statistically correlated, while in others, the cause-effect relationships are hypotheses that are validated through empirical observation.

For example, Cisco (profiled in Chapter 9) sets an annual target for overall customer satisfaction because it knows that customer satisfaction drives customer loyalty and revenues. It then identifies customer experience and functional metrics that drive customer satisfaction, correlating the relationship statistically. Doing this helps Cisco scientifically identify the key levers it can pull to improve revenues and profitability.

Strategy Management. While a management scorecard like Cisco's correlates metrics, a balanced scorecard correlates objectives. In a balanced scorecard, objectives come first, then metrics. "Don't go on a hunt for the right KPIs. That is not the answer," says Robert Kaplan in a 2004 presentation. "A successful balanced scorecard program starts with the recognition that it is not a metrics project. . . . It's a *change* process."

As a result, balanced scorecards start with a strategy map that links objectives in a cause-effect diagram. The strategy map tells the story of a company's strategy and makes it visible to everyone in the organization. Through a process known as cascading, each group in the organization creates its own strategy map with unique objectives, measures, and targets that show how it contributes to achieving the strategic objectives in the top-level strategy map. In a balanced scorecard ecosystem, strategy cascades down in the form of linked objectives. However, the metrics associated with the objectives often don't roll up because they are uniquely defined at each level of the organization.

To kick off a balanced scorecard program, a project team defines three to four major themes that embody the strategic direction of the organization. For example, a hospital might select the themes "Improve Quality and Patient Safety," "Grow Clinical Programs," and "Expand Community Health for Seniors." Then the leader assigns a cross-functional committee to create a strategy map for each theme. The committee identifies key objectives in the four perspectives (i.e., finance, customer, internal, and learning) and defines the cause-effect linkage among them. The combination of objectives across all themes represents the company's overall strategy map. (See Exhibit 6.8.)

Ideally, each theme team writes a profile of every objective in its strategy map. The profile contains:

- A description of the objective
- The name and contact information of the objective owner who is accountable for achieving the objective

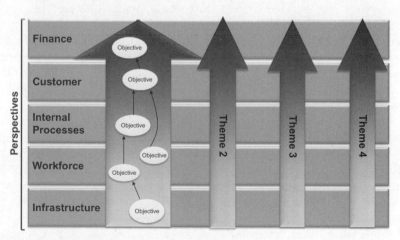

EXHIBIT 6.8 Themes and Strategy Maps
Source: Courtesy Insightformation, www.insightformation.com.

- A "from-to" scenario that describes the gap between the current and desired state of the organization
- Metrics and targets that measure progress towards accomplishing the objective
- Existing and future initiatives that are designed to close the gap between the current and desired states

Some scorecards now capture this information in a wiki for easier access and editing.

Metrics. The process of defining objectives, organizing them by themes and perspectives, and defining causal linkages is a powerful process that by itself can effect dramatic change within an organization. "Some organizations get all the ammunition they need to deliver breakthrough performance by simply creating a strategy map, and they never measure anything," says Bill Barberg, president of Insightformation, a provider of strategy management software and management consulting services.

Nonetheless, defining measures and targets for objectives is a key aspect of creating a balanced scorecard. Each theme team or objective owner brainstorms metrics for each objective, evaluates them by a set of criteria, and gets feedback from people who will be held accountable for the results. Since scorecards measure what an organization wants to be or do in the future, there often isn't data in operational systems to populate the proposed metrics. This is why more than half of all metrics in a typical scorecard are populated manually.

Targets. The KPI team will also need to establish targets for each metric. Many targets are established based on a standard benchmark, such as last year's performance or an industry best practice defined by a competitor. But in some cases, it makes sense to establish stretch targets to incent employees to achieve goals beyond what they think is possible. This is why many balanced scorecard metrics include a standard target and a stretch target for each metric. Once metrics and targets are defined, they are plotted on a scorecard along with color-coded stoplights that indicate performance against targets.

Ultimately, metrics and targets are about managing people. Companies need to take great care in establishing metrics and targets that motivate and inspire people to produce their best work for the good of the organization. Poorly designed metrics and targets, coupled with dysfunctional management and organizational structures, demoralize employees who spend most of their time dreaming up ways to circumvent the metrics and doing as little work as possible.

Navigation. Most scorecard software lets users drill from a summary view of top-level objectives and metrics to lower-level metrics by group or perspective. They also let users view objective profiles and associated initiatives. Most strategy maps incorporate metric stoplights that users can click on to view performance details over time.

For example, Exhibit 6.9 presents a scorecard that shows objectives and associated metrics grouped by the four classic balanced scorecard perspectives. Each metric shows color-coded values for the current (i.e., actual) period; a color-coded arrow indicating performance compared to the prior period along with a number indicating the number of months the trend has stayed the same; and links to comments and initiatives (or projects). Various icons indicate additional actions or views associated with each metric.

Alignment. Once an organization creates a top-level strategy map and scorecard, it then cascades the strategy to other parts of the organization. Each group is responsible for creating its own strategy map and scorecard that align with the top-level one. By cascading strategy maps in this manner, organizations theoretically can align everyone to the same strategy. In practice, most scorecards only cascade one or two levels in the organization.

Strategic Reviews. Barberg says the purpose of a strategic dashboard is not simply to display objectives and measures but to drive an organization in a new direction, changing fundamental behaviors and processes along the way. The most important use of a strategic dashboard is to guide discussions during quarterly strategic or operational review meetings where department heads present their portion of the corporate scorecard to top executives and strategize ways to improve performance and achieve goals.

The purpose of the meeting is to identify steps that leaders can take to shore up sagging performance highlighted in the scorecard. Another purpose is for executives and managers to review and refine the cause-effect linkages within the strategy maps. Each review meeting should reveal more about how objectives relate to and influence each other. Often executive teams discover that they need to insert an objective between two other objectives or refine or replace a metric that doesn't accurately reflect performance.

Collaboration. Prior to a strategic review, presenters annotate the scorecard with comments about that period's performance and recommendations for next steps. Executives can read these comments to prepare for the meeting to steer the discussion. After a meeting, an administrator will use the scorecard to document decisions and action items.

Strategic Expenditures. To sustain a strategy management program, enlightened companies allocate funds to support initiatives identified during strategy review meetings. To do this, the organization needs to create an Office of Strategy Management that oversees the people, processes, and technologies involved in the strategic performance management effort. For instance, this office helps business units and departments create strategy

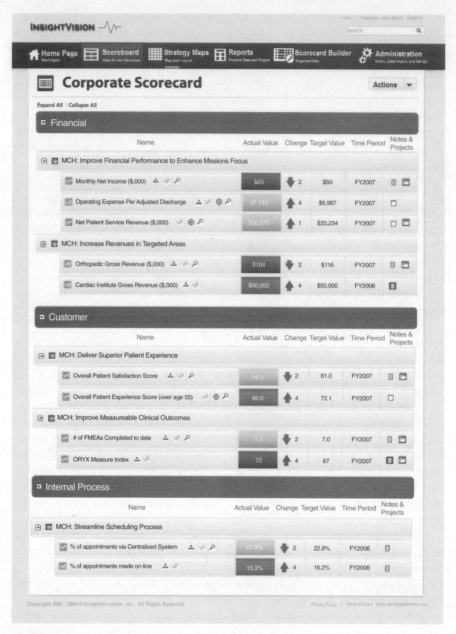

EXHIBIT 6.9 Scorecard

Source: Courtesy Insightformation, www.insightformation.com.

maps, cascade scorecards, and negotiate performance targets and incentives. It also prioritizes and funds strategic initiatives proposed by theme teams.

Summary

This chapter has presented a framework that describes three types of performance dashboards. It is not necessary to figure out which type of dashboard you want to build before beginning a project. In reality, many dashboards don't fit cleanly within the boundaries described in this chapter. Rather, the purpose of the framework is to help you understand the various purposes for which performance dashboards are built and the range of functionality that they can exhibit. Armed with this information, you can proceed more confidently when designing and delivering your performance dashboard solution.

CHAPTER 7

Operational Dashboards in Action

*E*very 15 minutes the executive dashboard at 1-800 CONTACTS gets updated with the latest sales and order information. The dashboard gives about 30 top executives and managers at the online supplier of replacement contact lenses a quick way to monitor performance metrics in context: They can view a time-series chart of sales, order count, or average order size by day, week, or quarter. They can also view current activity compared to the same 15-minute period last week, last year, or a four-week running average. (See Exhibit 7.1.)

Today, the dashboard shows a sharp spike in order volume and sales compared to the same day last week. An executive picks up the phone and calls the head of marketing, who confirms that the department ran an e-mail campaign this morning that offers existing customers a discount for ordering multiple boxes of contact lenses. The executive then checks the Daily Flash chart on the dashboard, which projects closing sales for the day and sees that the campaign will boost sales significantly, and he is pleased.

Meanwhile, the company's call center experiences an uptick in sales activity, which is good news for the 200 sales associates. They quickly check the call center dashboard, updated every 15 minutes, to see whether they are on track to meet individual and team goals for closing ratio, average order size, availability, and quality of calls. If not, they and their manager can make immediate changes to ensure they hit the target. They can also compare their performance to peers and see how their incentive bonus is shaping up.

Overview

Operational dashboards are used to control operational activity and make sure processes stay within prescribed limits for productivity, quality, and efficiency. Typically, front-line personnel use operational dashboards to monitor business events as they occur (every minute, hour, or day) by examining transaction data from core systems and acting immediately to address exception conditions. In this chapter, we examine two sets of operational dashboards, one from 1-800 CONTACTS and the other from the Richmond Police Department.

1-800 CONTACTS. 1-800 CONTACTS provides a great example of an incent-and-motivate dashboard, which is designed to improve the productivity of operations workers through friendly competition and personalized display of incentives. (See Spotlight 6.2 for a more detailed description of an incent-and-motivate dashboard.) The company supports three different operational dashboards, all of which are updated every 15 minutes via the company's data warehouse.

Like most operational dashboards, the ones at 1-800 CONTACTS don't contain complex visuals or navigation paths. They are designed to provide users with all the data they need in a single glance with minimal interaction. If users need to change perspectives, they can analyze data in place by selecting options from a handful of controls at the top of the display. What's also interesting is how 1-800 CONTACTS has evolved its dashboards. Initially, it used .NET and packaged charting controls to develop the dashboards; later, it switched to Microsoft's Silverlight and open source tools to deliver a cleaner, more appealing graphical interface.

Richmond Police Department. The operational dashboard at the Richmond Police Department is unique because it uses analytical models to predict crime throughout the city every eight hours. The models are fed with current crime data and real-time weather feeds, helping officers position patrolmen at the right place and time to deter crime. The use of predictive models is fairly common in most operational dashboards because they enable workers and managers to address issues proactively. In addition, the Richmond case study is interesting because it is a hybrid performance dashboard that combines both operational and analytical capabilities. The analytical module is very popular among officers who create short- and long-term plans because it enables them to view and interact with crime data visually at the speed of thought.

1-800 CONTACTS

1-800 CONTACTS, an online supplier of replacement contact lenses, began implementing operational dashboards in 2005, after it finished building its enterprise data warehouse (EDW). Although its business intelligence (BI) team had provided reports for executives and managers, it wasn't until the team deployed an operational dashboard that EDW usage took off.

Executives now view the company's dashboards and EDW as key competitive weapons.

The first dashboard that 1-800 CONTACTS built was in support of the company's call center. The dashboard dramatically improved the productivity of call center sales representatives, increasing closing ratios, average order sizes, and the quality of customer service. Jim Hill, director of Data Management at the company, estimates that the dashboard generates an additional $50,000 a month in revenue.

The company's executives have became so committed to a metrics-based approach that they purchased a second computer monitor for every sales associate so they can view the dashboard at all times. The executives also asked Hill's team to build an operational dashboard for them (described in the beginning of this chapter) and approved the creation of dashboards in other departments.

How It Works

Metrics. The first step in creating 1-800 CONTACTS's call center dashboard was to define a balanced set of metrics that would spur sales without diminishing customer service. Previously, associates were measured on sales output alone, which didn't always drive appropriate behaviors. The new dashboard now contains a "Quality" metric that scores an associate's customer service skills and phone conversations. Interestingly, some sales associates who were quite successful under the old regime didn't fare as well under the new "quality-driven" performance management system and subsequently left the company.

Trustworthy Data. The second step was to make sure that metrics were populated with accurate data so users would trust the numbers. Previously, performance metrics were calculated manually every week, and none of the staff believed the scores. As a result, the performance program didn't impact productivity. Now that the dashboard automatically populates performance scores every 15 minutes, sales associates no longer question the credibility of the numbers. This is another instance of how near-real-time data helps improve data quality.

Peer Competition. The call center dashboard turbo-charges productivity by engendering a spirit of friendly competition among sales associates. The dashboard scores the performance of all associates and teams every 15 minutes and displays everyone's rank for all to see. The dashboard channels the competitive energies of the sales associates in productive ways and helps managers identify individual associates who need assistance on a given day.

Visible Incentives. Finally, the dashboard provides visible and immediate reinforcement to sales associates. Every 15 minutes, the dashboard updates the amount of incentive pay each sales associate has earned, enabling them all to see the impact of their efforts immediately. By combining performance metrics, incentives, and immediate reinforcement, the dashboard boosts sales and productivity.

Architecture

Data Warehouse. The data warehouse at 1-800 CONTACTS runs on a Microsoft SQL Server database that stores 750 gigabytes of order, sales, and call data. The data warehouse uses a star schema dimensional design, and all dashboards query the data warehouse directly. In some cases, the dashboards access a summary table to accelerate performance. The data warehouse also populates Microsoft Analysis Services (MSAS) dimensional cubes, which are used by business analysts to examine historical trends and issues.

Initially, Hill's team refreshed the data warehouse daily, but once it built the call center dashboard, it accelerated the refresh rate to every 15 minutes. The team is now exploring ways to accelerate the loading process by migrating to near-real-time updates using change data capture, trickle feeding, and a services-oriented architecture. By updating the data warehouse and marts with delta changes instead of refreshing all the data, 1-800 CONTACTS will be able to scale the environment seamlessly as the company grows.

Dashboards. Hill's team built the call center dashboard using Microsoft's .NET programming environment and charting components from Dundas in about four months. Most of the time was spent establishing the data mart infrastructure and determining the best ways to embed parameterized charts and gauges into the .Net pages. Today, it can deploy new dashboards in half the time.

For its most recent dashboard, Hill's team employed Microsoft's Silverlight development platform, along with open source software called Blacklight for creating windows and panes in Silverlight. The new dashboards are more flexible and better looking. They give users more options for what components they want to display on the screen. The dashboards also have embedded text that appears with a mouse-over, enabling users to view definitions and rules for key metrics.

Agile Development. Following the lead of the information technology (IT) department, Hill's team employed agile software development methodology to develop the dashboards. Before it started, however, it spent three months creating a high-level data design, installing servers and tools, developing the initial extract, transform, and load (ETL) mappings, and resolving data quality issues.

Once the back-end infrastructure was in place, two developers created the dashboard in a series of weekly sprints. Each week the development team met with its business counterparts to prioritize story cards for the next three to four sprints and review work from the previous sprint. In some cases, the team needed to source new data and had to create an extended "ETL sprint," which took more than a week. On the whole, however, the agile approach has fostered a tighter partnership with the business and improved the deliverables. "We can respond quickly to how the business changes, and there are no surprises at the end," says Hill.

How It Looks

Executive Dashboard. The executive dashboard is a one-page display consisting of four graphical elements (i.e., three charts and a table) that users can filter with a series of buttons at the top of the screen. (See Exhibit 7.1.) Except for the Daily Flash chart in the lower right corner, the elements

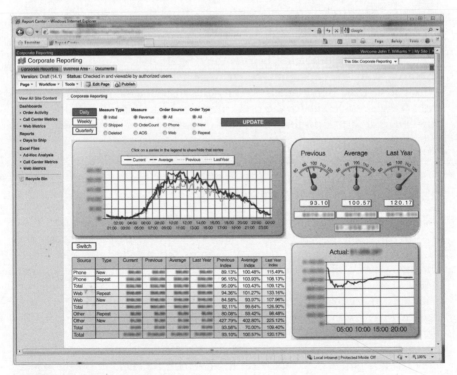

EXHIBIT 7.1 Executive Dashboard
Courtesy, 1-800 CONTACTS.

display the same data but in different formats. "Most people view either the time-series chart or the gauges," says Hill. "Only one person requested the table."

Executives can glean a lot of information from this deceptively simple display. Because the nature of online retail is so cyclical, it's critical that executives be able to compare current performance to the same period last week and last year as well as a running average for the past four periods. The line chart lets users select which comparison lines to display on the chart as well as what time span to display on the X axis: daily, weekly, or quarterly.

Monitoring. Although this is an executive dashboard, the data are updated every 15 minutes, which is what the executives desired. They can view performance trends by day, month, or quarter. The dashboard doesn't contain drill-downs to other displays, but the interactive filters at the top of the page enable executives to change views. If they want more detail, they will call a business analyst to explore the data in the dimensional cubes. "We typically don't do analysis in our operational dashboard environments," says Hill.

Prediction. The dashboard's Daily Flash chart (described earlier) incorporates predictive capabilities. It is a powerful tool that alerts executives to potential problems before they happen so they can mobilize resources to fix the situation. The chart estimates closing sales for the day by calculating the difference between sales from the same day a year ago and a weighted average for the previous four weeks. "By 10 a.m., we know how we're going to do that day," says Hill. The chart enables executives to take timely action to ensure the company hits its targets.

Prescription Incentives Dashboard

Following the success of its call center and executive dashboards, 1-800 CONTACTS built a dashboard for associates and managers in its prescription verification department. Associates are mostly part-time college students who verify prescriptions and talk to pharmacies and doctors' offices. The department wanted a dashboard that would make it easy for associates to compare their performance against each other and see their incentive pay. "We believe a little spirited competition is good for productivity," says Hill.

Built in Silverlight, the dashboard lets associates personalize the display. They select elements to display on their screen by clicking on the square icons in the left column. For instance, they can view their incentive pay formula; their quality, productivity, and availability scores; and the leadership board, which compares their performance to other associates for those

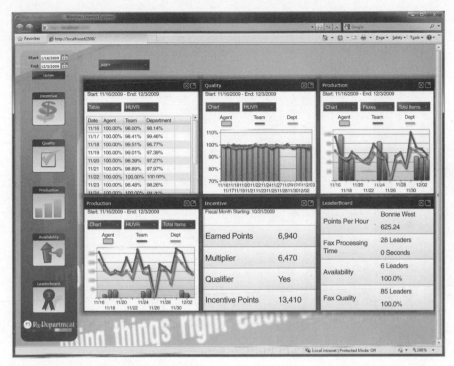

EXHIBIT 7.2 Prescriptions Dashboard
Courtesy 1-800 CONTACTS.

metrics, among other things. (See Exhibits 7.2 and 7.3.) Data is updated every 15 minutes.

How It Succeeds

The operational dashboards at 1-800 CONTACTS are deceptively simple. They provide just the information workers need to be productive and little else. For the most part, all the information that users need to view is placed on a single screen with controls that let them change the view in place. This is critical for a fast-moving business; users should be able to glance at a dashboard display to get all the information they need to do their jobs rather than navigate a complex data environment.

Keys to the success of the operational dashboards at 1-800 CON-TACTS are:

- **Near real-time updates.** 1-800 CONTACTS updates its data ware-house, data marts, and dashboards every 15 minutes. This provides

EXHIBIT 7.3 Prescriptions Leaderboard
Courtesy 1-800 CONTACTS.

actionable information to everyone, from executives to call center staff, so they can intervene to address issues before it's too late.

- **Agile development.** The agile methodology requires a small team of developers and business users to develop working code in short iterations. The company has used this approach effectively to develop dashboard screens.
- **Straightforward.** 1-800 CONTACTS avoided adding complex analytics or drill downs to the screens. Users can see all the data they need in a single glance. "We tried to design our operational dashboards to be intuitive and obvious," says Hill.
- **Analyze in place.** The executive dashboard has a number of controls that let executives change the perspective of the current view without leaving the page. This maintains the simplicity of the dashboard environment.
- **Prediction.** By estimating closing sales at the beginning of the day, executives can take action to achieve goals while there is still time to affect the outcome.

- **Friendly competition.** By displaying scores and rankings for every associate and team every 15 minutes, the dashboards engender friendly competition and turbo-charge productivity.
- **Visible incentives.** The operational dashboards enable call center and prescription verification staff to check their performance against goals and immediately see what they've earned in incentive pay.

Richmond Police Department

Police departments aren't typically known as savvy users of information technology, but that is changing. A number of big-city police departments are embracing new analytic technology that makes it easier to detect patterns in criminal behavior and deter crime.

In 2005, the city of Richmond, Virginia, implemented a state-of-the-art dashboard that integrates geographic information, exploratory analytics, and real-time statistical models that predict crime by type and location every four hours. At the time, the city was considered the fifth most violent city in America. Today, thanks to the dashboard and other crime prevention strategies, the city's rank has plummeted to 99, and it's still dropping.

"We have moved from being reactive to proactive to predictive," says John Buckovich, assistant chief of police. "The dashboard enables us to place police in the right places at the right times based on historical patterns of activity to deter crime."

Prediction. Before every shift, duty sergeants in each sector meet with patrol officers to map out a plan for the shift. Duty sergeants are responsible for executing strategic priorities defined by sector captains and lieutenants. Part of the strategy involves assigning officers to proactive work when they are not responding to 911 calls. The proactive work may involve community policing or addressing issues that often lead to crime later, such as abandoned cars and broken lights or windows. The duty sergeants factor in the predictive models when deciding where to position officers to best deter crime.

The predictive models, which predict crime by location, are updated every four hours for six types of violent crime: robbery, burglary, theft from motor vehicle, core violence excluding domestic incidents, and all other larceny. The statistical software processes five years of crime data, including data from the previous shift, as well as activities, such as paydays, holidays, day of week, and time of day. It also pulls in real-time feeds about city events, the weather, and moon phases.

Analysis. Besides its predictive capabilities, the dashboard enables about 30 lieutenants, precinct captains, duty sergeants, and crime analysts to explore the data on a self-service basis. Previously, only crime analysts could access the data or generate custom reports, which were complex and unwieldy to use. Now police officers can use a Web browser to explore the type and frequency of crimes committed by precinct, sector, and neighborhood with a click of the mouse. The dashboard enables them to develop highly effective 30-, 60-, and 90-day crime prevention plans and respond more appropriately to civic leaders and citizens about criminal activity in their neighborhoods.

How It Works

Summary View. The top-level screen of the Richmond Police Department's operational dashboard provides a quick summary of crime activity and performance trends. The left column displays alerts of current criminal activity and yearly totals of incidents and arrests for the past two years with variance encoded in green or red to indicate an upward or downward trend. The right column shows a table with built-in bar charts that plots incidents by crime type and allows users to filter two columns by a time period, such as last seven days. (See Exhibit 7.4.)

Map View. From the summary view, users can click on one of the six tabs at the top to analyze incidents, arrests, or crime. For example, users can choose to analyze incidents in a table or map. Some users prefer the

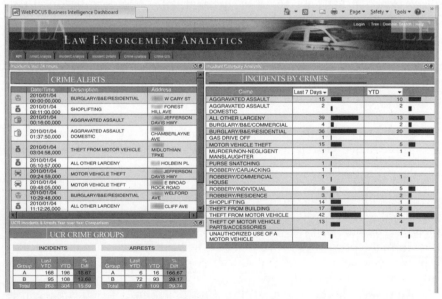

EXHIBIT 7.4 Richmond Dashboard Top Screen
Courtesy of Richmond Police Department.

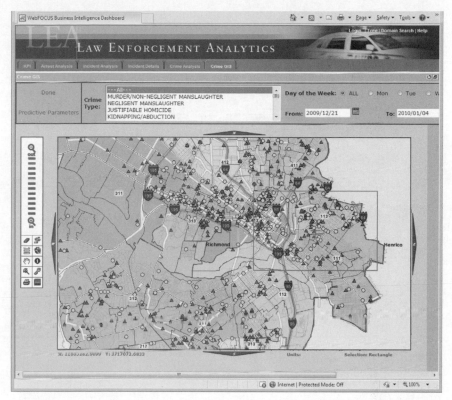

EXHIBIT 7.5 Spatial Analysis of Incidents
Courtesy of Richmond Police Department.

map view while others prefer the table format, where they can see numbers and variances.

Exhibit 7.5 shows incidents superimposed on a geographical map of the city. The crime types are represented by color-coded symbols representing property and violent crimes respectively. Users can use a cursor to lasso a number of incidents and display them in a detailed report, similar to the ones they used to receive before the dashboard.

The most popular part of the dashboard is the crime analysis module, which enables users to visually slice and dice crime statistics at the speed of thought. The summary view consists of six linked bar charts that show crimes by type (violent or property), description, and status and the locations where they occurred, by precinct, sector, and neighborhood. (See Exhibit 7.6.)

For example, a lieutenant may want to analyze details about motor vehicle theft. She clicks on that bar in the crime description chart (or lassos

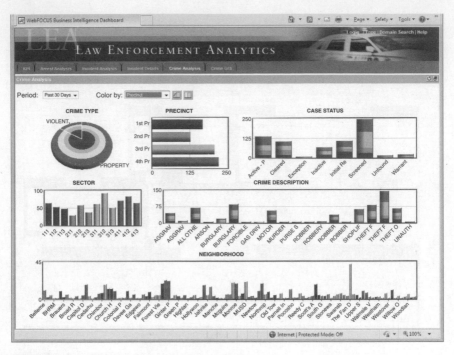

EXHIBIT 7.6 Visual Analysis: Top-level View
Courtesy of Richmond Police Department.

it with her cursor). This action filters the other charts that update automatically. Now she can see which precincts, sectors, and neighborhoods are
most affected by motor vehicle theft. (See Exhibit 7.7.)

Prediction. Finally, users can examine the output of the predictive
models on a geographic map. Users can select a day and time and see a
color-coded map that shows the level of criminal activity by neighborhood.
In this case, the map shows neighborhoods with "high" (red), "moderate"
(yellow), or "low" (green) levels of likely crime. (See Exhibit 7.8.)

Architecture. The operational dashboard uses data integration software from Information Builders to collect, cleanse, standardize, and load
source data every 15 minutes into a Microsoft SQL Server database. The
application uses analytical software from SPSS to build and execute the
statistical models, geographic mapping software from ESRI to display and
populate maps with data, and reporting and analysis tools from Information
Builders, which was the lead vendor on the project. All three vendors—
SPSS, Information Builders, and ESRI—worked closely together to build the
state-of-the-art application, which has since been duplicated in other police

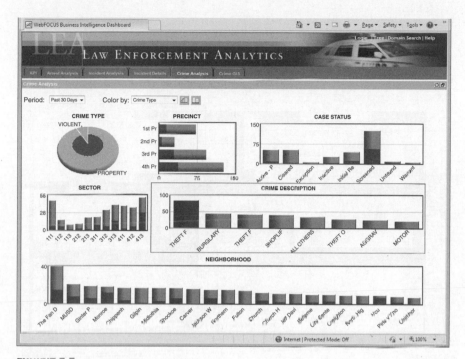

EXHIBIT 7.7 Visual Analysis: Drill #1
Courtesy of Richmond Police Department.

departments throughout North America. The dashboard takes about 80 man-hours a year to maintain, so it has a light footprint, which is ideal for a city agency. "It pretty much runs itself," says IT director Stephen Hollifield.

Why It Succeeds

The operational dashboard at the Richmond Police Department succeeds for many reasons:

1. **Integrated.** The application solves a domain specific problem by integrating four powerful analytic tools:
   a. Statistical software for predicting outcomes
   b. Reporting and analysis tools for exploring and displaying large volumes of complex data in a user-friendly way
   c. Geographic information system for displaying spatial data
   d. Data integration and database management products for capturing, storing, and transforming data

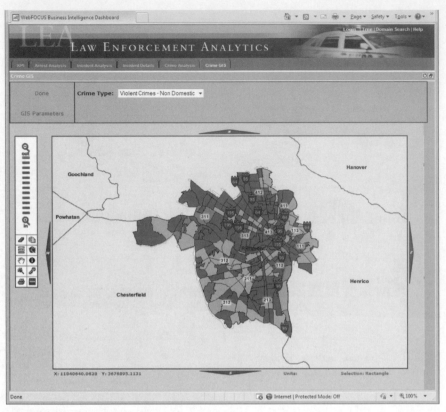

EXHIBIT 7.8 Predictions of Crime
Courtesy of Richmond Police Department.

2. **Easy to use.** The dashboard is so easy to use that most senior police officers can use the tool with minimal training. The dashboard displays existing metrics in a more accessible way.

3. **Self-service.** As a result, officers can access data directly through a Web browser instead of relying on a trained analyst to create reports for them.

4. **Analytical.** The visual analysis module makes it easy for officers to explore data visually, not just create static reports, to understand patterns of crime so they can create short- and long-term plans to deter it.

5. **Predictive.** The tool uses real-time statistical models to help officers anticipate crime hot spots every four hours.

6. **Low cost.** The solution didn't cost much to build and costs even less to maintain, which is perfect for a city agency on a tight budget.

The Future

Marketing. Ironically, the most powerful feature of the operational dashboard—its predictive models—is the least appreciated and used, according to Hollifield. "I know what's going on behind the scenes to create those predictions but others don't. It's something that's only possible with technology." Consequently, Hollifield is planning to work with media relations to create a marketing piece to explain the value of the models to the force and increase their use.

Mobile Use. Hollifield would also like to make the dashboard and its models available to officers in their patrol. The officers already have Web-based access in their vehicles, but there aren't enough WiFi hot spots in the city to make connectivity reliable, says Hollifield. At a minimum, he would like to send alerts to officers when they enter a neighborhood with elevated rates of predicted crime.

Extended Local Forecasts. The department would also like to predict crime levels every four hours on a weekly and monthly basis (instead of daily only) and apply what-if analysis to determine the best deployment tactics. It also wants to use statistical models to evaluate the effectiveness of past crime-fighting strategies. This knowledge would help the department identify the best strategies to apply in each neighborhood.

Summary

This chapter examined operational dashboards in action through case studies from 1-800 CONTACTS and the City of Richmond Police Department. Operational dashboards are used to manage operational activity of front-line workers and deliver near real-time data so users can work proactively to address problems before problems show up on the bottom line.

The call center dashboard at 1-800 CONTACTS has improved the productivity of call center staff and has had a huge impact on sales volume and revenues. Running against a data warehouse that is updated every 15 minutes, the call center dashboard enables workers to visually benchmark themselves against others and see how their work translates into merit pay. The dashboard was so successful that executives wanted one for themselves to track sales and order volumes in near real-time.

The operational dashboard at the Richmond Police Department uses analytical models to predict crime throughout the city every eight hours. The models are fed with current crime data and real-time weather feeds, helping officers position patrolmen at the right place and time to deter crime. Uniquely, the operational dashboard also contains a robust analytical module that helps senior officers develop one- and three-month resource plans.

CHAPTER 8

Tactical Dashboards in Action

*M*ichael M. Crow is a man on a mission. As president of Arizona State University (ASU), he is guiding the transformation of the university into one of the nation's leading public metropolitan research institutions. Since he took office in 2002, ASU has created more than 1 million square feet of new research space and established major interdisciplinary research initiatives, including the Biodesign Institute, the Global Institute for Sustainability, and MacroTechnology Works.

To keep this research juggernaut going, Crow periodically checks a tactical dashboard that tracks research proposals, awards, and expenditures by college, department, and principal investigator every month. In fact, Crow's desire to see a consolidated view of research-related information in one place triggered the development of performance dashboards at ASU.

Today, Crow scans a summary view of research information for the month of October. He sees that the number of proposals has climbed during the past 12 months but the number of awards has declined while expenditures have increased.

To understand who is generating research dollars for the university, Crow drills into the dashboard and sees that the Centers for Excellence in Genomic Science received a $4.4 million grant from the National Institutes of Health in October. He drills further to view the college that received the money and clicks on a link to read the biography of the lead faculty researcher.

Overview

Tactical Dashboards. Tactical dashboards are used to optimize business processes in various departments, such as finance, sales, marketing, and human resources, and, in some cases, provide an enterprise view across all departments. Departmental managers use tactical dashboards to analyze performance against goals using a combination of detailed and summary data, while executives view summary data for the entire organization.

A distinguishing feature of tactical dashboards is that they run against a data warehouse or departmental data mart and rely on standard reporting and analysis tools to display dashboard data. The top level of a tactical dashboard typically displays a dozen or so key performance indicators (KPIs) and provides links to various departmental dashboards and reports. Tactical dashboards often look like a metrics portal or mashup, consisting of a panel display of analytical and functional charts and tables. In general, the focus of tactical dashboards is what happened in the past and how to improve it.

In this chapter we examine two tactical dashboards, one from Arizona State University and the other from Rohm and Haas, now a subsidiary of Dow Chemical. Both leverage their organizations' data warehouse and business intelligence infrastructure to support the dashboards. But while Rohm and Haas tightly integrates its dashboards to deliver an enterprise view of data using common metrics, ASU does not.

Arizona State University. Although ASU's tactical dashboards don't share common metrics, they do share a common look and feel because they were designed with the same dashboard tool (Corda Centerview) and a common set of design principles for displaying quantitative data. In addition, ASU has done a great job providing users with a rich set of navigational options that enable them to drill into detailed data in the data warehouse and, in some cases, into operational systems where they can make changes.

Rohm and Haas. Rohm and Haas's business intelligence (BI) environment is designed to drive delivery of information from the top down, using a standard set of KPIs defined by senior executives and aligned with the company's strategic objectives. Today, more than 3,500 employees access more than 40 dashboards that span all business units, regions, and departments and provide seamless access to detailed reports. The data behind the dashboards and reports come from the data warehouse, ensuring data integrity and consistency.

Arizona State University

Arizona State University began implementing dashboards in 2006 once it realized that most staff members found the university's self-service reporting system too difficult to use. The goal was to convert the most widely used reports into dashboards and give everyone equal access to information.

"Our dashboards are designed to give users 40 percent to 60 percent of the information they need to do their jobs, regardless of the technical resources in their department," says John Rome, director of development and data warehousing at ASU.

The first dashboard ASU built was a big success. It tracked research proposals, awards, and expenditures by college, department, and principal investigator every month. For the first time, the university had a single source of truth about research dollars, a critical source of funding for the university. Once the president began using the dashboard, as described in the opening scenario, the deans, department heads, and faculty did so as well. "This was the tipping point for dashboards," says Rome.

How It Looks

With initial success, Rome's team of three full-time developers spent the next several years building dashboards for every department and subject area in the university.

What is unique about most of ASU's dashboards is that they enable users to drill from a high-level view of information to details with a minimum number of clicks. In some cases, users can drill all the way to the operational system where, if authorized, they can update information in effect, closing the loop between analytical and operational processes.

Admissions Dashboard. ASU's student admissions dashboard lets deans and admissions officers view data about students who have applied and been accepted by geography and school. The dashboard has played a key role in helping ASU improve student retention between freshman and sophomore years. In 2009, ASU achieved for the first time an 80 percent retention rate as defined by *U.S. News & World Report*. Says Rome, "The dashboard is helping us identify better-prepared students."

The top-level screen in the student enrollment dashboard displays a color-coded map of the United States that compares admissions data by state. Two accompanying tables show top 10 lists, in this case the top 10 high schools from which admitted students come, both in Arizona and outside Arizona. Top 10 lists are a great way to generate interest in dashboards. Each object contains two icons in the top-right corner of the pane. Clicking on the "i" icon enables users to view metadata properties for the object and the other enables users to export to PDF or Word. (See Exhibit 8.1.)

At the top of the dashboard are controls that let users analyze the data in place. By clicking on a radio button, users can filter the geographic map and tables by "Applicants" or "Admits." They can further filter the views using drop-down boxes to the right that contain variables for "Term," "Admit Type," and "College." In addition, the left-hand navigation column contains links to a half-dozen related dashboards. These links appear on every page in the Admissions dashboard.

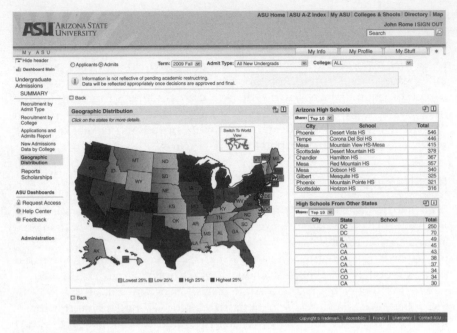

EXHIBIT 8.1 Student Enrollment Dashboard
Courtesy of Arizona State University.

To obtain more details, users can click on any state in the map to view admissions data for that state. Below each map is a table with data for people who prefer that mode of consuming information. They can continue drilling in this way to view data by county, city, and high school. At the lowest level, they can click on a student to view the individual's record in ASU's PeopleSoft student information system. (See Exhibits 8.2, 8.3, 8.4, and 8.5.)

How It Works

Architecture. Most of ASU's dashboards and reports run off the university's enterprise data warehouse, which was completed in 2002 and spans all major subject areas and departments. The data warehouse is updated daily. However, some dashboards run directly against operational systems. These dashboards are used primarily to facilitate the monitoring of employee compliance with human resource requirements, such as benefits sign-ups. ASU tunes the SQL in these dashboards so the queries don't interfere with the performance of the operational system.

The dashboards are built using visualization components from Corda. Developers first create reports in Oracle Hyperion Interactive Reporting

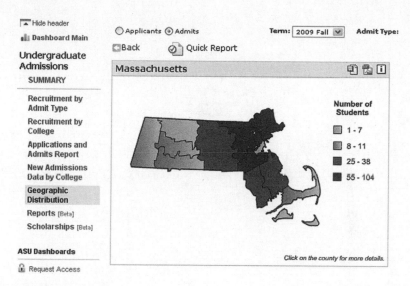

EXHIBIT 8.2 Drill Down #1: State View
Courtesy of Arizona State University.

(formerly Brio) and then copy the SQL into Corda components where they script variables for filtering.

Usability. ASU has invested a lot of time making the dashboards attractive and usable. Besides working with a design and usability expert in the information technology (IT) department, Rome and his team have learned visual techniques for displaying quantitative data, largely through books and conferences. For example, ASU dashboards use muted colors, vary intensity rather than color to highlight significant data values, and avoid using distracting decorative gauges, background colors, and frames.

Marketing. But even the best visual designs don't guarantee that users will use the dashboards. And since most tactical dashboards don't track activity related to bonus pay, they sometimes have a tougher time ensuring adoption unless they track performance of peer groups across the company. "Some of the best dashboards we've built aren't used very much," laments Rome.

To date, most users learn about the availability of dashboards from their department or the suggestion of a colleague. Some find the dashboards by clicking on the "dashboard" link that exists on ASU's intranet home page. Because ASU has single sign-on, users can automatically start browsing dashboards that they have permission to see. Some access is role based and other access requires the permission of a data steward granted through a workflow process.

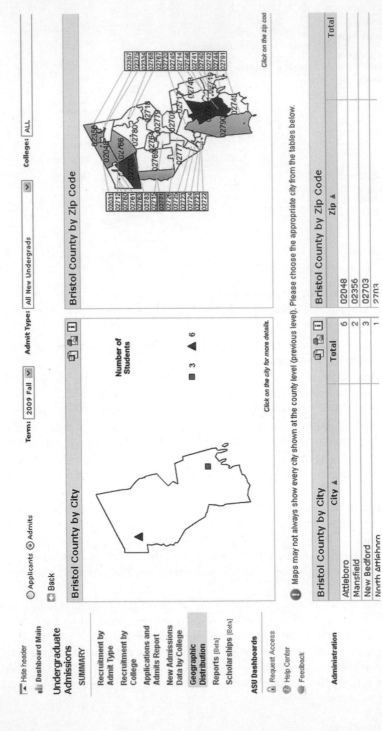

EXHIBIT 8.3 Drill Down #2: County View

Courtesy of Arizona State University.

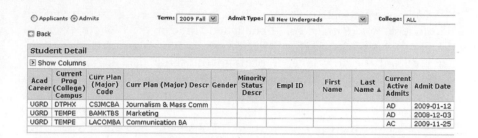

EXHIBIT 8.4 Drill Down #3: High School View
Courtesy of Arizona State University.

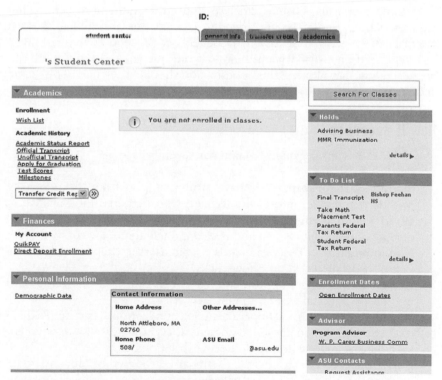

EXHIBIT 8.5 Drill Down #4: Student Record
Courtesy of Arizona State University.

To improve adoption, Rome will soon begin targeting users by title in departments where usage could be higher. His team has built an extensive dashboard that tracks usage so it knows exactly who is using the dashboard (or not) and for how long. It plans to use these data in more formal marketing campaigns. However, the team needs to make sure it can handle support calls that come from any expansion of the dashboard environment.

In addition, the team plans to add "bookmark" functionality that will let users save views of their favorite dashboards and access them from ASU's main portal page. ASU also plans to send e-mail messages that contain links to dashboard views that will foster greater usage.

Team. Rome has created a strong team of dashboard developers, leveraging university students where possible, and created an innovative, fast-paced environment that appeals to them. The developers hang out in "the cave," which, besides computer stations, contains bean bag chairs, a big-screen television, and game consoles.

In the beginning, the developers built dashboards soup to nuts, but now Rome is enlisting business analysts in each department to help gather requirements, define KPIs, and identify data sources and tables. "I don't want our developers to be experts in benefits code—and they're not really that interested anyway—I want them to write queries and build the dashboard screens," says Rome. This coordination should accelerate deployment and improve the quality of deliverables.

How It Succeeds

ASU dashboards have gained traction for several reasons:

- **Strong sponsorship.** They have strong support from the university president and chief information officer, who triggered the initiative.
- **Good visual design.** ASU's dashboard applies principles of visual display of quantitative data and is clean, uncluttered, and easy to read.
- **Easy navigation.** The dashboards enable users to drill from high-level views to detailed data in a few clicks.
- **Closed loop.** Where appropriate, users can drill from the dashboard into an operational system to take action.
- **Strong team.** ASU's dashboard team is young, enthusiastic, and skilled in dashboard design and development. It coordinates with departmental business analysts to build effective solutions.
- **Portal based.** Users access the dashboard through the company portal so they don't have to log on to a separate system.
- **High-quality data.** The dashboards run off a data warehouse that delivers accurate, trustworthy data.

- **Export to Excel.** Many ASU dashboards enable users to export lists (e.g., students or employees) to Excel to take action.
- **Help.** ASU provides on screen tips, a help page that answers frequently asked questions, and a support desk.
- **Usage monitoring.** ASU has built a dashboard to track usage at a detailed level.

Rohm and Haas

Rohm and Haas is a $9 billion specialty chemicals manufacturer that was acquired by rival Dow Chemical in 2009. Founded more than 100 years ago, Rohm and Haas has acquired 55 companies in the past decade, more than doubling its annual revenues. It now has more than 16,500 employees located in more than 100 operating sites around the world.

This rapid growth and organizational change made it difficult for Rohm and Haas to function as a single company. Prior to 2002, the Philadelphia-based company consisted of 13 business units that operated independently. There was considerable overlap and redundancy among the units. In the IT sector alone, the company maintained 300 disparate systems with redundant people, processes, and data.

Single View. To stem the bleeding, Rohm and Haas spent $300 million from 2002 to 2004 to replace its legacy systems with a single instance of SAP applications worldwide. The purpose of this mammoth investment was to create a common language and set of business processes to improve operational efficiency and deliver a single version of truth for decision making. As part of the investment, Rohm and Haas rebuilt its legacy data warehouse from scratch using SAP's data warehousing technology (SAP BW) and BI tools (BEx Analyzer and Web Application Designer) to serve as its decision-making platform.

"The goal was to create a 'one-number, one-process' culture among businesses and functional organizations," says Michael Masciandaro, director of BI at Rohm and Haas. Rather than have information and reports bubble up from the bottom using spreadsheets and other tools, the new BI environment was designed to drive delivery of information from the top down, using a standard set of KPIs defined by senior executives and aligned with the company's strategic objectives.

Today, more than 3,500 employees access more than 40 dashboards that span all business units, regions, and departments and provide seamless access to detailed reports. The data behind the dashboards and reports come from the data warehouse, ensuring data integrity and consistency. The BI environment now provides about 85 percent of the information business users need to do their jobs and has significantly reduced the number of renegade spreadmarts at the company. "We've stamped out all the competition," says Masciandaro.

How It Works

Dashboards to the Rescue. Early in the transformation process, Masciandaro discovered that producing a lot of reports was not enough. "We had 500 detailed SAP BW reports and people were having difficulty figuring out which one to use." The obvious solution, says Masciandaro, was to build layers on top of the reports using dashboards. "We started giving users information the way they like to see it and adoption took off."

Rohm and Haas uses a three-tier delivery framework, not unlike the monitor, analyze, and drill to detail (MAD) framework, to ensure tailored delivery of information and insights to business users. Information flows from a handful of KPIs at the top to detailed information at the bottom, giving executives clear line of sight up, down, and across the organization. The top tier in Rohm and Haas's framework consists of scorecards and dashboards; the middle layer, management reports and analytics; and the bottom layer, operational reports. (See Exhibit 8.6.)

Senior managers use scorecards and dashboards to view the overall health of the company and business unit performance but sometimes drill into management reports for more detailed information. Middle managers navigate all three layers of the framework, from summary views in

EXHIBIT 8.6 Rohm and Haas's Dashboard Framework
Courtesy of Rohm and Haas.

dashboards, to management reports of departmental performance, to operational reports for lists and other detailed data. Finally, operational staff use operational reports to monitor and control business processes, but they occasionally view management reports to get a broader view of performance.

KPIs, Targets, Thresholds. To deliver top-down line of sight, the company's executives selected 10 metrics that they wanted to track across every business unit, group, and region in the company, including volume (sold in) kilograms, net sales, and gross profit. To benchmark performance with these metrics, they chose to compare actuals to plan, prior year, and forecast. "We only got an hour of [executives'] time, and those are the metrics and targets they came up with," says Masciandaro. The metrics and targets weren't new to Rohm and Haas, but the company had never monitored every business group in the same way using the same metrics.

The impact was immediate and powerful. "People stopped arguing about the numbers and focused on what to do about them," says Masciandaro. "Like a laser, the KPIs focus people's attention on what's important. KPIs have a magical effect."

Time ran out before Masciandaro could get the executives to define percentage thresholds that would trigger stoplight alerts, so they decided to create the ranges themselves: a green circle would indicate performance exceeds plan; a yellow triangle would indicate performance is from 0 to 5 percent below plan; and a red square would indicate that performance is 5 percent or more below plan. "To my surprise, they adopted the scheme without pushback."

How It Looks

Display. The executive dashboard in Exhibit 8.7 shows the 10 KPIs displayed in table format in the middle of the screen. The data are updated monthly, and most but not all of the KPIs are financial. When a user highlights one of the KPIs, the two time-series charts below are updated to reflect the values for that KPI. Users can click on the associated check boxes to add or subtract comparison lines (i.e., current year, prior year, forecast, or plan) on the charts. "We let users muddy up the graphs as much or little as they want," says Masciandaro.

Filters. Executives can view the performance of any business unit or group in the company using these same 10 metrics by selecting items from one or more of drop-down list boxes in the filters section in the left column of the display. The filters are cascading, so making a selection in a top-level filter narrows the selections in lower-level filters. The filters change the data in the table and charts so users can analyze the performance of the entire company without changing pages.

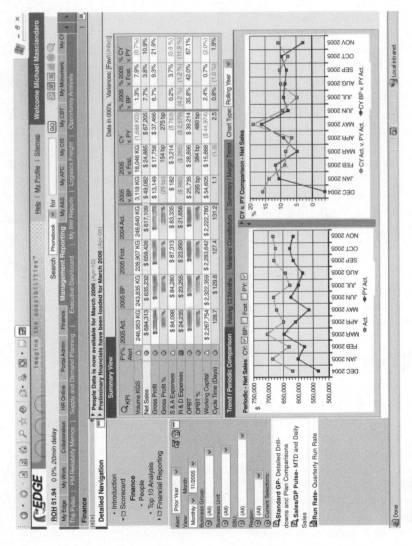

EXHIBIT 8.7 Executive Dashboard
Courtesy of Rohm and Haas.

Executives can also apply date filters to view performance by month, quarter, or year. They can select a specific date or change the variable for the color-coded alerts to current year, prior year, plan, or forecast. They can also select filters in a single display by clicking on the funnel icon. To see which filters are active at any moment, users can click on the "Current Selection" field in the filters section.

Navigation and Guided Analytics. The dashboard does a good job of showing users where they are in the dashboard and provides suggestions for related reports to view. The top section of the left column shows related dashboards and subpages within them. Clicking on an item takes the user to that dashboard. The current dashboard view is displayed in bold. The bottom section of the left column provides links to related reports or dashboards. These "suggestions"—which are hard-wired into each dashboard based on the developer's experience—guide users to related information in a single click. Users can also click on the small magnifying class in the top left corner of the table to create an ad hoc report using the current filters as a starting point. They can also access KPI definitions by clicking on the help button.

Decomposition View. One problem that afflicts top-level dashboards is that they often hide critical alerts or anomalies in lower levels of the business or metric hierarchy. To unearth what lies behind a KPI, executives can click on the "Decomposition View" tab at the top of the table. Exhibit 8.8 shows that the KPI "Gross Profit" is composed of "Standard Gross Profit" and "Total Other Cost." Standard Gross Profit is composed of "Net Sales" and "Standard Cost," which displays a red alert. Without a decomposition view or similar technique, these buried outliers would go unnoticed.

Management Reports. The middle manager's view has the same look and feel as the executive dashboard but is a lot busier. Exhibit 8.9 shows a daily sales dashboard, called the Sales Pulse, which helps executives and managers track revenue. Executives can use filters in the left column to drill down to view any group's revenues. Managers can create a bookmark of their view of revenue by clicking on the floppy disk icon in the label for the filters section so they don't have to reapply filters the next time they access the dashboard.

Operational Reports. Users can also drill down to a daily view by clicking on a hot spot in the chart. Or they can click the magnifying glass on a higher-level dashboard to view operational reports, which they can slice and dice by any dimension or filter available in a long list.

Common Look and Feel. All three levels of dashboards and reports have the same look and feel because they were created them using the same development tool, SAP's Web Application Designer. Rohm and Haas began developing the dashboards in 2005 when there weren't very many dashboard tools on the market so they decided to build their own. The

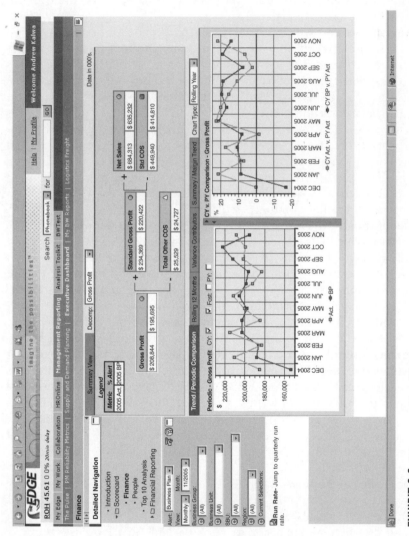

EXHIBIT 8.8 Decomposition View

Courtesy of Rohm and Haas.

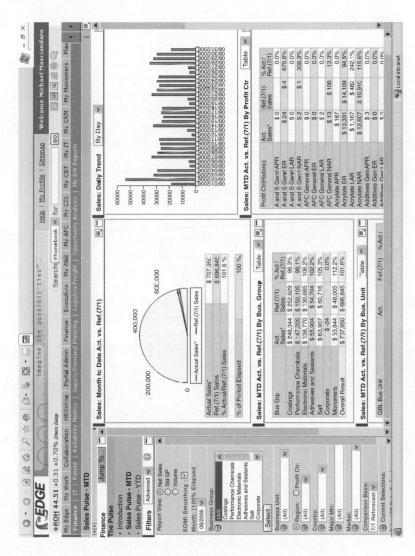

EXHIBIT 8.9 Daily Sales Dashboard

Courtesy of Rohm and Haas.

153

initial dashboard took six months and about $500,000 to deploy, which was mostly the cost of labor. Subsequent dashboards took one month and $100,000 to develop.

How It Succeeds

There are many reasons for the success of Rohm and Haas's tactical dashboard.

Data Infrastructure. For one, its dashboards are the visible expression of a robust, underlying data infrastructure. By standardizing its operating applications and BI environment on SAP, Rohm and Haas has been able standardize its business processes and data definitions and deliver a single version of truth for the enterprise. This has been a powerful proposition for a company that was fragmented by acquisitions.

Data Quality. Dashboards can improve data quality because errors are more visible. "If someone misplaces a decimal, people will see it and the problem gets fixed. That wouldn't have happened before. This empowers our front-line workers who enter data to know that what they do matters to the company," says Masciandaro. In addition, the BI team runs validations and applies Six Sigma processes to ensure the highest degree of data quality. "We have to explain why our data is different than someone's spreadsheet."

Portal. Rohm and Haas embedded its dashboards and reports into its corporate portal (also built on SAP technology). This means users don't have to learn how to use a BI tool; they simply log onto the portal and access all dashboards and reports via a Web browser that they are authorized to see. By simplifying access and delivering role-based views, the portal has greatly simplified training and accelerated adoption, says Masciandaro.

Performance. Performance has long been an issue with SAP's BI environment, but Rohm and Haas has made strides toward delivering consistent query performance. "Our average query response time is around 10 seconds," says Masciandaro, "but our goal is to for every click to deliver a response in 5 seconds or less."

Usability. Rohm and Haas has incorporated many features into its dashboards that promote usability:

- **Stickiness.** The dashboards display the filters that users last applied when viewing the dashboard. And users can bookmark pages to keep views intact.
- **Suggested reports.** Every page has a list of related reports or dashboards that users can access with a single click.
- **Mouse-overs.** Users can hover their cursor over an element on a chart to view the underlying data or text.

- **Zoom.** Users can click on a magnifying glass icon to create an ad hoc report starting with the current table or view.
- **Personalized alerts.** Users can select the variable they want to trigger KPI-based alerts.
- **Screen alerts.** Administrators can broadcast messages about relevant contextual details and alerts for each dashboard.
- **Cascading filters.** Cascading filters help users select the right filters quickly.
- **Slider.** Users can expand and collapse a chart with a single click.
- **Decomposition view.** Users can see the metrics that comprise a high-level KPI and their performance status.
- **Variance contributors.** Users can slice across dimensions to see contributors and detractors to the top-level KPI.
- **Top 10 list.** The dashboards incorporate top 10 lists, which always garner interest from users.
- **Open source.** Advanced Flash visualizations are easily incorporated into the dashboard via SAP's SDK.

The Future

Adapting to Change. Just when a BI program gets comfortable, something always happens that requires a major adjustment. Recently, Dow Chemical acquired Rohm and Haas, and the two companies are immersed in discussions about how to consolidate their respective BI environments.

In addition, like many SAP customers, Rohm and Haas is trying to create a strategic plan to accommodate SAP's road map for integrating BI products SAP and Business Objects, which SAP acquired in 2008. As one of SAP's most successful data warehousing customers, Rohm and Haas is working closely with SAP to incorporate Business Objects tools and functionality within its existing architecture.

Analytics. Before the acquisition by Dow, Rohm and Haas was delivering advanced analytics in areas like pricing optimization and product profitability. The analytics included advanced visualizations, such as bubble charts, band analysis, and motion charts. Unfortunately, the acquisition sidetracked some of this effort. "With the acquisition, people have been coming and going so now they are focused on basic blocking and tackling. We'll get back to it once the dust settles," says Masciandaro.

Mobile. The company is also experimenting with delivering basic reports to BlackBerry users. Currently, it delivers two reports to about 100 BlackBerry users. The reports are slimmed down to fit the smart phone. "Delivering business information, especially quickly changing information to an increasingly mobile workforce, helps us react faster to new situations," says Masciandaro.

Summary

This chapter examined tactical dashboards at Rohm and Haas, a division of Dow Chemical, and Arizona State University. There is a lot of diversity among tactical dashboards, which are generally used to deliver departmental information, although many embed departmental views within an enterprise or executive dashboard.

Rohm and Haas built a tactical dashboard from scratch, starting with an enterprise view that enables executives to view performance of every major operating group by a dozen or so metrics. The company now has 40 dashboards running against its enterprise data warehouse that span all business units, regions, and departments and provide seamless access to detailed reports. Its big challenge now is to integrate its IT infrastructure, including performance dashboards, with Dow Chemical, and migrate to SAP's new BI platform.

Arizona State University built a series of departmental dashboards that don't share metrics but do have a common look and feel since they run off the same dashboard platform and data warehouse and adhere to a common set of design guidelines gleaned from industry best practices. For good-looking tactical dashboards that enable users to drill to detail, including into operational systems if authorized, Arizona State University leads the pack.

CHAPTER 9

Strategic Dashboards in Action

*D*avid Hsiao, the director of quality data infrastructure at Cisco, just received an automated "Red Alert" e-mail message, indicating that there has been a spike in product returns from one of Cisco's top 250 customers. Hsiao knows that product returns directly correlate with customer satisfaction, which Cisco measures continuously via customer surveys. He also knows that a 10 percent drop in customer satisfaction can decrease Cisco's revenues from that customer by 40 percent in just one quarter. Thus, he must take swift action.

Hsiao immediately calls the customer's account manager, who also received the Red Alert. Together, they create a "Tiger team"—an ad hoc, cross-functional group of individuals who work to address a specific process, measurement, or performance issue. In this case, the Tiger team consists of specialists from sales, supply chain, engineering, and technical services. Within the next 48 hours, the team investigates the cause of the alert and reports to Cisco executives about the source of the problem and potential resolutions.

In this case, the Tiger team discovered a false alarm: The customer had been accumulating parts and shipped a big batch to Cisco to clear its loading dock. Nonetheless, the Tiger team proposes ways that Cisco can help the customer better manage its inventory in a volatile economy. The team's proactive attention to customers and quick response to a potential problem stems from Cisco's commitment to customer success and culture of metrics-driven performance.

Overview

Strategic dashboards—otherwise known as scorecards—typically are deployed in a top-down fashion to manage the execution of strategy on an enterprise scale. Executives use scorecards to review progress toward achieving strategic objectives in monthly or quarterly review meetings with business unit and departmental managers. The scorecards contain summary-level data updated monthly or quarterly either by individuals who compile data in spreadsheets or from operational systems. The focus of scorecards is the future (i.e., objectives and goals) and how to achieve it.

In this chapter we examine strategic dashboards from Cisco and the Ministry of Works in the Kingdom of Bahrain.

The Ministry of Works. The Ministry of Works is a classic example of a *balanced scorecard* that adheres to all major tenets of the Kaplan and Norton methodology. The ministry, which oversees construction projects, roadways, and sanitation infrastructure for the country, has institutionalized strategy management principles using balanced scorecards in every department. Today, the ministry has 17 sets of cascaded strategy maps comprising 200 objectives, 500 metrics, and 300 initiatives.

At the top level, the ministry's overall strategy map contains about 20 objectives that are linked using cause-effect logic and arranged in four major themes. Each theme and objective has an owner who is responsible for outcomes measured by multiple metrics. The overall strategy cascades to all departments, which maintain their own strategy maps, scorecards, and initiatives. To keep all this going, the ministry created a strategy management office of five people who help departments refine their strategic planning and scorecarding efforts.

Cisco. Cisco offers a great example of a *management scorecard* that focuses the organization on strategy without adopting a formal methodology. A top priority for Cisco is customer satisfaction because it knows that satisfied customers generate higher revenues. In fact, Cisco has validated this connection statistically, which is a major reason that it publishes the overall customer satisfaction score on its intranet home page alongside Cisco's stock price and includes customer satisfaction scores in the calculation of employee bonuses.

To improve overall customer satisfaction, Cisco maintains a bevy of dashboards and scorecards that track customer experiences, customer satisfaction, and customer loyalty. A corporate quality group works with each department to identify process measures that correlate with customer experience and satisfaction and establish performance targets for each. The departments launch Six Sigma and other projects to improve core processes and monitor whether these changes positively affect customer experience and satisfaction scores. By statistically correlating metrics, Cisco now knows what steps to take to improve customer satisfaction, loyalty, and revenues.

Cisco: A Metrics-driven Organization

Founded in 1984, Cisco is the worldwide leader in networking technology with $35 billion in annual revenues and 64,000 employees. The foundation of Cisco's culture is its all-abiding focus on the customer. Chairman and chief executive officer John Chambers preaches that "customers come first" and that Cisco's job is to make its customers successful. To do that, he exhorts employees to manage "the total customer experience" and "never let the customer down."

To embed this strategy in the fabric of the culture, top executives created the Corporate Quality department in 2004 to measure customer satisfaction and ensure compliance with regulations and industry standards. Today, the department works with functional groups to reengineer core processes around the customer experience and hold them accountable for results. This focus on quality has helped Cisco deliver an unrivaled experience for every customer, increasing customer loyalty and revenues.

Business Impact. Using regression analysis, the Corporate Quality team can now predict the degree to which a targeted improvement in an internal process will improve customer experiences and satisfaction with Cisco products and services, which, in turn, will drive a corresponding increase in revenues. Cisco has improved customer satisfaction significantly, and its supply chain now ranks fifth in the world after failing to make the top 25 five years ago, according to AMR Research. "We now know what levers to pull to increase customer satisfaction and revenues across all our products and services," says Hsiao.

Cisco's Quality Program

This transformation is remarkable considering that in 2004 Cisco did not have an enterprise-wide data model for quality metrics and standard definitions of organizational hierarchies. Having made 137 acquisitions in 25 years, Cisco was largely a collection of entrepreneurial business units with few common standards for cross-functional measurement. Every business unit had its own data marts and defined or interpreted quality metrics in different ways.

Quality Data Infrastructure. Today, Cisco has a common set of metrics, hierarchies, and sources of record for measuring quality and customer satisfaction across all of its product lines. A 4-terabyte Oracle data warehouse now provides a single source of truth for all quality-related, performance measurement and forms the foundation of its Quality Data Infrastructure (QDI) program. The warehouse pulls data from 20 transaction systems across the company on a daily basis to deliver a comprehensive, cross-functional view of quality metrics. The data include orders, shipments, bookings, hardware deliveries, service contracts, product replacements, software defects, service requests, technical services, and customer satisfaction.

Rolling Survey. Cisco collects customer satisfaction data in a survey that it runs continuously throughout the year. Last year, it received more than 110,000 responses to the survey, which takes less than 18 minutes to complete and is tailored to the level and role of the individual taking it. The survey captures customer satisfaction with Cisco's account team, partners, pre- and postsales technical support, order fulfillment processes, and Cisco hardware and software. It also gauges their perception of Cisco as a valued partner, technical innovator, and customer-focused supplier, among other things.

Scorecards and Dashboards. More than 3,500 Cisco employees now access the QDI data warehouse through five enterprise dashboards and dozens of functional scorecards, trend charts, and Pareto drill-downs. The Corporate Quality group maintains enterprise-level dashboards that monitor customer satisfaction (i.e., the subjective perception of quality), customer experience (i.e., the objective experience of quality), and customer loyalty. Users can drill down in these dashboards to view scores by individual customers, products, or services.

Functional groups keep balanced scorecards to monitor their progress toward achieving strategic objectives targeting customer satisfaction, customer experience, and financial performance, among other things. They also maintain operational and tactical dashboards to track internal processes and employee satisfaction scores that correlate with customer satisfaction and experience.

Although all dashboards and scorecards are built on the same platform (i.e., Oracle BI Enterprise Edition) and run against the same data warehouse, they are built by various internal information technology [IT] organizations that tailor dashboards to conform to the way their departments want to view and use the data. Although few dashboards and scorecards share a common graphical interface, they are easily linked, allowing users to navigate from one dashboard to another via menu tabs at the top of each page.

Getting Started

Metrics and Dimensions. For Cisco, the first step in creating a metrics-driven organization was to define meaningful and actionable metrics. This was no small undertaking in a company the size of Cisco. To get started, the Corporate Quality group focused on measuring hardware quality from the perspective of customers, working closely with the company's engineering and manufacturing organizations. It has since broadened its scope and now measures software quality, order fulfillment, technical services, and the effectiveness of Cisco account teams and partners.

True to its customer-focused culture, Cisco turned to customers to help prioritize and identify quality (i.e., customer experience) metrics. Cisco used its 30-member Global Customer Advisory Board to brainstorm measures, which were winnowed down to about two dozen that best correlate with customer satisfaction. Every year, the Advisory Board reviews the metrics and suggests new ones that better capture their experiences in doing business with Cisco.

Cisco uses several criteria to evaluate potential metrics:

- **Scalable.** Can we apply this measure universally and collect it consistently in an automated fashion?
- **Normalized.** Can we normalize the data so it can be compared across functional areas? (e.g., parts per million).
- **Accountable.** Can we measure with enough granularity to assign someone to be accountable for results?
- **Goalable.** Can we attach a market-driven target to say how much more or less will drive loyalty and revenue?
- **Actionable.** Do users know what to do to improve the performance of this metric?

Metadata. A cross-functional team then hammered out detailed definitions for each metric as well as common dimensions and hierarchies by which Cisco employees would view the measures. Common dimensions include geography, theater, platform family, product, component, customer network, technology group, business unit, role, time, and supplier, all of which come with their own hierarchy of elements.

The QDI team then created an online metadata library to house the definitions. Every QDI dashboard is linked to the library so users can examine definitions at any time and better understand the meaning of data they are viewing. Each metric has a page in the online library that contains the metric's description, business owner, IT steward, goals, data sources, refresh rate, business rules, and other attributes. Stakeholders can quickly update definitions in the library as needed. The metadata library provides a vehicle for data governance and fosters data transparency. (See Exhibit 9.1.)

Correlating Performance. With metrics and data in place, the Corporate Quality team segments customers into one of four loyalty categories: Truly Loyal, Trapped, Accessible, and High Risk. It knows that Truly Loyal customers will increase purchases of Cisco products and recommend them to others. Cisco's current goal is to sustain at least 75 percent of its customers in the Truly Loyal quadrant. (See Exhibit 9.2.)

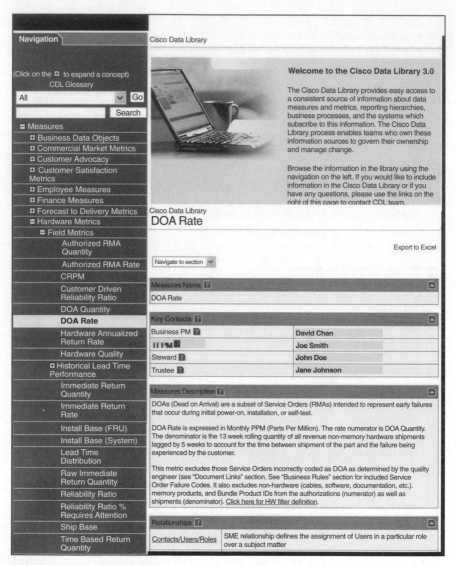

EXHIBIT 9.1 Cisco's Data Library
Courtesy of Cisco.

Cisco then analyzes the degree to which various customer attitudes and perceptions of Cisco correlate with customer loyalty. Currently, "customer focused" (33 percent), "overall satisfaction" (23 percent), "technologically advanced" (20 percent), and "value" (16 percent) correlate most with loyalty scores.

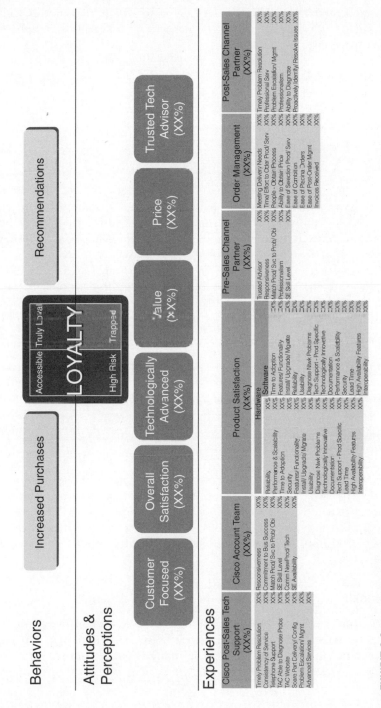

EXHIBIT 9.2 Drivers of Loyalty

Courtesy of Cisco.

163

From there, the team analyzes the degree to which customer experiences correlate with overall customer satisfaction. Customer experiences span six dimensions:

1. Account team relationship
2. Order management
3. Hardware quality
4. Software quality
5. Network availability
6. Technical services

Some key customer experiences that Cisco monitors are account team responsiveness, on-time delivery, hardware returns, software defects, network outages, and problem resolution times. Cisco calculates the degree to which each type of customer experience impacts customer satisfaction.

Finally, Corporate Quality works with each functional area to identify internal process metrics that are most likely to drive the customer experiences. For instance, a statistical analysis might show that 22 percent of an overall customer satisfaction score for hardware quality is explained by hardware reliability. Hsiao says:

> *Then we go to Cisco's supply chain management [department] and ask, "Which internal process measures best predict hardware reliability in the field?" They might hypothesize that it's "product complexity" or "first pass yields." They'll conduct linkage analysis to verify relationships in the data and then potentially kick off Six Sigma initiatives to "move the needle" on those internal measures.*

Afterward, Corporate Quality measures whether gains in the functional process metric produce corresponding improvements in customer experience and satisfaction measures. If there is a correlation, Cisco keeps ratcheting up the targets for those metrics to yield the customer satisfaction levels it seeks. If there is no correlation, it searches for another metric that correlates better.

How It Looks

Top to Bottom. Cisco posts an overall customer satisfaction rating on its intranet home page, right next to its stock price. This reinforces Cisco's customer-centric strategy and culture. The rating is updated in real time as survey responses come in and shows performance against an annual target.

Every employee's bonus is based in part on achieving the company's overall goal for customer satisfaction.

From the rating, users can link to dashboards that examine customer loyalty, customer satisfaction, product satisfaction, or sales bonus information. In addition, there is a "Low Score Follow-Up" dashboard that highlights customers with downward-trending satisfaction or experience scores. The dashboard embeds a workflow process so the appropriate individuals working as a team can address the issue.

Exhibit 9.3 depicts a customer satisfaction dashboard that shows overall customer satisfaction scores for the entire company across five dimensions (overall, software quality, hardware quality, Cisco account team, and technical support). The bottom table shows overall customer satisfaction scores versus targets with a link to detailed information about

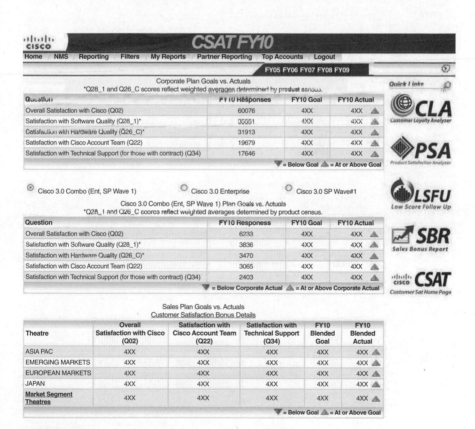

EXHIBIT 9.3 Cisco's Customer Satisfaction Dashboard
Courtesy of Cisco.

how the scores affect employee bonuses. On the right there are quick links to other enterprise dashboards that track customer loyalty, product satisfaction, customers with low satisfaction scores ("low score follow-up"), and the sales bonus report.

From these top-level dashboards, users can drill down to view customer satisfaction scores and targets for any of Cisco's 250 major accounts. These dashboard views enable Cisco account managers to monitor their clients' perception of Cisco, their experiences dealing with Cisco, and overall satisfaction. Likewise, it enables Cisco product managers to evaluate how customers perceive the quality of the products they are responsible for.

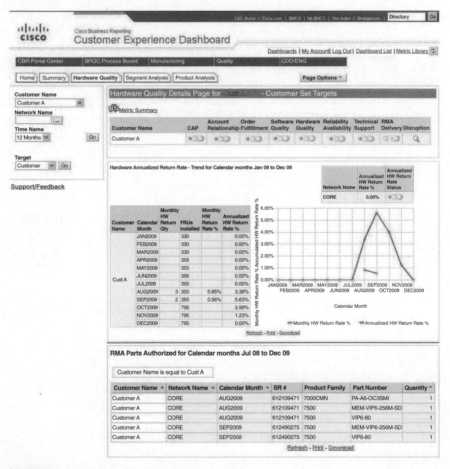

EXHIBIT 9.4 Customer Satisfaction by Account
Courtesy of Cisco.

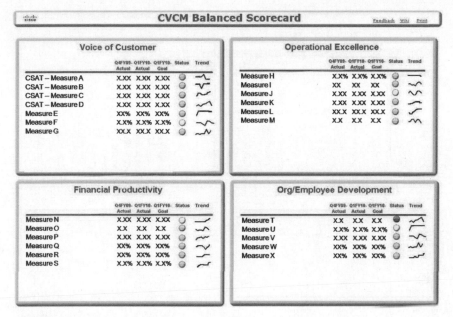

EXHIBIT 9.5 Functional Balanced Scorecard
Courtesy of Cisco.

For instance, Exhibit 9.4 shows hardware quality details for a single customer. The page shows customer satisfaction scores and customer experience data relevant to hardware quality, such as number of returns. An account manager can check this information before visiting an account.

Functional Scorecards and Dashboards. Nearly all functional groups at Cisco maintain a balanced scorecard that contains customer satisfaction and other metrics germane to their domain. Every fiscal quarter, executives and managers in the functional areas hold a one- or two-day operational review meeting to discuss the results in the scorecard. Exhibit 9.5 displays a balanced scorecard from the Customer Value Chain Management (CVCM) functional area, which groups metrics by the classic balanced scorecard perspectives, although the names are slightly different: Voice of the Customer, Operational Excellence, Financial Productivity, and Organization/ Employee Development.

Users can click on a perspective label to view lower-level details, including a table and chart that shows performance over time and metadata describing the highlighted metric. If they need more information, they can click on the metric label and link to an interactive operational dashboard that tracks lower-level metrics and enables users to filter the view via

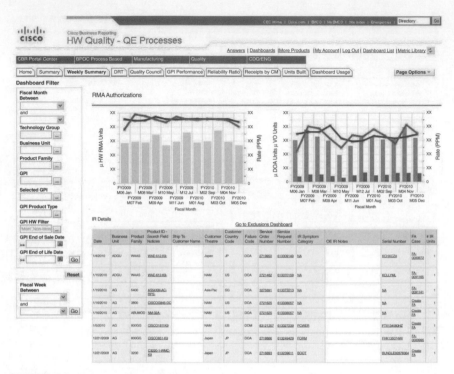

EXHIBIT 9.6 Functional Dashboard Metric View
Courtesy of Cisco.

multiple parameters. (See Exhibit 9.6.) Although the scorecards and dash-boards have different graphical interfaces, all the data come from the QDI data warehouse.

Navigation. Because QDI has so many interrelated scorecards and dashboards and detailed views, it's easy for users to get lost in the maze. To alleviate this problem, most dashboards incorporate a set of menu tabs at the top of each page that provide quick links to relevant dashboards and scorecards. In addition, some dashboards incorporate active site maps to show users how to navigate the detailed views within the same dashboard.

For example, Exhibit 9.7 shows a hardware quality dashboard with a menu bar that contains links to other dashboards and portals. In addition, the Welcome Page (depicted) incorporates a site map that visually shows the navigation path by which users can drill from high-level views to lower-level details. For example, the white line depicts how users can check the status of Immediate Returns (IR), drill to an analysis layer where they can select different views of IR status, and then drill again to interact with a variety of Pareto charts that examine root causes of IR.

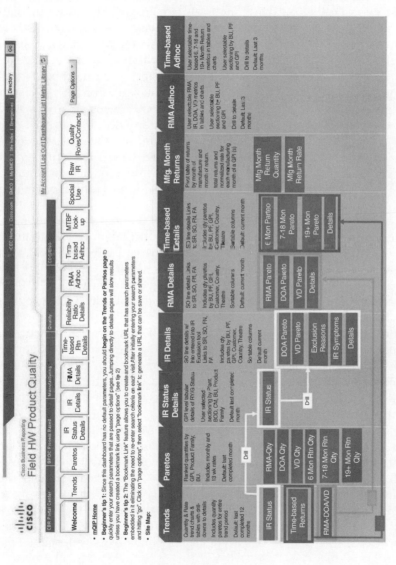

EXHIBIT 9.7 Dashboard Site Map

Courtesy of Cisco.

How It Succeeds

Governance. The key to Cisco's quality initiative is the governance program
it implemented to oversee the effort. The QDI program is managed by a
cross-functional team that spans four levels of management and seven functional areas, including Corporate Quality and the IT department. Cisco is
keen to foster this type of cross-functional collaboration to bridge organizational silos that have been a vestige of its growth-by-acquisition strategy.

At the Sponsor level, vice presidents from the seven functional areas
meet quarterly to approve funding and direction of the program. Next, a
Steering Committee of directors meets every other week to review and
approve strategy, business architecture, and platform decisions. Below this,
a Core Team of managers from each functional area meet weekly to identify
and prioritize projects and enhancements to the QDI. Each manager on
the Core Team has a Subteam that provides assistance and undertakes
special projects. Together, the Core Team and Subteams form the working
group that manages QDI operations.

Like any good BI governance program, QDI is run by the business.
Members of the QDI governance body allocate a portion of their time to
QDI, which becomes part of their job description. Each functional area
contributes people and money to the program, which is supported by the
IT department. The business side sets the strategy and direction and defines
measurement and reporting requirements, while the IT department builds
and maintains the systems and applications.

Compensation. Employees understand the importance of meeting
customer needs because their bonuses are based in part on achieving
specific customer satisfaction scores displayed in the QDI. Top executives
have defined five customer satisfaction metrics upon which the bonuses
are based: overall satisfaction, account team, postsales technical support,
hardware quality, and software quality.

Setting targets for the bonus metrics involves a delicate negotiation
between Corporate Quality and each business function. The targets are then
presented to an internal Quality Experience Board, which has cross-
functional representation, and subsequently to John Chambers and the
executive staff for approval. In addition, some functional groups have
defined common metrics with associated targets to manage their own processes. In Engineering, for example, five of the QDI dashboard metrics are
used to calculate a portion of an engineer's bonus based on operational
performance.

Metrics. Typically, Cisco prototypes a metric before deploying it. The
team uses Excel to collect data on a few products and PowerPoint to display
the data in dashboard format. However, Cisco doesn't try to achieve metric
perfection. Often the data populating a metric may have some anomalies,

but this doesn't stop it from putting the metric into production. "It's okay to create a metric with nuances, because it will still drive dramatic improvements in performance," says Hsiao. "And often, publishing a metric will cause the business to clean up the data."

Accountability. In addition, every metric has a business owner and an IT steward who are responsible for it. The business owner is responsible for results, while the IT steward is responsible for the data that populates it. These responsibilities are published in the Data Library so there is visible accountability. Data integrity issues are escalated through the sponsor hierarchy, and performance is reviewed in each of the business functions during operations review meetings.

Actionability. Since Cisco has correlated the metrics in its QDI program, it understands the importance of taking action when any metric exceeds control limits. Cisco can take action from the outside in or inside out. Outside-in action is when the customer experiences a problem that registers on Cisco's Customer Experience dashboard, such as the Red Alert described in the scenario at the beginning of this chapter. Inside-out action occurs when a Cisco functional area notices an internal process metric has veered out of control and will soon affect the customer experience. (Cisco also identifies key customer issues through direct contact via advisory boards, account teams, technical support centers, and executive briefings.)

In either case, when a metric exceeds a predefined threshold, Cisco employees know they need to act. As described earlier, the relevant managers form a Tiger team to understand the cause of the issue and recommend actions to fix it. By working proactively, Cisco can address problems that the customer may not even have recognized yet. This helps Cisco provide superior service and cement customer loyalty.

Self-Audits. The QDI program eats its own dogfood by holding itself accountable to high standards of customer satisfaction and quality. It regularly asks employees to rate their satisfaction with the QDI dashboards and support services, and it tracks the results in a dashboard. One key QDI metric is adoption, which has nearly doubled in the past two years. Other key customer satisfaction metrics are availability, performance, operational excellence, meeting business need, change management, and on-time project delivery. In addition, the QDI team establishes stringent service-level agreements with clients and conducts 40 daily data audits to ensure it delivers a high-level of data quality to users.

The Future

Cisco increasingly sells products through channel partners. While this is good for business, it makes it difficult to track who the customers are and what their experiences have been buying, implementing, and using Cisco products. The QDI team currently is exploring data interfaces with several channel partners to facilitate the exchange of information and standardize metrics. It is also working with its suppliers, at the behest of some of Cisco's largest customers, to capture and report on supplier quality.

Kingdom of Bahrain

The Kingdom of Bahrain takes strategy management seriously. This island nation in the Persian Gulf with just over 1 million people has one of the fastest growing and freest economies in the Arab world. Despite its remarkable rise, its enlightened leadership now seeks even greater changes. In 2007, the government unveiled a strategic plan titled *Bahrain Vision 2030* that calls for dramatic economic and social transformation. To make its vision reality, all 16 government ministries must create and document strategic plans that fully align with the country's vision for the future.

The Ministry of Works, which oversees construction projects, roadways, and sanitation infrastructure for the nation, already had a head start on the strategic planning process. It began implementing balanced scorecards in 2006.

How It Works

Corporate Strategy Map. Today, the Ministry of Works has a corporate strategy map that consists of 19 objectives linked via cause-effect logic. (See Exhibit 9.8.) The objectives are organized into the four perspectives: Stakeholder, Customer, Internal, and Learning and Growth. These mimic the classic balanced scorecard perspectives set forth by Kaplan and Norton with one difference: Since the kingdom is a government entity whose goal is to serve citizens and not make a profit, the ministry subsumed the classic finance perspective within a broader "stakeholder" perspective.

The strategy map links objectives using arrows to create a cause-effect diagram that visually represents the ministry's strategy. The diagram depicts how objectives relate to each other so that improving one objective positively influences the ones connected to it. The ministry continues to refine the cause-effect linkages in its strategy map as it gains empirical evidence about what factors drive desired results.

Risk. Currently, the Ministry of Works has extended its balanced scorecard with a risk management framework. Now each objective measures both performance and risk and objective owners are responsible for both. The language of risk management can be useful for the public sector when discussing aspects of strategy, says Mark Ranford, who is a key member in the Strategic Planning Section team, andworked in conjunction with other

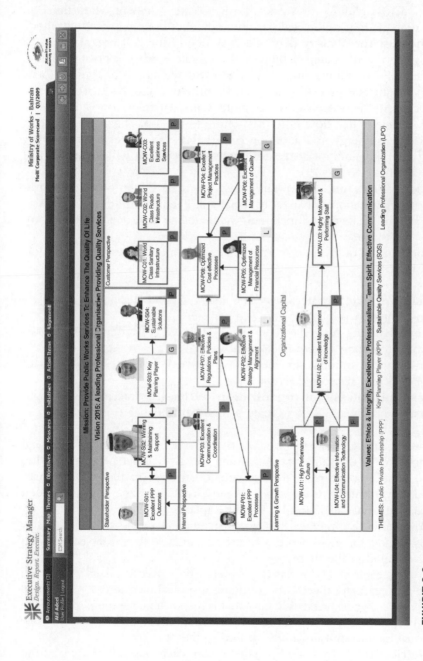

EXHIBIT 9.8 Strategy Map

Courtesy, the Kingdom of Bahrain.

SPS members in architecting the balanced scorecard and managing the strategy across Ministry of Works. "Risk is a key element when thinking about strategy; in fact you really cannot talk about one without the other."

Themes. The Ministry of Works was one of the first organizations to employ the use of strategic "themes" in a strategy map, a practice that is now endorsed by Kaplan and Norton and widely embraced. Themes focus on specific areas of transformation and represent a group's strategy at the highest level. When depicted on a strategy map, themes consist of sets of linked objectives that flow from the bottom to the top. Themes channel an organization's energy and attention on a handful of strategic ideas rather than spread them across dozens of objectives, many of which can get lost in the shuffle.

Themes cross functional boundaries. This makes them powerful instruments of organizational change, especially if, like at the Ministry of Works, organizations create cross-functional "theme teams" that oversee the execution of the theme.

The Ministry of Works has four strategic themes, represented by color-coded boxes:

1. **Public private partnership** (blue lines). Expand the amount of private investment in public projects and services.
2. **Key planning player** (green lines). Improve collaboration and coordination among government agencies.
3. **Sustainable quality services** (purple lines). Improve the quality of projects and services delivered.
4. **Leading professional organization** (red lines). Attract and retain high-quality professionals and create a high-performance organization.

In an unusual twist, one of the themes, "Leading Professional Organization," is the same as the learning and growth perspective. In other words, it cuts horizontally through the objectives on the strategy map instead of vertically like the other themes. This approach has since been proposed as a viable option by Robert Kaplan.

To ensure that themes are not just ethereal concepts, the ministry assigns owners for each theme who are accountable for the objectives and initiatives listed in the theme.

In turn, each objective has an owner, whose face is visually depicted on the strategy map; there is no dodging responsibility here! Like themes, the objective owner oversees a team that is responsible for the performance of the objective. The owner assigns members of the team responsibility for individual metrics and initiatives related to the objective.

Metrics. The color-coded squares below each objective represent the overall status of the objective compared to the current year's target. Each objective is represented by one or more measures with time-based performance targets. The color-coded squares make it easy for individuals to assess the performance of each objective at a glance. The ministry uses these codes:

- Red squares with letter "P" mean "poor."
- Yellow squares with letter "L" mean "lower than targeted."
- Green squares with letter "G" mean "good."
- Blue squares with letter "B" (not pictured) mean "breakthrough."

Objective View. Users can click on an objective in a strategy map to view its details. The objective sheet includes a description of the objective, the owner's name, a list of risk metrics, a heat map that plots the metrics by likelihood and consequences, and time-series charts. It also contains information derived from quarterly review meetings, including actions taken and their status, a performance analysis (not shown), recommendations for action, and a list of initiatives. (See Exhibit 9.9.)

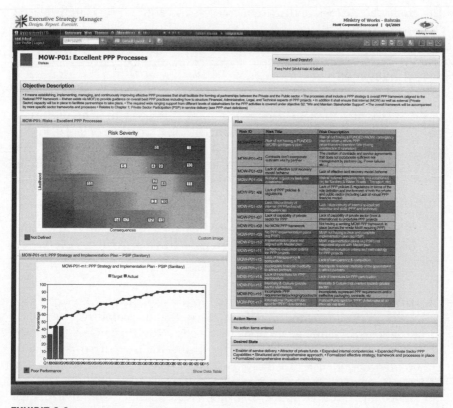

EXHIBIT 9.9 View of an Individual Objective
Courtesy, the Kingdom of Bahrain.

Navigation. From within an individual objective, users can drill on individual metrics, initiatives, and action items to glean more information about each and view current status and trends. Thus in a few simple clicks, users can drill down from a top-level strategy map to detailed views of each objective's underlying components.

Users can also use the menu bar on the strategy map to navigate directly to a summary view of performance across all perspectives, objectives, metrics, and initiatives. This is the scorecard view. (See Exhibit 9.10.) Or they can use other menu items on the strategy map to navigate directly to themes, objectives, measures, initiatives, or action items that they want to see.

Cascading. Finally, users can click on the Alignment menu item in the strategy map view to see more than a dozen cascaded scorecards. To ensure that all departments and groups aligned their efforts and activities to the corporate strategy map, the ministry required each to create their own strategy map and scorecard. Today, the ministry has 17 cascaded strategy maps comprising 196 objectives, 503 metrics, and 327 initiatives that guide the actions and investments of every group and individual in the organization.

How It Succeeds

Challenges. One problem with strategy management in general and balanced scorecards in particular is that they can lose momentum when the original sponsor leaves or changes jobs or the organization is turned upside down by an acquisition or major market change. When push comes to shove, strategy often loses to operational exigencies. In addition, people are often fearful of having their performance exposed to the rest of the organization and will do anything to resist or sabotage such programs.

To ensure adoption of its strategy management initiative, the Ministry of Works took a number of steps to make strategy everyone's business:

- **Office of Strategy Management.** To drive strategy into core processes and sustain the initiative long term, the ministry established a Strategic Planning Section to oversee the balanced scorecard program. The chief reports directly to the minister of works, indicating the importance that the organization places on the initiative. The group, which has five permanent staff members, helps all departments and groups in the ministry create, refine, and utilize their scorecards.

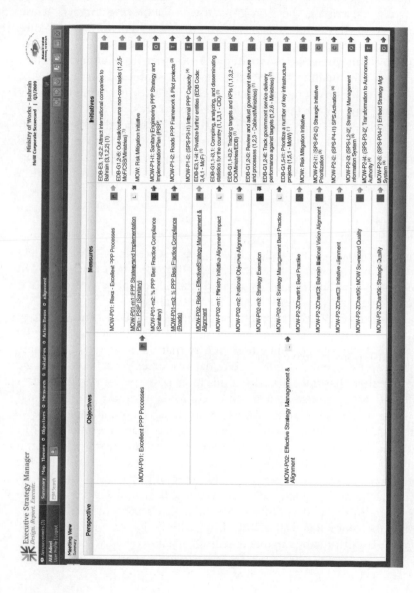

EXHIBIT 9.10 Scorecard View

Courtesy, the Kingdom of Bahrain.

- **Quarterly reviews.** Every quarter, the ministry holds a series of "Sector Business Reviews" culminating in a "Corporate Business Review" in which objective owners must deliver a presentation to the minister of works describing their progress toward achieving targets. These presentations have created a visible and dramatic improvement in commitment and ownership among the objective owners.
- **Monitor the process of strategy.** The Strategic Planning Section evaluates the quality of every department's scorecard and gives it a score, which shows up on their scorecard. The group audits every scorecard and evaluates the objectives, measures, targets, initiatives, and timeliness of reporting. These scores become the basis of an ongoing dialogue between the Strategic Planning Section and the departments. The dialogue helps departments understand the importance and value of strategy management and how it can help them.

Summary

Strategic dashboards—otherwise known as scorecards—are typically deployed in a top-down fashion to manage the execution of strategy on an enterprise scale. This chapter examined strategic dashboards from Cisco and the Ministry of Works in the Kingdom of Bahrain.

The Ministry of Works adopted the balanced scorecard methodology to create 17 strategic dashboards consisting of 200 objectives and 500 metrics. It took time to convince the Ministry that the strategic dashboards would be used to help it secure additional resources to achieve strategic objectives rather than as a tool for punishing poor performance. With a dedicated strategy management office to coordinate the development and use of strategic dashboards, the Ministry has achieved significant success.

Although Cisco didn't apply the balanced scorecard methodology, its strategic dashboards have cultivated a strong "customer-first" culture in a company formed from hundreds of acquisitions. And by statistically linking customer perceptions and experience with internal processes, Cisco knows exactly what impact an increase in customer satisfaction scores will have on customer loyalty and revenues. As such, Cisco uses metrics to drive changes in behavior that will enable it to achieve its strategic objectives. In short, it's a performance management all star.

Critical Success Factors: Tips from the Trenches

Part III provides tips and techniques for creating and deploying performance dashboards. Chapter 10 outlines the strategies and steps for launching and managing a performance dashboard project; Chapter 11 explains how to gather requirements and create effective key performance indicators; Chapter 12 provides tips for designing attractive dashboard displays; and Chapter 13 explains how to architect and integrate performance dashboards.

CHAPTER 10

How to Launch, Manage, and Sustain the Project

Launching a performance dashboard project is easy if you are a senior executive with a vision for a metrics-driven organization. But what if you are a mid-level manager or information technology (IT) professional? How do you convince executives and the rest of the organization about the value of performance dashboards? How do you obtain sponsorship, funding, and staff resources? How do you fight cultural resistance to change and quiet the naysayers? How do you set up a team and define the project scope? And how do you sustain momentum and ensure success? In short, how can you translate your vision into a tangible reality?

This chapter outlines three major elements of a performance dashboard project and offers strategies and tips for succeeding in each of them:

1. **Sell the project.** You can't deploy a performance dashboard unless someone pays for it and people use it. Thus, the first step is to find a visionary executive and get the buy-in of mid-level managers and staff whose output will be measured by the performance dashboard. Success here requires strong communications skills and political savvy.
2. **Manage the project.** Once you get a green light, you need to create a team, scope the project, and keep it on track. This requires excellent team-building and project management skills and the ability to manage user expectations.
3. **Sustain the project.** Finally, a performance dashboard project is never done. You need to continually monitor usage, adapt metrics and user interface to changing business needs, and coach managers how to use the performance dashboard to motivate employees, not punish them.

Sell the Project

Find a Sponsor

The first step in implementing a performance dashboard is to find an energetic, committed business sponsor and sell him or her on the value of the project. The best sponsors exhibit numerous characteristics that can make or break a project. (See Spotlight 10.1.)

There are two types of potential sponsors: (1) enlightened executives who instantly understand the benefits of a performance dashboard and immediately agree to sponsor a project and (2) skeptical executives who need convincing. Unfortunately, the number of enlightened executives are few, although their ranks are growing as younger executives trained in data management and analytical techniques take charge.

Enlightened Executives. Enlightened executives are either drawn to the light by their own knowledge and experience or they are pushed there through a crisis that threatens their careers. These visionary executives understand how to harness information technology to transform the business. They aren't intimidated by technology and see it as a powerful tool to help them achieve their goals. Often these executives are easy to spot: They are new to the company or business unit and have experience leveraging IT in a previous position. Visionaries often find you before you find them.

This was the case at Hewlett Packard (HP) when a new vice president of customer service in the European service division "drove some new thinking" into the program, according to Martin Summerhayes, who was a program director at HP at the time. The executive asked Summerhayes to spearhead a new measurement framework, which quickly turned into a strategic dashboard using a balanced scorecard approach.

Ascetics. When an executive does not come looking for you, the next best option is to look for an executive who is suffering from lack of timely, accurate, or consistent information and turn him or her into a visionary. These executives often feel they are flying blind without accurate data to make good decisions. They are frustrated that their organizations run on spreadsheets and reports whose numbers never line up. They are tired of mid-level managers spinning the numbers in their favor. Most would like to expose performance to the light of day and engender some friendly competition among peer groups but are frustrated by lack of consistent reporting. Others feel they are drowning in data yet starved for information. Executives who feel this kind of pain often jump at the chance to sponsor a performance dashboard project.

Spotlight 10.1 Characteristics of a Good Sponsor

Is there a litmus test for good sponsors? Although sponsors come in all sizes and shapes, the best sponsors exhibit these seven characteristics:

1. **Respected.** The sponsor should be well known in the company and have a solid track record for making positive contributions over the years. The sponsor's opinion should carry significant clout on the executive steering committee.

2. **Knowledgeable.** The sponsor should understand the company inside and out, having served in numerous capacities over many years. The person should also know how technology can be applied to improve the company's competitive position in the marketplace.

3. **Well Connected.** The sponsor should have many allies and few, if any, foes. The sponsor should know the key players whose support is required for the project to succeed. Avoid sponsors with an archenemy who will try to sabotage the project.

4. **Established.** The best sponsors are well established in their positions and will not abandon the project in midstream. Avoid recruiting young executives eager to climb the corporate ladder or veterans a year or two from retirement. "Losing a sponsor midstream was the worst thing that happened to us," laments one manager of business performance.

5. **Committed.** The sponsor needs to commit his or her most precious commodity to the project: time. Avoid sponsors who have a vision but are too busy to evangelize the project, attend meetings, make decisions, and allocate resources. They also must be willing and able to commit other people's time to the project, especially a trusted lieutenant to drive the project and business analysts who can interpret data and business requirements for the technical team.

6. **Good communicator.** A good sponsor knows how to communicate the project's rationale effectively to every constituency in the company and how to galvanize enthusiasm for the project on a sustained basis.

7. **Good role model.** A good sponsor backs up words with actions and uses the performance dashboard to manage the business, either directly or indirectly.

Although few executives possess all seven characteristics, strive to find executives who exhibit most of them or at least do not have any glaring weaknesses.

Skeptical Sponsors

Not everyone is lucky enough to have a visionary executive or one who is feeling sufficient pain to jump at the chance to sponsor a performance dashboard project. In this case, we have to work a lot harder to make a formal case for a performance dashboard. The mantra for skeptics is "Show me the money," so you'll need to craft a strong cost-benefit analysis. (Truth be told, you'll need to do the same with visionaries, but the process is more a formality than a requirement.) But after that, you'll need to size up your executive to determine the most suitable sales technique.

Educate. Sometimes executives just need to hear the right presentation in the right context to turn formative ideas into a concrete vision and plan. For example, the chief information officer (CIO) of a large wireless telecommunications firm attended a workshop delivered by Robert Kaplan, professor at Harvard Business School and co-creator of the balanced scorecard methodology. The CIO was so impressed that he recruited the company's chief financial officer (CFO) to attend the next workshop session, and both of them then sold the concept to the rest of the executive team.

Prototypes. A picture is worth 1,000 words. Showing a prototype of the performance dashboard is a quick way to demonstrate the benefits. For example, one ambitious project manager spent months wheeling a computer across a corporate campus before he found a sponsor willing to commit to the project. (This was before the advent of Web applications!) But don't just show pretty pictures; show a dashboard that meets the explicit needs of potential sponsors. For example, if sponsors are concerned about equipment utilization rates, make sure the dashboard displays metrics that monitor those rates. One word of caution: Make sure potential sponsors realize that the prototype is not a finished application and requires additional time, money, and staff before it can be transformed into a production application.

Benchmarks. If education or a prototype fails to do the trick, it often helps to show a skeptical executive what the company's direct competitors are doing with performance dashboards if such information is available. There is no quicker way to educate and motivate an executive than to show that a close competitor is achieving an advantage by harnessing information via a performance dashboard. Many industry groups, associations, or consultancies publish benchmarking data. If none exists, consider commissioning a research firm to conduct a custom study.

Cost-Benefit Analysis. It's true that the biggest benefits of a performance dashboard are intangible and difficult to quantify: quicker access to information, better decisions, and more effective plans. However, it usually isn't too difficult to justify a dashboard project based on tactical cost savings.

A performance dashboard often can replace dozens if not hundreds of existing reports and reporting systems and free up people's time to focus on more value-added activities.

For example, the project team at International Truck and Engine Corporation estimated that a performance dashboard would save the company the equivalent of 10 full-time staff positions by reducing the number of hours financial analysts spent each month collecting and formatting financial data. Martin Summerhayes justified a $1 million balanced scorecard implementation at HP in 2004 by creatively estimating that it would save the company $26 million in three years. He said the company would save $11 million by reducing the time people spent looking for reports, $9 million by eliminating dozens of reporting systems, and $1 million by reducing training on reporting tools.

Obviously, some of these cost savings are soft, involving people's time. So you will need to bolster your case with firsthand testimony from spreadsheet or reporting jockeys who can describe the cumbersome process they use today to assemble reports on demand. This type of color commentary from people in the trenches sometimes can sway skeptical executives.

Wait for a Catalyst. Sometimes the best cost-benefit analysis, prototype, or strategic rationale is not enough to gain executive commitment. In that case, you have to wait for an external catalyst to reshape the business landscape and change the way executives perceive the value of the project. The most common catalysts are mergers and acquisitions, deregulation, and economic downturns.

For example, a large telecommunications company in Canada struggled for years to put together a balanced scorecard in its operations group without luck. But in short order the company was buffeted by industry deregulation, several mergers, and an economic downturn. In the wake of these events, the board brought in new executives from nonregulated enterprises who were much more receptive to the plan, which was designed to increase the productivity of the operational workforce by 5 percent and save the company millions of dollars. "The company had always pursued efficiency improvement, but now there was no choice," said the company's manager of business performance.

Sell to Staff

Mid-level Managers. If you succeed in getting an executive sponsor, don't celebrate just yet. Most people fail to appreciate the fact that mid-level managers can make or break a project. These managers control departmental budgets and funds and influence whether their staff members take an executive mandate seriously. Mid-level managers may also feel threatened by a performance dashboard that displays their group's performance to the entire company in an unvarnished fashion. If they are used to spinning the numbers in a spreadsheet that they personally present to an executive, they will try to slow down or sabotage a dashboard project.

To corral mid-level managers, you need a carrot and a stick. The stick is easy: an executive mandate to implement the system. But a stick alone is not enough; if the mid-level managers aren't enthusiastic supporters of a new project, they will bleed it to death with a thousand nicks and cuts. So it's imperative that you bring along a few carrots. The most important is the information that the new dashboard will provide that will improve department operating efficiency by freeing up staff time and lower costs by eliminating legacy reporting systems. Ideally, the dashboard addresses a pet project of the most influential department.

An executive sponsor is also critical here. These sponsors have the clout to open up doors and facilitate dialogue between you and the departmental teams. "You have to become a persistent, visible, and vocal advocate of the project," says Jim Rappé at International Truck and Engine. "I'll go to the vice president or director and get 50 minutes at their staff meetings to provide background on our project, explain what's in it for them, and demonstrate the application. I also spend a lot of time talking one-on-one with people to market and sell the project."

To win mid-level managers, you need to start small and demonstrate that the dashboard is their friend, not their enemy. Mid-level managers often fear that the dashboard will expose their weaknesses or make them look bad to their superiors. They often don't realize that a dashboard is designed to help business groups obtain the resources and attention needed to improve poor performance not penalize them for it. For example, one manager in the Ministry of Works in the Bahrain initially resisted balanced scorecards because he was afraid it would make him and his department look bad. But when he realized that red flags on his scorecard convinced senior executives to allocate additional resources to his department to achieve performance objectives, he became an ardent supporter of the dashboard initiative.

Staff Buy-in. It is also critical to gain the support of the front-line staff when the dashboard will be used to monitor key facets of their performance. In many organizations, staff members are understandably jaded and cynical. Many believe, rightly or wrongly, that management will not give them enough resources to meet the goals and objectives in the performance dashboard or enough freedom to optimize performance using strategies and tactics that aren't officially sanctioned.

"Our initial performance management system was built at a time when the prevailing thinking was that you use it to go and beat up the [workers]," says a senior vice president at a services company who asked not to be named. "Quickly, workers questioned the validity of this metric or that data and you begin debating the accuracy of the data, and it's a downward spiral from there."

Another senior director who wished to remain anonymous says, "We had strong support from the top, but I don't think we've done enough to get the folks at the level below them to become really invested. There is a lot of skepticism with front-line employees. Many don't believe the numbers that [departments] report and vigorously comment [on] why some directors get performance bonuses [based on those numbers]."

Both managers said it was important to include staff in the process of developing metrics and targets to get their buy-in. It is important to tell the staff in advance about the project and give them the opportunity to provide feedback both during the design and development stages as well as after the application is deployed through online feedback links or formalized review sessions. Staff members are best positioned to understand whether the key performance indicators (KPIs) measure the correct activity and can't be gamed, and whether they have the resources, authority, and skills to influence the outcome. They can also provide feedback on whether the targets are reasonable to achieve.

Secure Funding

The main job of a sponsor is to secure adequate funding for a project. Without adequate funding, most projects will fail to take root. To ensure sufficient funding, the project plan needs to accurately estimate the costs of staff, services, software, and hardware and the time to roll out the first application. Does the project call for 9 metrics and 800 users or 32 metrics and 5,000 users? The scope of the project will dictate schedules, staffing, and costs. Without accurate scoping, the project will overrun its budget and undermine its credibility and any chances of future funding.

Bootstrapping. Although every performance dashboard requires funding, there seems to be little correlation between money and success. In fact, it appears that new projects sometimes fare better on a shoe-string budget. Some initial hardship forces teams to get creative and go slowly, giving them time to align plans and metrics with reality and gain the trust and support of those who are most likely to resist its deployment.

One advantage of bootstrapped projects is that they usually are driven by small teams of highly motivated business and technical people. They know the only way to kick-start the project is to deliver a quick win and generate some momentum. "I started with no dedicated budget, no full-time staff, and no hardware or software," says Martin Summerhayes, a former scorecard project manager at HP.

To get by until he could secure formal funding, Summerhayes "stole" two part-time developers from other projects and "found" some hardware they could use to build the system. In seven weeks, his makeshift team delivered the first version of the scorecard, which contained 9 metrics and supported 800 users. Because of his initial success, Summerhayes was able to divert money from other projects and hired 11 developers and 2 project leads. Within 18 months, the new system contained 120 metrics and supported 5,500 HP users worldwide.

Perils of Big Budgets. In contrast, larger teams with bigger budgets often take on bigger projects with bigger expectations that are challenging to meet. With more staff to coordinate, more users to satisfy, and more requirements to meet, they often experience problems.

For example, in early 2004, the District of Columbia purchased an integrated business performance management solution and began developing more than 1,200 scorecards for 56 agencies covering 19,000 employees. The application was scheduled to go live in November 2004, but the district postponed the rollout date indefinitely. Doug Smith, director of strategic planning and performance management, said at the time, "We bit off a little more than we can chew, but we are making progress."

Manage the Project

Where to Start? One of the most common questions that people ask is "Where is the best place to start a performance dashboard project?" The best place to start is where there is an energetic, committed sponsor. However, a sponsor is not enough to guarantee the success of a project. It is also important to evaluate the group the sponsor represents to determine how receptive it is as a whole to using a performance dashboard. The readiness assessment checklist in Chapter 5 is a good way to compare and contrast several groups in an organization to find the best place in an organization to launch a project.

The type of dashboard dictates the starting point to some degree. Operational dashboards by definition start within a department at an operational level. Tactical dashboards are enterprise in scope, serving multiple departments, so they usually start in the IT department or occasionally the finance department. Strategic dashboards start at the executive level, usually the chief executive officer or CFO, although some people think a strategic dashboard should never be held hostage to an individual department, especially the finance department whose output metrics have long dominated business reporting. "A scorecard project needs to balance all constituent parties," says Summerhayes.

Create Teams

Once a performance dashboard project gets approved and funded, the next step is to create a capable team to define the metrics, create the dashboard, and train the users.

Project Champion. The project first needs a champion or business driver who either pitched the idea to the business sponsor or was asked by the sponsor to spearhead the project. The project champion doesn't run the project—champions are usually senior-level managers or executives—but must possess a versatile mix of skills. They must have strong knowledge of the business and performance management concepts and excellent communications skills. They must be enthusiastic and relentless promoters, excellent team builders, consummate salespeople and politicians, and superb managers of time, resources, and projects.

It's also important that the champion have strong knowledge of the data and technology so he or she can communicate effectively with the technical team. The champion needs to explain business requirements in technical terms and make sure that developers build solutions that meet the requirements. In effect, they need to be comfortable straddling the worlds of business and information technology.

Steering Committee. The first thing a champion does is create a steering committee to oversee the project. The steering committee consists of the business sponsor, the project champion, and representatives from every group or business unit that ultimately will use or support the performance dashboard. The steering committee for an enterprise dashboard will have representatives from across the company, while a departmental dashboard will have representatives from various working groups. The purpose of this committee is to resolve definitions of critical metrics, prioritize applications, approve scope, and ensure funding. Committee members should have clout in their own organizations so they can effectively evangelize the value and importance of the project back home.

Politically, it is wise to invite executives and managers who might have reservations about the project to sit on the steering committee. This gives you more opportunity to sell them on the value of the project and helps you proactively develop work-arounds to things they might find objectionable. You can also keep them better apprised of project developments that affect their area and intercept rumors or hearsay that might adversely color their opinion. Even if they decline to join the group, they will be flattered by the invitation. You usually can get them to agree to be on the committee mailing list to receive meeting summaries and updates.

KPI Team. The project champion or steering committee needs to recruit a team to define KPIs for the performance dashboard. This team usually is composed of between three and five subject matter experts who are authorized to make decisions on behalf of their group. It also usually contains an IT person who can evaluate the technical feasibility of proposed KPIs.

The KPI team defines requirements, including the strategic objectives the project is supposed to support and the questions the dashboard should answer. The team also defines metrics, dimensions, targets, drill paths, and behavioral outcomes. The IT representative investigates whether data exists to populate proposed KPIs and the condition and quality of the data. It's important to perform this assessment up front before the KPI team spends too much time on a particular KPI.

In terms of scope, the KPI team should strive to model between five and seven objectives, each of which may constitute multiple KPIs. This will take several days to complete. Many KPI teams use an external facilitator to ensure that they create a balanced set of metrics that accurately portray and predict performance. The KPI team then works with the technical team to encode the KPIs in software and populate them with data. Depending on the quality and condition of data, the project should take between three weeks and three months.

Many dashboard managers underscore the importance of going slow and doing things right. "Start small and take time to define the most important KPIs for your business," wrote one respondent. "The fewer the KPIs, the more you can evaluate the impact of each KPI and make refinements to ensure it drives the right behavior."

Technical Team. The technical team translates metrics into a working application. If the technical team uses a commercial tool, it should hire a vendor consultant or tool specialist to get team members up to speed quickly on the tool. The best developers interact continuously with business users and other members of their team. They feel comfortable conducting interviews or calling subject matter experts to get clarification.

The best technical teams have few members and work in close proximity to each other, ideally in the same room. This enables the team to work quickly and efficiently to meet user requirements and deadlines. "We keep ETL [extract, transform, and load] developers, report developers, and Web developers in the same room so they work collaboratively, which is ultimately more efficient than an assembly-line approach where one group hands off work to another," says a manager of business performance at a telecommunications firm.

The longer a technical team stays together, the more efficient it becomes. Technical team members learn each other's strengths and weaknesses and develop pride in their collective accomplishments. "I find developers with lots of drive and enthusiasm and give them plenty of freedom to experiment, which makes them excited to come to work every day. Also they can be very creative in developing solutions, where the business can only outline the issue," says Summerhayes.

Develop the Dashboard

The dashboard project needs an experienced project manager to create a project plan, coordinate resources, manage scope and requirements, and keep the project on track and in budget. Much has been written about how to manage technical projects in other books so we will not dwell on that here.

Dashboard Tool. Once requirements are gathered and prioritized, the KPI team should select a dashboard product or commission the technical team to build the dashboard from scratch. Research shows that about half of organizations still build their dashboards using custom code while the remainder either buy a dashboard tool or customize one to deliver a dashboard application. (See Exhibit 6.4 in Chapter 6.) Unfortunately, many teams purchase a dashboard tool too early in the process, short-circuiting the requirements process. Teams should purchase tools only after they have developed a rich set of requirements to guide their selection. Otherwise, they'll be force-fitting their requirements into a tool.

Parallel Development. With requirements and tools in hand, the technical team then sources data and develops the dashboard. Most development teams work on parallel tracks using an agile or spiral development methodology that involves frequent iterations and weekly meetings with the KPI team to review progress and priorities. Half of the technical team sources and models data to populate a data warehouse or metrics mart, while the other half works develops mock-ups of dashboard screens.

The two groups of developers need to keep each other abreast of changes in requirements or issues to ensure the project stays on track. For example, if the dashboard designers decide to drop a metric in response to user feedback, they need to inform the data developers so they don't spend extra time profiling and sourcing data that are no longer needed. Conversely, if the data developers discover that a source of data is unusable, they need to alert the dashboard designers so they can brainstorm with users a suitable replacement.

Review and Testing. The final stage of development requires testing the software to ensure it meets user requirements. Prior to writing code or installing software, the KPI and technical teams should work together to define criteria for testing whether the dashboard is delivering accurate data. The teams should define ranges for acceptable data for each metric and create use cases to validate the output. Once the dashboard is built, developers need to conduct appropriate unit, functional, and data quality tests, run the use cases, and obtain sign off by the KPI team and steering committee.

Sustain the Project

After the KPIs are encoded in a dashboard, the real work begins. Building the dashboard and getting sign-off from users simply gets you to the starting line. Now you have to make sure that it gets used and improves organizational performance. To ensure the success of a performance dashboard, project teams need to market the project, monitor usage, periodically revise KPIs, govern the system, and coach managers. Let's examine each one briefly. Chapter 15 provides additional detail.

- **Market the project.** If users don't know the dashboard exists, they won't use it. It behooves the KPI team to create a marketing plan that defines target groups of users, key messaging for each group, and the frequency and channel for delivering the messages. Training and support also needs to be woven into the marketing program. It may be wise to consult a marketing manager in your own company to help you set up the plan, which can make or break your project.
- **Monitor usage.** It's rare to define KPIs correctly the first time or design the perfect dashboard on the initial rollout. Thus, it's critical that the KPI and technical teams closely monitor usage to see what users like and don't like. This means creating a dashboard about the dashboard. A good usage monitoring system helps the technical team work proactively with the user community. If usage drops in a particular department, the technical team can call or meet with users to find out the cause of the decline and make changes. They can also use usage patterns to target marketing initiatives to groups that are underusing the dashboards.
- **Revise metrics.** More important, the KPI team and KPI owners need to track whether the KPIs are driving the desired outcomes. Besides tracking usage, the team needs to track overall performance against targets for every metric. Is performance improving or declining? Has performance peaked? Are employees gaming the system?

  "You really don't know what impact a KPI will have until you put it into practice," says one dashboard manager. "You need to be ready to make adjustments to ensure you drive the right behavior."

  Most organizations discover that KPIs have a finite shelf life and need to be rejuvenated or retired at some point before they start dragging down the rest of the metrics. A periodic purge helps refocus employees on what's important and give them new goals to shoot for.

However, unless the technical team monitors usage and performance, it can't ascertain where each KPI is in its life cycle.

- **Govern the process.** The KPI steering committee and project team shouldn't disband after the dashboard is delivered. They should form the basis of a KPI governance team that monitors the effectiveness of the dashboard and its KPIs, authorizes new KPIs, revises existing ones, and sets direction for the program. Some companies hire a chief performance officer whose job is to oversee performance processes and technical implementations and guide the governance committees.

    The technical team creates the "standard" dashboard or report that is used for decision making in every department. The technical team can be a central business intelligence/data warehousing (BI/DW) team or departmental group with requisite skills or some combination. If designed properly, these performance dashboards should meet 60 percent to 80 percent of the needs of most casual users. For the remaining 20 percent to 40 percent, superusers in each department—technically savvy business users—are authorized to create ad hoc reports and dashboards on behalf of their colleagues. The content of these ad hoc reports shouldn't overlap with the standard dashboard but rather provide information where none exists.

    The central team trains and supports the superusers to create the ad hoc reports using the company's standard BI or dashboard tool. These superusers are also part of the company's BI Competency Center (BICC) and help chart the direction of the BI program and submit recommendations for extending the boundaries of the standard performance dashboard serving their department. They also sit on a governance board that reviews requests for new standard dashboards and reports and decides whether to create new dashboards, expand the boundaries of existing ones, or deny report requests altogether because they overlap with existing reports. (See Exhibit 10.1.)

    The BICC is responsible for creating the data infrastructure to support BI and performance management applications and maintaining the semantic layer of business objects (e.g., entities, metrics, dimensions, and hierarchies) used in all reporting applications. Most important, it defines and documents best practices for developing and managing BI solutions and educates the rest of the organization about them. By recruiting superusers to serve on a corporate governance committee (i.e., the BICC and related groups), an organization leverages the strengths of both centralized and distributed development.

- **Coach managers and users.** One of the most important but overlooked elements of a performance strategy is to teach managers how to use performance dashboards as a coaching tool. By itself, the dashboard won't necessarily change behavior, especially if the metrics

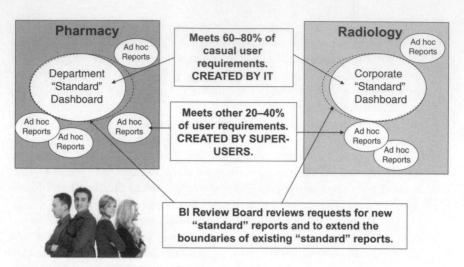

EXHIBIT 10.1 Dashboard Governance

represent a new strategy and way of doing business. "Measures without meetings are useless," says a team leader. "Unless managers hold regular sit-down meetings with their staff to review performance, nothing will change. Managers need to ask 'What are you doing about this number? How will we avoid this happening next time?'"

On the flip side, some managers overreact to every dip and ripple in performance captured by the dashboard. They call meetings with their staff and initiate projects to bolster performance. Unfortunately, knee-jerk reactions usually backfire, exhausting managers and staff alike. Managers need to learn to take a longer-term view of performance. They need to react to trends, not individual data points.

Managers also need instruction on how to use performance dashboards to motivate employees, not penalize them. Managers need to go out of their way to inform employees that a "red light" or negative performance is not an indictment but a request for help. Perhaps the employee doesn't understand how metric works or have the resources or authority to take actions that would positively impact the metric. Or maybe the employee has encountered a difficult customer or situation and needs assistance.

The same is true for executives and managers. For example, the director of a public works agency responsible for roads, bridges, and other infrastructure initially resisted the idea of a performance dashboard for fear that it might expose problems within his division and reflect badly on him. With coaching from the company's strategy management office, the director recognized that a red flag wasn't a penalty but an opportunity to shore up a sagging maintenance budget. Using a balanced scorecard approach, the director defined objectives for maintaining the country's infrastructure. Soon enough, the division garnered lots of red flags, which caught the attention of top officials, who subsequently agreed to increase the division's maintenance funding.

- **Build and maintain a metrics-driven culture.** In addition, managers need to build the discussion of KPIs into management meetings and personal performance reviews. The whole point of a KPI is to foster dialogue between manager and employee. Poor performance gives the manager license to discuss goals and strategies and investigate whether the individual or team has the skills and resources to achieve the targets. Or the manager could determine that the metric or target is unrealistic and needs revision.

- **Celebrate success.** Finally, make sure you take the time to celebrate success. Recognize those who support the performance measurement system and strive to achieve established targets and goals, even if performance falls short. Also reward teams that have made gains in performance over a given period by making significant or subtle changes to the way they employ people, processes, or technology. Communicate these successes in monthly newsletters, quarterly reports, and corporate Web sites

Summary

A performance dashboard project shares many traits with other IT projects, although it has some unique characteristics that are important to know. Rarely is a dashboard project "required" for running the business. For many executives, it's a nice-to-have resource, unless they truly want to run the business by the numbers. Thus, to launch a project, you need to have consummate sales and marketing skills. And creating the dashboard is never as straightforward as an online transaction processing project since the dashboard must be flexible enough to answer business questions that continuously evolve as the business changes. And finally, there is no corporate edict that tells employees, "You must use the BI environment to make good decisions." Thus, ensuring adoption and sustaining usage is a critical element of a successful performance dashboard project.

CHAPTER 11

How to Create Effective Performance Metrics

One of the most common questions people ask about performance dashboards is "How do we create effective metrics?"

Change Agents. Metrics are important because they govern how employees do their jobs. The adage "What gets measured gets done" is true. Metrics focus employees' attention on the tasks and processes that executives deem most critical to the success of the business. Metrics are like levers that executives can pull to move the organization in new and different directions. In fact, among all the tools available to executives to change the organization and move it in a new direction, performance measures are perhaps the most powerful.

For that reason, executives need to treat metrics with respect. As powerful agents of change, metrics can drive unparalleled improvements or plunge the organization into chaos and confusion. If the metrics do not accurately translate the company's strategy and goals into concrete actions on a daily basis, the organization will flounder. Employees will work at cross-purposes, impeding each other's progress and leaving everyone tired and frustrated with little to show for their efforts. In short, the company will be efficient but ineffective.

A trucking company, for example, that measures performance by the percentage of on-time shipments may drive hauling costs skyward because the metric does nothing to discourage dispatchers from sending out half-empty trucks to meet their schedules. To keep costs in line, the company needs to add a second metric that measures the percentage of unused cargo capacity in outgoing trucks, and it needs to revise the first metric so it emphasizes meeting customer expectations for fast, reliable shipments rather than just on-time deliveries. This combination of metrics gives dispatchers leeway to contact customers and renegotiate shipping schedules if they know the customer may be flexible.

More Art than Science. Crafting sound metrics is more an art than a science. Although a metrics team may spend months collecting requirements, standardizing definitions and rules, prioritizing metrics, and soliciting feedback—in short, following all the rules for solid metric development—it still may not succeed. In fact, there is a danger that metrics teams will shoot for perfection and fall prey to analysis paralysis. In reality, KPI teams can get only 80 percent of the way to an effective set of metrics; the last 20 percent comes from deploying the metrics, seeing how they impact behavior and performance, and then adjusting them accordingly.

"Only when you put the metrics out there, do you really understand what behaviors you are driving," says John Lochrie, former senior vice president of Direct Energy Essential Home Services.

Understanding Metrics

Types of Metrics

Metrics versus Indicators. A metric is a measurement of business activity, such as a "number of new customers," "average mean time between repair," or "total sales." But in a performance management system, we want to do more than just measure business activity; we want to measure how well we are executing business strategy.

To measure business strategy, we compare business activity to a goal defined in a plan designed to achieve the strategy. In the examples just listed, goals might be "25 new customers per month," "10,000 hours between repairs," or "$10 million in sales this quarter," respectively.

A metric that measures business activity against a goal is called a performance indicator. If designed properly, a performance indicator embodies the organization's or group's strategy. It measures what is important and compares performance to time-based targets. Performance indicators show how closely the output of our business activity is tracking to plan and "indicates" whether we are on course to achieve our strategic objectives.

There are two major types of performance indicators: outcome metrics and driver metrics. There are also diagnostic or activity metrics that don't have goals attached but are nevertheless important to measure. In addition, there are risk indicators that measure risk instead of performance. Finally, there are key performance indicators (KPIs), which are few in number (i.e., "key") but have widespread impact on the business.

Outcome Metrics. Outcome metrics—sometimes known as lagging indicators—measure the output of business activity that a strategy is designed to achieve. So, if the organization's strategy calls for a 12 percent return rate, the outcome metric might be "return rate per month." Outcome metrics are generally backward looking. They measure past activity that has already happened and cannot be changed.

A majority of outcome metrics are financial in nature—revenues, profits, return on equity—because most commercial organizations define their strategy and success in financial terms. But this is not always the case. Cisco, for example, displays its overall customer satisfaction metric alongside its stock price on the company's intranet home page, reflecting how deeply the company believes customer satisfaction and loyalty are the key to the company's success. Nonprofit and government agencies have many nonfinancial outcome metrics because their mission is to serve the public good in some way. For instance, a hospital might have "patient safety" as an outcome metric while a public works department might have "quality of roads."

Driver Metrics. Driver metrics—sometimes known as leading indicators—measure business activity that influences the results of the outcome KPIs. Driver metrics are tactical in nature: They measure activity that happens between the periods in which outcomes are measured. So if an outcome metric is monthly sales, a typical driver metric might be weekly or daily sales. The purpose of driver metrics is to track current activity so people can make necessary adjustments to meet or exceed outcome goals for the period. Driver metrics foster proactivity.

Actionable. The best types of driver metrics are actionable. They give workers enough time to make necessary adjustments to affect the desired outcomes. For example, if monthly sales drops, executives might realign vacation schedules to ensure there are enough salespeople working at all times. Or they can ask salespeople to schedule more meetings with clients and prospects during the next two weeks.

Predictive. Often, organizations use regression algorithms to predict future outcomes based on current levels of activity so workers can see whether they are going to meet targets by the end of the period. For example, an online mortgage company identified two driver metrics that correlate with the ability of its salespeople to meet daily quotas: (1) the amount of time they spend on the phone with customers and (2) the number of clients they speak with each day. The company now displays these two "current-state" metrics prominently on its dashboards. It also created a third driver metric based on the other two that projects every 15 minutes whether salespeople are on track to meet their daily quotas.

Brainstorming Drivers. It behooves organizations to spend time brainstorming activities and behaviors that correlate with outcome drivers. The more an organization aligns drivers and outcomes, the better it can adapt to changes in the marketplace and achieve its goals. So, in our last example, an organization might determine that the best driver metric for monthly sales is the number of salespeople on the street. Or they might get more granular and determine that the best driver is the number of face-to-face meetings that salespeople have scheduled with customers in the next two weeks.

Five Whys. There are two techniques for brainstorming driver metrics. One is the "Five Whys." Here a metrics team starts by identifying key outcomes aligned with strategy that it wants to achieve. Then a facilitator selects one outcome and asks the team, "What drives, causes, or contributes to that outcome?" The team brainstorms potential drivers and selects one. The facilitator then asks, "What drives that metric?" The process repeats itself three more times until the team comes up with a few good candidate metrics.

Sensory Perceptions. Stacey Barr, a performance management specialist in Australia, suggests that a group take a more "sensory" approach. She says a team should identify an outcome and then describe how it would "look, feel, and sound" if it were happening. Then the team could brainstorm ways to count whether the outcome was happening. These counts become the driver metrics. For example, a manufacturing organization that wants to reduce injuries might envision a limber, flexible employee who participates in daily stretching exercises. To count such behavior, the team decides the only reasonable approach is to have the floor supervisor check a daily form to indicate that workers have stretched. Spotlight 11.1 provides examples of how to correlate outcome and driver metrics.

Other Metrics

Activity Metrics. Activity metrics measure business activity related to performance indicators but don't have goals associated with them. They provide additional context about performance that helps businesspeople make informed decisions. For instance, activity metrics include top 10 lists, such as top 10 customers by revenue or bottom 10 suppliers by on-time delivery performance. Activity metrics might also include 360-degree views of customers or suppliers as well as counts that indicate demand for some resource, such as number of cell phones issued, number of shuttle bus runs, or number of procurements processed.

Risk Indicators. Unlike performance indicators, which measure how well something is being done, risk indicators measure the riskiness of a business activity or how it might adversely affect operations. A risk indicator measure provide an early warning sign to identify events that may harm the continuity of existing processes. Like performance indicators, risk indicators have goals associated with them. For instance, the Ministry of Works in Bahrain profiled in Chapter 9 has numerous risk objectives and associated metrics.

Key Performance Indicator. A KPI is a performance indicator that has a profound impact on the business. David Parmenter, author of the book *Key Performance Indicators: Developing, Implementing, and Using*

Spotlight 11.1 Cause-Effect Relationships

It is easy to define outcome metrics, but it takes imagination to identify driver metrics. One must follow the trail backward from results measured by an outcome metric to a first-mover driver. Because each outcome metric has numerous drivers, the key to defining effective drivers is to find the one or two that have the greatest impact on results desired by executives. Here are a few examples of driver metrics and the outcome metrics indicators they influence.

Driver Metric	Outcome Metric
Complex repairs completed successfully during the first call or visit	Customer satisfaction
Number of signed, positive employee suggestions each week or ratio of positive to negative comments	Employee satisfaction
Number of part for which orders exceed forecasts within 30 days of scheduled delivery	Per unit manufacturing costs
Number of days with lowest prices for comparable products	Market share
Number of customers who are delinquent paying their first bill	Customer churn
Number of loyalty rewards cashed in each month	Customer loyalty

Eyes of the Beholder. Truth be told, often there isn't a lot of difference between an outcome metric and a driver metric. "One man's outcome measure is another man's value driver," says Neal Williams, founder of Corda, a dashboard solutions provider. "An outcome KPI in one dashboard could be a driver KPI in another." For example, a business intelligence (BI) team's outcome metric is "number of active BI users per month." But this is simply a driver metric for the overall information technology (IT) organization, whose outcome metric might be "return on assets" or "customer satisfaction" or "cost efficiency."

Winning KPIs (John Wiley & Sons, 2007), says a KPI is a nonfinancial metric that is measured frequently and affects most of the company's critical success factors and performance metrics. Most important, he says, a KPI is monitored directly by the chief executive officer (CEO).

Parmenter recounts the story of Lord King, chairman of British Airways, who reportedly turned around the ailing airline in the 1980s using a single

KPI: the timely arrival and departure of airplanes. "[Lord King] was notified, wherever he was in the world, when a British Airways plane was delayed more than two hours. The British Airways airport manager at the relevant airport knew that if a plane was delayed beyond this threshold, he or she would receive a personal call from the chairman. It was not long before British Airways planes had a reputation for leaving on time," says Parmenter.

Of course, British Airways, or any airline for that matter, needs to make sure it doesn't value on-time arrivals and departures at the expense of safety and customer satisfaction. Employees ranging from flight attendants, pilots, mechanics, and bag handlers, who are under pressure to achieve time-based metrics, may be tempted to cut corners in ways that could have serious consequences. If bags are lost, customers harassed, pilots fatigued or ill, or safety compromised, the airline's brand could be seriously tarnished. Therefore, KPIs must be balanced by a host of performance and risk indicators to ensure the business maintains an even keel.

A well-designed KPI triggers a chain reaction of process improvements throughout the organization. In the British Airways example, late planes increase costs because airlines have to accommodate passengers who miss connecting flights; customer satisfaction declines because customers dislike missing flights; worker morale slips because workers have to deal with unruly customers; and supplier relationships are strained because missed flights disrupt service schedules and lower quality. When Lord King focused on late arrivals and departures, managers and staff figured out ways to change business processes and behaviors so they didn't receive a career-limiting call from the CEO. As a result, a single operational KPI monitored by the CEO created a ripple effect of process improvements that produced rapid and dramatic gains in performance.

Metric Components

Six Attributes. A performance indicator—whether an outcome or driver metric—has six primary attributes. Some of these attributes are visually depicted in Exhibit 11.1.

1. **Value.** A performance metric contains an actual value or number that represents the measurement of performance. The bold line in Exhibit 11.1 represents total sales each month. Ideally, if a user moved the cursor over a point in the line, the chart would pop up the actual numeric value for sales during that period.
2. **Time frame.** Performance metrics have a time frame by which they are measured. A time frame includes the end date when the target must be achieved and interval dates that are used to gauge progress along the way. The chart in Exhibit 11.1 measures performance monthly but does not indicate an end date.

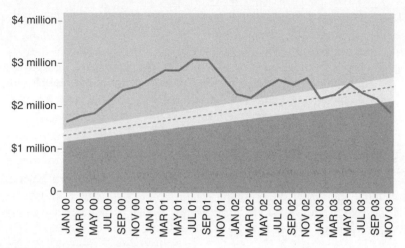

EXHIBIT 11.1 Sales Performance Chart

3. **Benchmark.** A performance metric compares actual values to some benchmark or baseline. A most common benchmark is the result from the same period last year. The benchmark could also be an arbitrary number, such as a budgeted or forecasted number. Or a metric could have multiple benchmarks (i.e., prior year, plan, and forecast), which is often the case with financial numbers. Benchmarks can also be external measures, such as the performance of an industry leader.

4. **Targets.** Each metric is associated with a target defined by executives in a planning or budgeting session. The target represents a tangible goal in context of the benchmark. For example: "We want sales to exceed last year's number by 10 percent this period." There are end targets, which typically are measured annually, and interim targets, which are measured in smaller intervals, such as daily, weekly, or monthly. The chart graphically depicts how the interim target increases at a steady rate each month. Presumably, the end target is defined annually.

5. **Ranges.** Targets are divided into ranges of performance, usually "above target," "on target," or "below target." Ranges commonly are based on percentages, although more complex rules can be used as well. For example, performance that is 5 percent above target might be considered "above target," while performance within 5 percent of target is considered "on target," and performance below 5 percent of target is deemed "below target."

Most metrics teams apply three or four ranges to each metric, although some apply more. For example, the operations department of a U.S. railroad had 16 ranges for each metric. Organizational culture seems to be the biggest factor in defining the number of ranges. Most executes and managers are fine with three or four, while engineers and operations staff prefer more.

6. **Visual encodings.** Finally, a dashboard visually encodes ranges so users can quickly grasp how close or far away they are from achieving the target. Most metrics encode ranges using traffic lights: green, yellow, and red. The chart shows graphically how targets and ranges change by a steady percentage each period.

Targets

Performance metrics derive much of their impact from the targets associated with them. The visual encoding of those targets into ranges causes users to "jump" when they see a red light. Ranga Bodla, senior director of enterprise performance software at SAP, defines five types of targets.

1. **Achievement.** With an achievement target, performance should reach or exceed the target in an upward direction. Anything over the target is desired but not required. An example is revenue, where you want to grow sales to at least 100 percent of the target, but more revenue is better as long as you maintain quality and customer satisfaction.

2. **Reduction.** A reduction target is the opposite of an achievement target. Here, performance should reach or exceed the target in a downward direction. Anything less than the target is valuable but not required. An example is overtime, where you need a certain amount of overtime to get work done, but less overtime is desirable as long as you don't sacrifice other goals, such as on-time deliveries.

3. **Zero.** A zero target is an extreme form of a reduction target in which the goal is zero. Basically, zero means that there is no circumstance in which a positive number is a good thing. Examples are number of injured employees or product defects.

4. **Absolute.** With an absolute target, the goal is to come as close as possible to the target value without exceeding it in either direction. For example, a manufacturing plant wants suppliers to ship goods as close as possible to an agreed-on delivery time. If a part ships too soon, the plant has to store it as inventory at considerable cost; if the part ships too late, the assembly line has to shut down until the part arrives; if it ships on time, the plant achieves maximum efficiency.

5. **Min/Max.** Min/max is like an absolute target but with more leeway in what is acceptable. Instead of shooting for a fixed number, performance should exist within a range of values. Anything above or below the range is not good. An example is mean time between repairs in which a manufacturer wants to deliver products that require repair only every 24 to 36 months.

Setting Targets. Business users should be able to define targets and thresholds for metrics using Boolean rules (i.e., if, then, or else) or by inserting values. The rules are applied to the metrics whenever the underlying data is updated. Many commercial dashboards, especially strategic dashboards, now enable authorized business users to define targets and thresholds via a point-and-click graphical interface.

Setting Alerts. The system should also let business users define personalized alerts when a metric exceeds a certain threshold. The alerts may be one and the same as the traffic lighting system (see Rohm and Haas example in Chapter 8) or a special icon or ticker tape animation that scrolls across the screen when the alert is triggered. The best alerts notify users through a preferred channel (e.g., wireless phone, e-mail, or land-line phone) so they don't have to log on to the dashboard to see significant events. In complex event processing systems, intelligent alerts can even trigger predefined actions, such as updating a database or sending e-mail messages. (See Chapter 6.)

Displaying Metrics

Conveying the Full Story. Performance dashboards display multiple attributes of a performance metric to give users a comprehensive view of performance. The number of attributes displayed depends on the application and user requirements. The goal is to provide the key information in a quick glance.

The chart in Exhibit 11.2, which comes from a balanced scorecard, shows six metric attributes: name, trend, status, target value, actual value, and variance percentage. Notice that it uses symbols to indicate trend and status so that color-blind people can interpret the encodings correctly.

The metric name usually is hyperlinked so users can click on it to drill down and view a time-series chart. Status measures performance against the target and usually is shown with a colored stoplight. Trend measures performance against the prior interval or another time period and often is

Name	Trend	Status	Target	Actual	Variance %
📄 **Finance**					
⬤ Decrease European Discounts	+	✅	16.00%	15.53%	-3%
⬤ Keep APAC discounts < 17%	—	❌	17.00%	24.77%	31%
⬤ Keep N.A. discounts < 17%	—	✅	17.00%	15.66%	-9%

EXHIBIT 11.2 Displaying Performance Metrics

displayed using sparklines (a miniature time-series trend line without a scale), arrows, or in this case plus/minus signs. The actual and target values are self-explanatory and usually are displayed as text. Variance (not depicted) measures the gap between actual and target values and usually is displayed using text or a bullet chart (or a variance chart if users drill to a separate page). Variance percentage divides the variance against the target so users can interpret variance quickly.

Interpreting Variances. Variance, by itself, is tricky to interpret. Its meaning depends on the type of target. For example, most people automatically assume that a positive variance is a good thing. But if the metric uses a reduction target, a positive variance could be bad. For example, a positive 5 percent variance in overtime means workers are taking more overtime than desired, which dramatically increases costs. The difficulty of interpreting variance is why most metrics designers display a combination of attributes for each metric, including status, trend, and variance. The combination of attributes usually gives viewers an accurate impression of overall performance.

However, sometimes the attributes give mixed signals. For example, what does it mean if status is red but the trend is green? Should people take action to address the red status, or should they relax because someone has already addressed the problem and progress is being made? A dashboard that enables users to annotate metrics with comments would help in these situations. It would also behoove organizations to train employees how to interpret metrics properly, either through formal classroom instruction or an apprenticeship or mentorship.

Buried Scores. However, sometimes a performance dashboard disguises the true state of performance. This occurs when a compound metric displays a positive status even though one underlying metric is negative. The negative score of the single metric is outweighed by the positive scores of the other metrics. So, unless users dig below the surface of the compound metric, they will never see that a major problem is brewing.

The problem arises because most compound metrics today calculate overall status by averaging the percentage variance from target of underlying metrics. Some designers are circumventing the law of averages by giving added weighting to negative scores so they have more impact on overall status. Others will display an alert next to the compound metric that indicates that there is problem with one of its underlying metrics.

Number of Metrics

No Hard-and-Fast Rules. Many people ask, "How many performance metrics should we display on a dashboard?" In general, the fewer metrics the better, but there is no hard-and-fast rule about how many to display on a single dashboard screen. Ultimately, you are trying to help business-people manage processes and solve problems. The less work they have to do to get the information they need to do their jobs effectively, the more useful they will find the dashboard.

There is a natural tendency among organizations to keep adding metrics and never delete any. Over time, the metrics lose their power to grab the attention of employees and focus their behavior on key value-added activities. "When people have too many metrics to track, the message gets blurred," says the director of customer management at an energy services provider.

The number of performance metrics depends on many factors: the type of users, the nature of the data, the complexity of the processes being monitored, and the skill and maturity of the users. In general, business executives and managers work effectively with about 5 to 7 metrics displayed as charts or more if the data are arranged in tables. The executive dashboard at Rohm and Haas (see Chapter 7) displays 12 metrics in a table with two associated line charts.

Engineers and service managers prefer densely packed dashboards with lots of metrics and text. Front-line workers, such as salespeople and field technicians, need simpler displays with a handful of easy-to-understand metrics as well as charts to help them calculate their incentive pay. 1-800 CONTACTS, for example, provides a simple, one-page dashboard for its call center salespeople. (See Chapter 7.)

Hiding Complexity. Monitoring complex processes from end to end may take dozens or more metrics. For example, a repair call resolution metric might require five submetrics to capture performance accurately at each stage of the repair process, from taking an order, scheduling the repair, and validating the repair to receiving customer payment. One metric will not shed enough insight to help managers know what part of the process is experiencing problems.

Obviously, it is difficult to display this many metrics on a single dashboard page without overwhelming users. One option is to group metrics by category and place them on different tabs (i.e., pages or folders) within the same dashboard. Another option is to house related metrics on different dashboards and then interlink the dashboards so users can navigate easily from one to the next.

For instance, if users want to examine a single departmental process from top to bottom, you can place strategic, tactical, and operational metrics on different dashboards and link them together. Or if the process crosses departmental boundaries—such as order to cash or procure to pay—you can link different departmental dashboards or create a single dashboard for the entire process, nesting metrics using tabs or radio buttons if needed.

If you aren't sure how many performance metrics to create, err on the high side. What does not get measured does not get done, and what does not get done can hurt the organization. The key to selecting metrics judiciously is to validate that they are aligned with strategic objectives and distribute them to performance dashboards at the appropriate level in the organization. Not all metrics need to appear on the top-level scorecard; most, in fact, should be delegated to lower-level ones.

According to research from TDWI, most organizations adhere to the less is more rule regarding KPIs. On average, organizations deploy 12 metrics on the top-level screen of their dashboards and 159 metrics overall. Operational dashboards have fewer top-level metrics (11) and fewer total metrics (141) than the average; tactical dashboards have the same number of top-level metrics as the average (12) but fewer overall metrics (110); and strategic dashboards have more top-level metrics (14) and total metrics (183) than the average. (See Exhibit 6.3.)

Metric Ecosystems

Balancing Metrics. When creating performance metrics, it's important to make sure they are aligned. Typically, one metric is not enough to drive performance in the right direction. It usually takes an ecosystem of metrics to ensure proper balance.

For instance, a call center may want to increase the productivity of its customer service representatives by measuring how many customers they talk to per hour. The unintended consequence of this measure is that it will discourage service representatives from spending enough time with customers to solve their problems. To avoid a precipitous drop in customer

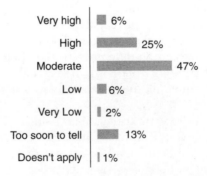

EXHIBIT 11.3 To What Degree Have Your KPIs Improved Performance in Your Organization?

satisfaction, the call center needs to balance its productivity metric with one focused on quality or customer satisfaction.

"We've seen our staff take unexpected actions to boost a metric that undermined other areas," says one director of BI.

Ironically, a balanced measurement ecosystem often consists of contradictory metrics. In our call center example, a balanced ecosystem might consist of a productivity metric (e.g., "Make as many calls per hour as possible.") and a quality metric (e.g., "Take as much time as you need to solve customer problems."). Humans have the capacity to manage this tension between opposites to some degree. But the metrics inevitably will spawn new procedures that resolve the tension more effectively. For example, the call center might divide agents into two groups, one that is incented to handle lots of easy calls quickly and forward harder calls to a second group, which is encouraged to spend more time with each customer.

Characteristics of Effective Performance Metrics

Organizations create many performance metrics, and most may exhibit the attributes we've discussed to this point. However, a well-constructed performance metric doesn't mean that it's an effective one. Exhibit 11.3 shows that a third of performance metrics have a "very high" or "high" impact on performance, while almost half (47 percent) have a moderate impact.

As I said at the outset, creating performance metrics is as much art as science. To guide you in your quest, here are 12 characteristics of effective performance metrics:

1. **Strategic.** To create effective performance metrics, you must start at the end point—with the goals, objectives, or outcomes you want to achieve—and then work backward. A good performance metric embodies a strategic objective. It is designed to help the organization monitor whether it is on track to achieve its goals. The sum of all performance metrics in an organization (along with the objectives they support) tells the story of the organization's strategy.
2. **Simple.** Performance metrics must be understandable. Employees must know what is being measured, how it is calculated, what the targets are, how incentives work, and, more important, what they can do to affect the outcome in a positive direction. Complex KPIs that consist of indexes, ratios, or multiple calculations are difficult to understand and, more important, not clearly actionable.

   "We hold forums where we show field technicians how our repeat call metric works and how it might impact them. We then have the best technicians meet with others to discuss strategy and techniques that they use to positively influence the metric," says a director of customer management at an energy services provider.

3. **Owned.** Every performance metric needs an owner who is held accountable for its outcome. Some companies assign two or more owners to a metric to engender teamwork. Companies often embed these metrics into job descriptions and performance reviews. Without accountability, measures are meaningless.

4. **Actionable.** Metrics should be actionable. That is, if a metric trends downward, employees should know what corrective actions to take to improve performance. There is no purpose in measuring activity if users cannot change the outcome. Showing that sales are falling isn't very actionable; showing that sales to a specific segment of customers is falling compared to others is more actionable.

   Actionable metrics require employees who are empowered to take action. Managers must delegate sufficient authority to subordinates so they can make decisions on their own about how to address situations as they arise. This seems obvious, but many organizations hamstring workers by circumscribing the actions they can take to meet goals. Companies with hierarchical cultures often have difficulty here, especially when dealing with front-line workers whose actions they have historically scripted. These companies need to replace scripts with guidelines that give users more leeway to solve problems in their own novel ways.

5. **Timely.** Actionable metrics require timely data. Performance metrics must be updated frequently enough so the accountable individual or team can intervene to improve performance before it is too late. Some people argue that executives do not need actionable or timely information because they primarily make strategic decisions for which monthly updates are good enough. However, the most powerful change agent in an organization is a top executive armed with an actionable KPI.

6. **Referenceable.** For users to trust a performance metric, they must understand its origins. This means every metric should give users the option to view its metadata, including the name of the owner, the time the metric was last updated, how it was calculated, systems of origin, and so on. Most BI professionals have learned the hard way that if users don't trust the data, they won't use them. The same is true for performance metrics.

7. **Accurate.** It is difficult to create performance metrics that accurately measure an activity. Part of this problem stems from the underlying data, which often need to be scanned for defects, standardized, deduped, and integrated before displaying to users. Poor systems data create lousy performance metrics that users won't trust. Garbage in,

garbage out. Companies should avoid creating metrics when the condition of source data is suspect.

Accuracy is also hard to achieve because of the way metrics are calculated. For example, a company may see a jump in worker productivity, but the increase is due more to an uptick in inflation than internal performance improvements. This is because the company calculates worker productivity by dividing revenues by the total number of workers. Thus, a rise in the inflation rate, which artificially boosts revenues—which is the numerator in the metric—increases worker productivity even though workers did not become more efficient.

Also, it is easy to create metrics that do not accurately measure the intended objective. For example, many organizations struggle to find a metric to measure employee satisfaction or dissatisfaction. Some might ask users in surveys, but it's unclear whether employees will answer questions truthfully. Others might use the absenteeism rate, but this might be skewed by employees who miss work to attend a funeral, care for sick family members, or stay home when child care is unavailable.

8. **Correlated.** Performance metrics are designed to drive desired outcomes. Many organizations create performance metrics but never calculate the degree to which they influence the behaviors or outcomes they want. Companies must refresh performance metrics continually to ensure they drive the desired outcomes.

9. **Game-proof.** Organizations need to test all performance metrics to ensure that workers can't circumvent them out of laziness or greed or go through the motions to make a red light turn green without making substantive changes. "Users always look for loopholes in your metrics," says one BI manager. To prevent users from fudging customer satisfaction numbers, one company hires a market research firm to audit customer surveys.

10. **Aligned.** It's important that performance metrics are aligned with corporate objectives and don't unintentionally undermine each other, a phenomenon called suboptimization. To align metrics, you need to devise them together in the context of an entire ecosystem designed to drive certain behaviors and avoid others.

11. **Standardized.** A big challenge in creating performance metrics is getting people to agree on the definitions of terms, such as sales, profits, or customer, that comprise most of the metrics. Standardizing terms is critical if organizations are going to distribute performance dashboards to different groups at multiple levels of the organization and roll up the results. Without standards, the organization risks spinning off multiple, inconsistent performance dashboards whose information cannot be easily reconciled.

12. **Relevant.** A performance metric has a natural life cycle. When first introduced, the performance metric energizes the workforce and performance improves. Over time, the metric loses its impact and must be refreshed, revised, or discarded.

"We usually see a tremendous upswing in performance when we first implement a scorecard application," says a program manager at a major high-tech company. "But after a while, performance trails off. In the end you can't control people, so you have to continually reeducate them about the importance of the processes that the metrics are measuring or you have to change the processes."

Designing Effective Metrics

Gathering Requirements

Chapter 10 discussed how to sell, manage, and sustain a dashboard project and examined the different teams required to design, develop, and manage the project. This section provides additional detail about how the KPI team gathers and prioritizes requirements for creating performance metrics and creates a blueprint for development that the technical team can implement.

KPI teams use a variety of methods to capture requirements for dashboard metrics. Chief among these is to "review and prioritize metrics used in existing reports" followed closely by "interviews and joint design sessions" selected by 55 percent and 51 percent of respondents respectively to a 2008 TDWI survey. (See Exhibit 11.4.)

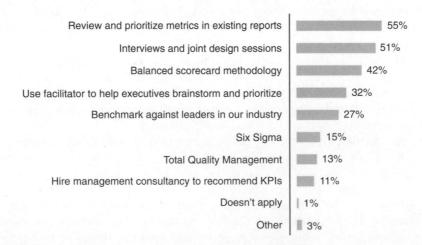

Review and prioritize metrics in existing reports	55%
Interviews and joint design sessions	51%
Balanced scorecard methodology	42%
Use facilitator to help executives brainstorm and prioritize	32%
Benchmark against leaders in our industry	27%
Six Sigma	15%
Total Quality Management	13%
Hire management consultancy to recommend KPIs	11%
Doesn't apply	1%
Other	3%

EXHIBIT 11.4 Approaches to Gathering Metric Requirements

Leverage Existing Metrics. Rick Sherman, president of Athena IT solutions, a Boston-based BI consultancy, says, "In the discovery process, you learn that there are almost no green fields. If an executive has an idea for a metric, the company is probably already measuring it somewhere in a spreadsheet or report." Sherman first interviews executives and managers and then the analysts who create existing reports. He identifies gaps between what the business wants and existing metrics deliver, and then works with the data to ensure it meets user requirements for timeliness, accuracy, and cleanliness, among other things.

Start with Objectives. Robert Kaplan, cofounder of the balanced scorecard methodology, takes a different tack. He says executives should take all their existing measures and "lock the [metrics] in a room" while they hash out the strategic objectives that they want to drive the organization. Once they've completed their strategy and mapped out interdependencies among objectives, then they can go "unlock the room" and see which existing metrics can be reused. This process ensures that strategy drives metrics, not the reverse.

"Don't go hunt for the right KPIs," says Kaplan. "That is not the answer. A successful balanced scorecard project is not a metrics project. It's a strategy and change management process."

Bill Barberg, president of Insightformation, a strategy management consultancy and software provider, estimates that half of the metrics in a typical balanced scorecard solution already exist and half are designed from scratch. He says companies have already defined most of their executive-level and operational metrics. The fertile ground for new metrics comes from the process of creating cross-functional strategic themes. Themes are collections of related objectives in a strategy map and represent an organization's overall strategy.

Interviews. Regardless of the approach, most KPI teams use interviews to gather requirements. Interviews usually are done by business analysts who ask a series of predefined questions to top executives about the business strategy, objectives, goals, and expectations for the project, among other things. The analysts then gather additional detail by interviewing mid-level managers and subject matter experts who can fill in the details of specific processes, identify data sources, and point out metrics used in current reports, what those metrics mean, and how they are calculated.

Some KPI teams like to create use cases to discover metrics and test their validity. These use cases can be solicited by asking users to create day-in-the-life-of stories about how they manage a particular process. For example, a use case might define a series of steps that a business user goes through to manage the sales pipeline, for example. Use cases are good ways to understand the core processes performance metrics are designed to measure.

Group Sessions. Some KPI teams supplement individual interviews with facilitated group sessions. The group sessions can help teams achieve consensus on the key purpose and goals of the dashboard project and define key metrics. The group might use brainstorming techniques to generate driver metrics (see "The Five Whys" section) or work through multiple use cases to flush out core metrics. Neal Williams has developed a 9-step facilitated workshop to help KPI teams create a metrics blueprint that developers can use to build dashboards. (See Spotlight 11.2.)

Spotlight 11.2 KPI Design Workshop

Neal Williams, president of Corda, developed a nine-step workshop to accelerate the deployment of performance dashboards. Before then, groups would purchase Corda's dashboard software and start implementing the tool before they knew what they wanted to measure. Says Williams, "Many teams get a mandate to implement a dashboard and then struggle through many product iterations before they figure out what to measure and how to display it."

The two- to three-day workshop enables a KPI team comprised of three to five businesspeople and an IT professional to create a detailed blueprint that comprises a complete set of specifications. Williams says the blueprint reduces the number of product development iterations by 80 percent to 90 percent and significantly accelerates dashboard delivery times.

The KPI team writes the output of each step *in English sentences*. There is no coding during the workshop, and prototypes are done on a whiteboard or sketch pad. Once the workshop is finished, the team hands the blueprint, including prototype sketches, to the technical team, which uses it to develop the dashboard and metrics.

The nine steps are:

1. **Frame.** Write a framing statement that defines one or more strategic objectives that the performance dashboard is designed to support. Each dashboard project tackles a maximum of three to four objectives, each of which will generate multiple metrics.
2. **Elaborate.** Write business questions for each strategic objective that you want the dashboard to answer.
3. **Define metrics.** Define measures and dimensions that will help you answer each question; for example, show sales by product, region, and channel.
4. **Define targets.** Describe benchmarks and targets for each metric.

5. **Diagram drill paths.** Diagram the drill paths needed to answer each question. What information should appear on the top page? How might users navigate from a summary to detailed views? These diagrams can be created with pencil and paper if desired.

6. **Define behaviors.** Define type of indicator (outcome or driver) for each metric and describe the behaviors that each is supposed to drive. Define the actions users should take to achieve the objective the metric supports.

7. **Check data.** Check the availability and condition of data for each performance metric.

8. **Check for compliance and balance.** Check to make sure metrics adhere to standard definitions and rules in use across the organization. Make sure each metric doesn't undermine key objectives or conflict with other metrics, and that it cannot be easily circumvented by users.

9. **Assign owners.** Assign a business owner and data steward for each metric. The business owner is responsible for the definition and meaning of the metric while the data steward certifies that the data populating each metric is accurate.

Requirements Forms. To guide business analysts during interviews, most KPI teams create a requirements form to capture responses from business managers in a standardized way. This ensures that analysts ask a consistent set of questions and gather a comprehensive set of information that is easily synthesized and standardized.

One high-tech company, for example, uses two forms to define metrics for its strategic dashboard: one to gather business requirements and another to define technical specifications. The business requirements form asks for a general description of the metric, how it aligns with corporate strategy, the name of the metric, its owner, its target and stretch goals, and how the metric is calculated, among other things. (See Exhibit 11.5.)

The technical specification document provides technical details for each proposed metric. For example, it asks for data sources and formats, extraction logic, scorecard layouts, target specifications, analytical layouts (including columns, rows, data types, formats, and formulas), chart views, and security requirements. Most important, the form asks for the names of the business and technical owners of the metrics so project team members can follow up with additional questions, if needed.

Surveys. Some KPI teams use surveys to gather user requirements. This method is a more efficient way to gather input from large numbers of people. It also gives users more time to provide thoughtful responses

EXHIBIT 11.5 Request Form

P M M S	**Metric Request Form** Submitted By: _____ Date: _____
Business or Function	*What business or function do you request a metric for?*
Region/Country Scope	*What is the geographical scope of the metric?*
Metric Perspective	*What balanced scorecard perspective does the metric fit in: Customer, Financial, Internal, Learning?*
Metric Title	*Give a brief name to the metric (fewer than 20 characters)*
Metric Description	*Describe the metric in business terms.*
Business Justification & Strategic Importance	*Specify whether the metric is a strategic metric or an operational excellence measure, and justify your selection. How does the metric measure progress toward strategy execution?*
Metric Business Owner, Subject Matter Expert, Business IM Owner	*Specify the owners of the metric, either from the business or the function that will be measured on the results (can be name or job title). Also, who collects, reviews, approves, and reports the data?*
Metric Goals	*Specify both the target and stretch goals for the metric (indicate over what time period) Also, how is the goal selected and who approves the goal?* **Target:** **Stretch:** **Goals-setting process and approval from:**
Definition, Calculation, and Criteria	*How is the metric calculated? What criteria are used? Identify any differences between worldwide or sub-region definitions.*
Data Source and Availability	*What is the data source for the actual results, and how are data collected? When is the data available (i.e., which workday, every six months, annually, etc.)?*

Supporting Reports	*What detailed reports are available to support the metric results?*
Related Metrics	*List upstream metrics influenced by this metric. List downstream metrics that have influence on this metric.*
Additional Information	*Specify additional information related to the metric.*
Status	*Status of the metric request from the PMMS worldwide program office team (approved, pending additional info), targeted implementation date, etc.*

to questions compared to a one-on-one interview. Users can skim through the survey questions and collect their thoughts before submitting an answer. In contrast, a one-on-one interview puts users on the spot, unless they have received the questions in advance and spent time reviewing them prior to the interview.

Prioritizing Metrics. Once the KPI team has gathered requirements, it needs to cull the number of performance metrics to a manageable number. The easiest way to do this is to create a list of criteria to evaluate each proposed metric. For example, the team might want to use the 12 characteristics of effective performance metrics defined earlier or some other relevant criteria. Cisco, for example, uses 5 criteria to evaluate potential metrics: scalability, normalization, accountability, goalable, and actionable. (See Chapter 9.) The team should weight each criterion on a scale from 0 to 1 and then score each metric on a scale of 1 to 5 with 5 equal to "closely meets the criterion." Exhibit 11.6 is an example of template used to evaluate performance metrics.

Validating Metrics

Once a KPI team has defined and prioritized its performance metrics, it should present them to the individuals whose performance will be measured to get their feedback. This is a critical part of the process that shouldn't be shortchanged.

Nuances. Sometimes it is difficult to define a metric that accurately captures the nuances of a business process. For example, it took Direct Energy Essential Home Services considerable time to create a repeat call metric. The metric tracks the efficiency of field service technicians who repair residential furnaces and air conditioning systems and is designed to

EXHIBIT 11.6 Culling Performance Metrics

Measures	Criteria	Linked to Strategy	Drives Behavior	Action-oriented	Easy to Understand	Condition of Data	Standard Definition	TOTAL
	Weight	1.0	1.0	0.8	0.7	0.5	0.7	
Financial perspective								
Measure 1								
Measure 2								
...								
Customer perspective								
Measure 1								
Measure 2								
...								
Internal Operations								
Measure 1								
Measure 2								
...								
Learning and Growth								
Measure 1								
Measure 2								
...								

Instructions: Rate each measure on a scale from 1 to 5, with 5 = "Closely meets requirement."

Source: Adapted from Karen Degner.

218

encourage technicians to fix problems on an initial site visit instead of making repeated trips, which occurs if technicians don't stock the right parts in their repair vehicles.

When the KPI team presented the metric to service technicians, the team discovered that they not only fix equipment but are encouraged to sell it as well. The team then struggled to define when a repeat call is a good or bad thing and how to measure that. If the technician makes a repeat trip to bring literature about a replacement system, is that good or bad? What if a homeowner only permits a technician to make minor repairs to an aging system, but then the system breaks shortly afterward and the technician returns to fix or replace it?

To flesh out these nuances, KPI teams need to get feedback from the people who are closest to the process the metrics measure. These people know best whether a performance metric accurately represents a process as well as how easy it might be for employees to circumvent or game the metric. A KPI team that implements performance metrics without getting feedback and buy-in from front-line staff risks stirring up a hornet's nest of trouble, especially if incentive pay is tied to metric results.

Standardizing Terms

Gaining Consensus. The hardest part about creating metrics is defining the meaning of common terms that they are based on. It is ironic that the terms used most frequently in an organization are the hardest to pin down. For example, most organizations have difficulty defining exactly what a customer is and is not. Is a customer someone who has purchased product sometime in the past or just within the last 12 months? Is a customer someone who has registered on a Web site and downloaded documents but has never purchased anything? In the same way, every industry has difficulty defining core terms. An airline often can't get agreement on the definition of a flight segment and a manufacturing firm has difficulty achieving consensus on the meaning of the word *part*.

The challenge in standardizing terms increases with the scope of the project and the number of departments supported by a performance dashboard. It's easy to standardize terms and rules within a single department because everyone views the business in much the same way. But when you cross departmental boundaries, achieving consensus on a common term, such as *sales*, is surprisingly difficult. For example, a "sale" to the finance department occurs when payment is received and deposited in the bank; but the sales department sees it differently: A "sale" occurs when a customer signs a purchase order. And marketing believes a "sale" happens when a customer pays for an item with a credit card or check.

CEO Intervention. The more groups and people, the more divergence there will be in the definitions of terms, rules, and calculations that compose a metric. Sometimes the only way to resolve these differences is for the CEO to call a meeting of top executives and force them to hash out standards with which they all can live.

"We have two distinct businesses, commercial and government, and the measurements each uses are very different, which makes it very challenging to develop corporate-wide standards," says a senior manager of reporting at a major U.S. consultancy. "We've had strong backing from our CEO to make this work and we've made a lot of progress. But even with that, it takes a lot of time and our partners recently decided to postpone trying to resolve the issues until a later time."

A high-tech company faced a similar situation. Says the program manager:

> *We wanted a worldwide metric for cost reduction, and we discovered that the operation and finance people had 32 ways to measure cost reduction. Some of these were duplicates, others measured different facets of costs. The project team arranged a meeting between two top financial executives, and they agreed to standardize on 6 metrics for cost reduction.*

Collecting Data

Poor-Quality Data. Sometimes the data to support a metric simply do not exist, or they are in poor condition. The most well-defined performance metrics are irrelevant if there are no data to populate them. To get a handle on data issues early in the process, the KPI team needs to appoint a systems analyst to participate on the team and scout out data sources for proposed performance metrics. If the analyst reports that the data don't exist or are full of missing or invalid values, duplicate records, or inconsistencies that might take weeks or months to clean up, the KPI team has a decision to make: If the metric is important enough, the team can kick off a major data reconditioning project or build a new system to automate data collection. If the proposed metric isn't that critical, the team can revise or scrap it. The key here is that the KPI team builds metrics in context of available data so that they don't waste time and money defining metrics that can't be supported.

Distributed Data. Another common problem is that the data required to populate a metric are spread across multiple systems that capture and format data differently. Even if the distributed data are in good condition, which they usually are not, the project team must expend significant effort to integrate the data in a consistent fashion. Thus, the dashboard project turns into a data warehousing project. Obviously, dashboards that leverage metrics in an existing data warehouse are much easier to build and deploy than dashboards that must acquire data natively.

"Data integration is critically important but it is often overlooked, especially by the business side of the house," says a manager of performance management. "Businesspeople often don't know there is a problem until the technical team reports back that it can't deliver all the relevant performance metrics. The larger the organization, the bigger the data integration challenge."

Setting Targets

One of the toughest challenges of a KPI team is to set realistic targets. Targets should not be so challenging that they discourage workers, nor should they be too easy, which leads to complacency. Often setting targets is a matter of trial and error. However, it is best to identify realistic targets up front to avoid problems later on. Many times this requires an organization to establish formal policies and procedures for setting targets.

Get Buy-in. It is important not to set targets in a vacuum. Executives and managers often are tempted to set targets based on their own experience and knowledge of the business. But such unilateral goal setting does not engender goodwill among the staff responsible for achieving the goals. It is critical that the KPI team gathers input from employees to understand what targets are reasonable and gains their buy-in to the project. Ultimately, employees are doing the work and should feel that the goals are reasonable.

Cisco, for example, has a Corporate Quality team that negotiates performance targets for customer satisfaction scores with every department in the company. The targets are then reviewed by an internal cross-functional board and sent to the executive team for approval. Such elaborate negotiation is necessary when a portion of employees' incentive pay is based on achieving the targets, which is the case at Cisco. (See Chapter 9 for more details.)

Calculating Metrics

A final thing that metrics designers need to consider is in what layer of the architecture they should write metric calculations. Some metrics may be quite complex, requiring aggregating data across multiple dimensions and levels in an organizational hierarchy or combining one or more metrics in a ratio or compound measure. In addition, most dashboards display metrics over time and calculate variance from period to period. Such time-series calculations can consume a lot of processing power and slow query performance significantly.

When physically creating metrics, dashboard designers have three choices. They can define and calculate metrics in (1) the dashboard, (2) a BI semantic layer, or (3) the database.

The easiest and most natural approach for developers is to create metrics within dashboard applications since most dashboard products support calculation and rules engines. The downside is that embedding rules inside a dashboard creates a spreadmart (dashmart?) since every developer is likely to define the same metrics differently. It also creates a maintenance nightmare: When a developer wants to revise a metric, he or she needs to update the metric in every dashboard that uses it. Finally, dashboards that calculate metrics on the fly in the application layer will suffer poor performance, especially when they display time-series charts for complex metrics.

The second option—a BI semantic layer—abstracts the metric from the dashboard application and makes it available to any application that can read the semantic layer. Designers write the metric once and deploy it many times. The fact that the metric is maintained centrally ensures that any revisions are automatically available to downstream applications. The downside here is that many dashboard applications don't support BI semantic layers and performance still can be an issue, especially if queries to populate the metric are executed dynamically.

The third option involves executing the metric inside a database. This requires data designers to incorporate the metric inside the data model and then create transformations to populate the model with relevant data and apply the appropriate calculations. Like a BI semantic layer, this method manages the metric centrally, which ensures consistency. It also provides better performance because designers can calculate the metric in advance as data are transferred from source systems to the database and store the time-series data locally. The downside is that changes to the metric require designers to change the data model, which can be tricky and time consuming.

Summary

Performance metrics are powerful agents of organizational change, but creating them is challenging. To create effective performance metrics, organizations need to understand the components of a performance metric and create a KPI team that gathers requirements, prioritizes, validates, and standardizes metrics and sets realistic targets after getting buy-in from individuals whose performance will be measured.

CHAPTER 12

How to Design Effective Dashboard Displays

Overview

Good Design. This chapter examines how to design the "look and feel" of a performance dashboard so that it is easy to use and visually appealing. The visual interface—what users can see and do on the screens—can determine whether a performance dashboard succeeds or fails.

Visual design is important because business users don't have to use a performance dashboard; in most companies, it is not a requirement for doing their jobs. They will use it if it makes them more productive and effective, but they will shun it if it is not intuitive or consumes too much time and effort for the value it delivers. They will go elsewhere to obtain the information they need, or they will rely on intuition and gut feel alone.

Good dashboard design instantly connects users to actionable and relevant data. Stephen Few, a visualization expert and author, writes: "The dashboard does its primary job if it tells you with no more than a glance that you should act. It serves you superbly if it directly opens the door to any additional information that you need to take that action."[1]

Challenges. Creating dashboard displays is challenging, and few report designers—the people who create dashboard screens in most organizations—have sufficient background in visual design to do a good job. Most rely on their own visual sensibilities combined with feedback from business users, who also lack knowledge of basic visual design principles. The process of mocking up dashboard screens is often a case of the blind leading the blind.

The result is a visual interface that is cluttered and unnecessarily complicated, forcing users to work too hard to discern pertinent facts and navigate to relevant underlying detail. Unless business users can consume dashboards at a glance—or in "big visual gulps," as Few says—they will abandon dashboards and revert to former, less than optimal habits of consuming information.

Despite the challenges, designing dashboard displays is rewarding. It is the fun part about building performance dashboards, the icing on the cake, if you will. Dashboard design is where all the elements of a performance dashboard system come together to address business issues. It's like the grand finale when systems architects finally see the fruits of their efforts and business users get excited about using the new system.

Before You Start

Although it's tempting to jump right into selecting layout designs, chart types, color palettes, fonts, and navigation controls, there are a number of things that you should keep in mind before beginning the design process. Some of these are fundamental principles of information delivery that bear repeating; others are overlooked steps in a dashboard project plan.

Focus on Requirements and Data First

The quickest way for a magazine to boost sales is to put a picture of a pretty woman on the cover. The same holds true for performance dashboards. A surefire way to get funding for a dashboard project is to show executives a mock-up of a dashboard screen with their metrics wrapped in appealing graphics. However, selling and delivering a performance dashboard are two different things.

Says a performance manager at a major telecommunications company:

> *It's often too easy to create a fancy-looking dashboard and get executive support. But if you don't have real data to put into it, it's really just smoke and mirrors. It's important that you do the necessary work to get to the point where the glitz is functioning properly. That includes defining metrics and targets as well as getting systems data. If we had gone in with glitz and glamour before building the infrastructure, we would have set unrealistic expectations and wouldn't be as far along as we are now.*

Requirements. When gathering requirements for a performance dashboard project, it is critical to focus on what information users need and how they plan to use the dashboard rather than how they want to view the data it contains. Focusing on screen layouts too early in the process restricts your ability to design an optimal visual interface; it is best to show a screen mock-up at the end of the requirements process, once developers have a solid understanding of the information that users need to do their jobs. For example, the nine-step dashboard design workshop described in Chapter 11 produces a requirements document written in English that defines goals, questions, metrics, targets, drill paths, and data, among other things, that developers need to build a dashboard prototype.

Data. It's also critical to ensure that you populate the dashboard with high-quality data that business users trust. Business users always underestimate the time and money required to source, clean, and integrate data for dashboard and BI projects. Often data acquisition consumes 80 percent of the work involved in delivering a performance dashboard. This is especially true if the dashboard does *not* source most of its content from a data warehouse that adheres to a rigorous data cleansing and validation process.

Prototypes. Without a strong data foundation, a performance dashboard is just a pretty face without much personality: intriguing at first, but quickly dissatisfying. Even a dashboard prototype should incorporate accurate data. Otherwise, you'll be on the defensive during most of the prototyping session, explaining the origins of your data and why it's not accurate. And you'll have missed a brilliant opportunity to gain traction for the new system. I've known cases where business managers hurriedly began making calls to fix operational problems that they spotted while providing feedback on a dashboard prototype.

Know Your Users

It is one thing to build a visually elegant performance dashboard, and it is another to get business users to use it. As discussed in Chapter 2, it is important to segment users by their technical and analytical capabilities and preferences. Just because one segment of users finds the screens easy to use does not mean that all segments will. To encourage adoption and use, performance dashboards need to be tailored to the needs of each target group.

For example, some executives today prefer to receive reports via e-mail, while others like to print out various screens, and some desire offline electronic versions that they can examine while traveling. To address these types of requirements, one BI team trained each executive's administrator to use the dashboard and generate output in the executive's preferred method. "We told executives, don't worry about accessing the tool, we'll train your assistants to get you the information for you," the team lead said. At another company, the project leader spent 30 to 60 minutes with each executive describing how to use the tool. The project lead also configured the dashboard screen to match the executive's preferences to ensure adoption and buy-in for the project from the top.

Executives may need extra hand holding, but power users need additional leeway. Power users usually are not satisfied with functionality geared to casual users, who primarily want to monitor data, not analyze it. Although well-designed dashboards let users drill from high-level views to detailed transactions, the pathways are fairly structured and circumscribed. To satisfy power users who want unlimited freedom to explore, it is often necessary to let them access data and information directly using whatever tools they want. These could be online analytical processing, visual analysis, or ad hoc reporting tools.

Enlist Visual Designers

Report developers who design dashboards tend to overcomplicate the display, using too many colors, borders, frames, and images. As developers, they take pride in understanding and exploiting all the features and functions in a software tool. Unfortunately, this backfires with dashboard displays.

When left to their own devices, report developers overemphasize the design at the expense of the data. This creates cluttered, overdecorated displays where everything competes for attention and thus nothing of importance gets communicated. "Focus should always be placed on the information itself, not on the design of the dashboard, which should almost be invisible," writes Few.[2]

Interior Decorating. Designing dashboards is not unlike decorating a room in your house. Most homeowners (like me!) design as they purchase objects to place in the room. When we buy a rug, we select the nicest rug; when we pick out wall paint, we pick the most appealing color; when we select chairs and tables, we find the most elegant ones we can afford. Although each individual selection makes sense, collectively the objects clash or compete for attention.

Smart homeowners (with enough cash) hire interior decorators who filter your tastes and preferences through principles of interior design to create a look and feel in which every element works together harmoniously and emphasizes what really matters. For example, the design might highlight an elegant antique coffee table by selecting carpets, couches, and curtains that complement its color and texture.

Recruiting Design Experts. Thus, to optimize the design of your performance dashboard, it is important to get somebody on the team who is trained in the visual design of quantitative information displays. Although few teams can afford to hire someone full time, you may be able to hire a consultant to provide initial guidance or find someone in the marketing department with appropriate training. Ideally, the person can educate the team about basic design principles and provide feedback on initial displays.

But be careful: Don't entrust the design to someone who is a run-of-the-mill graphic artist or who is not familiar with user requirements, business processes, and corporate data. For example, a Web designer will give you a professional-looking display but probably will garble the data—he or she might use the wrong type of chart to display data or group metrics in nonsensical ways or apply the wrong filters for different user roles. And any designer needs to take the time up front to understand user requirements and the nature of the data that will populate the displays.

Partnership. Ideally, report developers and design experts work together to create an effective series of dashboard displays, complementing their knowledge and expertise. This partnership can serve as a professional bulwark against the misguided wishes of business users. Although it's important to listen to and incorporate user preferences, ultimately the look and feel of a dashboard should remain in the hands of design professionals. For example, most companies today entrust the design of their Web sites and marketing collateral to professional media designers who work in concert with members of the marketing team. They don't let the chief executive dictate the Web design (or they shouldn't anyway).

Books. There are many good books available today to help dashboard teams bone up on visual design techniques. Stephen Few's *Information Dashboard Design* book is a must read. He delves into greater detail in two other books, *Show Me the Numbers* and *Now You See It*. Few and others have drawn inspiration from Edward R. Tufte, whose book *The Visual Display of Quantitative Information* is considered a classic in the field. Tufte has also written *Visual Explanations, Envisioning Information*, and *Beautiful Evidence*.

Create a Prototype

Once you have gathered all the information requirements and defined the metrics and targets, you are ready to design the look and feel of the performance dashboard. The best way to get the process going is to create a prototype that you've developed in conjunction with a visual designer or based on knowledge you've gained from reading selected books.

Soliciting Feedback. Then get users' feedback. But don't ask questions like "Do you like how this looks?" Rather, have users focus on whether the dashboard makes it easy to find the most important information. For example, ask "Do the items that need attention stand out?" Or "When scanning the revenue section, can you easily detect the trend?"

Allow users to tweak the layout and design, but do not let them overhaul it completely (unless it is really poor). Also, do not start with a blank screen or let users create the prototype on their own. They have fixed ways of viewing information, usually limited by what they've grown accustomed to seeing and doing in the past.

However, sometimes there is no way around user biases. In one company, executives insisted that the opening scorecard screen look exactly like the paper scorecard they had created during the strategy mapping process. Although this made sense in many ways—the company had published posters of the initial scorecard and hung them in the hallways throughout the organization—it forced the team to create a custom solution, which both the business users and technical team did not want to do.

How Much Data? The prototype should contain a modicum of real user data. Perhaps it's only a row or two, but it should be enough to lend the dashboard an air of reality and give users a sense of ownership of the prototype and project. Meanwhile, a subset of the development team should be working on a parallel track, sourcing and preparing data that was defined in the requirements-gathering session. Working on the back and front ends of the dashboard simultaneously accelerates deployment and brings to the surface problems that might derail the project if development is done sequentially.

For instance, the prototyping sessions might reveal that a particular dimension or attribute is no longer needed and that new dimensions or fields have to be added. This knowledge can save the back-end team considerable time if it hasn't already sourced the data.

Employ Usability Labs

Fine-tuning. Once the prototype is finalized and populated with data, then you need to test the dashboard display in a real-life setting. In the best of all worlds, your company has a usability lab that enables you to observe workers using the performance dashboard in a laboratory setting. Usability labs employ cameras and recorders to document users' hand, eye, and body movements and record their verbal comments. The labs also interview users to get their reaction to the application. Ultimately, the labs help determine how intuitive an application is and where users get hung up in the visual interface. They can rescue poorly designed dashboards from oblivion but also polish well-designed dashboards to make them even more accessible and usable.

Says an IT director at a financial services company:

> We used [our company's] usability lab twice. We went initially to get advice about how to design the interface and get the dashboard up and running. Then we went a few months after our dashboard went live to test it with real users. Some of the advice involved making small cosmetic changes, such as moving some icons and cleaning up the layout. But other advice gave us a better understanding of how the system behaves from the perspective of business users, where they find it confusing. We

learned that people had difficulty drilling down into our data using parameterized drop-down lists. So now we're trying to address these issues in subsequent upgrades.

Do It Yourself. If your company doesn't have a formal usability lab, don't despair. You can create an informal lab on your own and still glean a lot of valuable insights. Simply recruit a handful of people from different segments of your user population to test the dashboard prototype for 15 minutes. The best candidates are ones who are gregarious and can provide a running commentary of what they see and experience.

When you put these people in front of a screen, most immediately will begin examining the data and interacting with the dashboard. Ask them to verbalize everything they do, think, or experience. Just in case, have a few tasks for them to perform based on their role. For example, ask an executive to print the current view or export to Excel, a manager to filter the data, and power users to calculate a new column and change chart types. Take copious notes or record the session and transcribe the dialogue later.

Once the session is finished, talk with the test subjects and get them to summarize their experiences, identifying what they liked and didn't like and where they got confused or lost. Once you conduct several sessions, you'll identify several things that you can do to tweak the visual display to improve its usability.

Iterate

Like key performance indicators (KPIs), a dashboard display is never finished. Even with prototypes and usability testing, you are not likely to build the perfect display the first time. In addition, user preferences and requirements change over time, which will force a rewrite, and you'll devise new ways to visualize data after watching how users interact with the dashboard or examining dashboards at other companies. After a while, you'll need to redesign the dashboard display to keep it relevant, fresh, and attractive.

"Designs are iterative," says John Rome, associate vice president at Arizona State University. "We keep dreaming up new ways to visualize data to enhance adoption and usage." Rome spent considerable time learning the basics of visual design and now employs a staff member who has a visual design background. They've redesigned the look and feel of several dashboards in the past several years.

Guidelines for Creating Displays

First impressions make a big difference, today more than ever. In our busy, fast-paced lives, if something does not catch our eye immediately and draw us in, we ignore it and move to something else. For this reason, it is imperative to spend time and effort designing the initial screen of a performance dashboard. This view conveys the breadth, depth, and usability of the entire performance dashboard. If it does not resonate with users or portray the right information, they may not use it, or may use it only begrudgingly.

Less Is More. However, this does not mean that we need to apply painterly touches or create a visual masterpiece. The art of visual design is working sparsely, making sure that every element and figure on the screen is there for a purpose. Visual designers are ruthless in stripping out colors, shapes, images, or decorations that distract users or do not convey vital information.

Although few of us have training as artists or visual designers, there are easy things we can do to enhance the visual appeal and usability of the dashboard and scorecard screens we create. General guidelines for creating dashboard displays that jump out and grab users rather than force them to study a display to discern important facts are presented next.

Display Information on a Single Screen

The first and toughest goal of a dashboard designer is to squeeze relevant information onto a single screen. Users should not have to scroll down or across a screen to view critical data. That is too much work when all users want to do is glance at the screen to monitor what is going on.

Out of Sight. Similarly, users should not have to click on a radio button to compare data that should be logically grouped together on a single display. All information needed to make an immediate assessment should be instantaneously viewable. Data that are out of sight are out of mind.

Few writes:

> *The fundamental challenge of dashboard design is to display all the required information on a single screen, clearly and without distraction, in a manner that can be assimilated quickly. If this objective is hard to meet in practice, it is because dashboards often require a dense display of information. You must pack a lot of information into a very limited space, and the entire display must fit on a single screen, without clutter. This is a tall order that requires a specific set of design principles.*[3]

Top-level Display. Of course, this doesn't mean that the entire performance dashboard should consist of a single page of information. A good dashboard summarizes all relevant information on a top-level display so users can monitor performance at a glance. But then, if desired, users can navigate to detailed data or related views with a single click to explore underlying causes of problems or issues surfaced in the monitoring layer.

Balance Sparsity and Density

Some experts say that dashboard screens should only have between three and seven metrics to have the greatest visual impact. However, few people want to arbitrarily restrict the number of metrics and risk excluding those that meet bona fide business requirements or should be viewed together to deliver the full story.

How Many? What is the ideal number of objects to place on a dashboard screen? Should we design sparse, uncluttered displays with a minimum of objects to optimize at-a-glance monitoring and enhance retention? Or should we pack the dashboard with enough objects to give the complete picture?

The answer is that dashboard designers need to balance the twin demands of sparsity and density. There is always a trade-off between these two, but following good design principles can help you create a dense dashboard layout that is also highly accessible and legible. Thus, you shouldn't limit the dashboard to a fixed number of objects, but you should always be aware when the display reaches its saturation limit.

The ratio between sparsity and density often varies by type of user and individual preference. Although there are no hard-and-fast rules, operational workers typically prefer denser displays of data, packed with detail and containing as much text as charts. In contrast, managers or executives prefer to scan a dozen or so metrics highlighted with stoplights and accompanied by an associated chart or two.

Evolving Perceptions. In addition, users who are intimately familiar with the data and processes represented on the dashboard can consume more information than those who are new to the space. Experienced users will get frustrated if they have to click multiple times to view information that belongs together. In fact, they might prefer a spreadsheet, despite its ungainly aesthetics and endless tables, because it gives them all the information they need in one ungainly gulp.

In contrast, novice users or people unfamiliar with a dashboard's business domain can't absorb as much information all at once. They prefer a simpler display with fewer items. Over time, as they gain more experience and become more familiar with the dashboard elements, they, too, will find the display limiting. At this point, savvy dashboard designers deliver a more advanced view by exposing more objects and functionality.

Eliminate Decoration

Preserving Real Estate. The way to pack a lot of information onto a single screen is to abbreviate or summarize it. This is usually done by representing metrics as graphical elements. "That's because graphics convey more information in less space and we process visual information more rapidly than other types of information," says Few.

However, most dashboard developers get carried away with graphical elements, spurred by vendors who populate their dashboard solutions with eye-popping graphics that do a good job of catching attention but a poor job of communicating information quickly. Part of the problem is that most vendors try to simulate an automobile dashboard on a computer screen and try to outgizmo each other with graphical effects. Thanks to evangelization by Few and other design experts, vendors have reined in some of their more egregious design instincts but still make these capabilities available to unsuspecting dashboard developers.

As a rule of thumb, every dashboard developer should ask: "Do the graphics provide the clearest, most meaningful presentation of the data in the least amount of space?" For example, radial gauges waste a lot of space due to their circular shape. Stoplights and thermometers that look like their real-life counterparts also consume too much real estate.

Nothing Signifies Something. Few says, "Don't waste visual content with an entire stoplight, just show a single icon (for example, a circle) next to a metric." He goes one step further and recommends not showing a symbol or icon at all if performance is acceptable. Users subconsciously recognize that the absence of an object carries meaning, like "no news is good news."

Use an Intuitive Layout

Many developers stare at a blank dashboard screen and don't know where to begin. Or they rush into the job without thinking at all. It's safe to say that most need guidance about where to place various components, including metrics, charts, filters, tabs, help text, and other controls, on a dashboard screen to optimize the visual design.

Templates. Although there are no definitive rules, one place to start is to examine designs used by well-known, information-rich Web sites visited by millions of people, such as Yahoo, Amazon, and others. These sites have been scrutinized by Web site designers and redesigned numerous times to optimize usage and navigation. Although Few disagrees that Web site templates make good dashboard designs, imitating such templates gives users a familiar look and feel and ensures that they know how to navigate your dashboard. For example, Arizona State University patterns its dashboards after common Web site templates. (See Exhibit 12.1.)

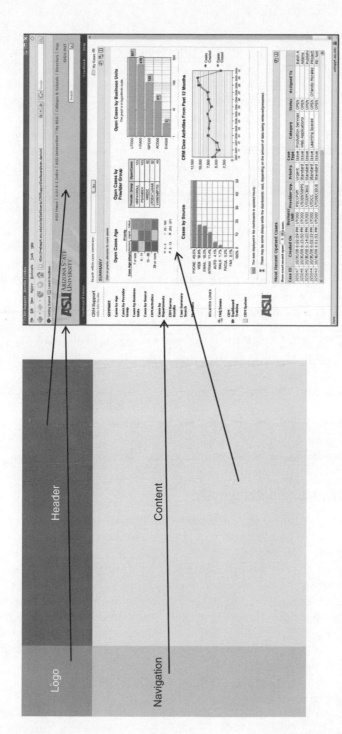

EXHIBIT 12.1 Web Site Templates
Courtesy of Arizona State University.

233

Predefined Layouts. Some dashboard products use a Web publishing metaphor that lets users drag and drop components anywhere on the screen. Although this method offers tremendous flexibility, it can be overwhelming without a template to follow. Some dashboard products provide templates that offer predefined combination of panes, such as 2 × 2 or 3 × 4. Although these can accelerate deployment, they may also limit your ability to match the design to user needs, so employ them with caution.

Position and Placement. The way objects are positioned on a dashboard display tells a story and communicates meaning. For example, elements in the top left quadrant receive the most attention, followed by the upper right and lower left quadrants. The bottom right quadrant gets the least attention.

Therefore, designers place elements that deserve the greatest prominence in the upper left quadrant, followed by less prominent information in the other quadrants. Sometimes designers use arrows to step people from one section of the display to another if there is a logical sequence or flow to the data. Or they number elements to indicate a visual flow.

The center of a dashboard can also serve as a major focal point, especially when a graphic placed there is set apart visually from what surrounds it using a border or white space. However, few designers place objects in the middle of a dashboard because this makes the remaining space too narrow to display other items.

Groupings and Flows. Designers also group like elements together to show that they are related. The same goes for items that need to be compared. Placing them too far apart makes the user's eyes work too hard to see and compare items. When designers cannot place items together, they use hues, shapes, or fonts to link related elements on the page.

Arrange Components Intelligently

Besides panes and charts, a performance dashboard contains other components that need to be arranged on the screen in an optimal fashion: tabs, filters, help menus, and bread crumbs.

Tabs. Folder tabs at the top of dashboard are an appropriate way to differentiate content based on a user's role. Since most users wear many hats in an organization, they need quick access to multiple dashboards, each representing a different role they play. Tabs group functional content that belongs together, enabling users to switch quickly between roles instead of having to scroll through a hierarchical folder structure to launch a new dashboard or report.

Tabs also make it easy for dashboard architects to build a dashboard once and deploy it many times. Each dashboard is simply a role-based view of the same content running on the same platform. This method saves time and money compared to creating a new dashboard each time a user or group requests one.

However, users should not be shown tabs that don't pertain to their role. For example, a poorly designed dashboard might show tabs for sales, marketing, maintenance, and flights—functions that a single person is unlikely to be responsible for. This clutters the display and tempts users to waste time. A good dashboard platform enables an administrator to select the appropriate tabs to display to each user or group.

Filters. Filters enable users to change data in a chart by refining a query against a set of data. They represent the most basic form of dashboard interactivity. Filters let users drill down a hierarchy to view more detail, drill up to view aggregated data, or drill across to view different dimensions (e.g., sales by product versus sales by region). When a user applies a filter, every graphic associated with the filter refreshes with new data.

A classic design mistake is to place filters (or other controls) in an ambiguous location on the screen. The problem arises because filters can apply to every chart on a page, a selected group of charts, or an individual chart. Without proper visual cues, viewers can't discern to which charts a filter applies.

Typically, universal filters are placed in close proximity to their associated charts, which should be grouped together and enclosed by a light border. Filters for individual charts usually are placed above the object— sometimes in a chart-specific toolbar—so it's obvious that the filter applies to that chart alone.

A visual analysis tool may have dozens of universal filters for each page in the dashboard. By selecting and deselecting filters, users can rapidly explore data from different perspectives. To facilitate such exploration, these filters should always be visible and activated with a single click. The best way to display these types of universal filters is in a navigation band, usually on the right- or left-hand columns of the dashboard screen.

Filters can be controlled by radio buttons, check boxes, or drop-down lists. Radio buttons are used when viewers can select only one filter at a time, whereas check boxes and drop-down lists enable users to select multiple filters at once. Drop-down lists hide filters behind an icon and are more compact than check boxes but harder for users to manipulate. Users usually must hold down the control key to select multiple items in a drop-down list.

Bread Crumbs. Bread crumbs enable viewers to keep track of where they are and where they've been while navigating a multilayered dashboard environment. Essentially, bread crumbs document the filters users have applied to a chart or page of charts and the pages they've viewed. Ideally, the items in a bread crumb list are active, making it easy for users to return to a previous view.

Text. Text can be a valuable addition to a performance dashboard. Sometimes text is the only way to communicate important information, such as top 10 customers, bottom 10 products, projects at risk, or highest-performing salespeople. Text also works when it is dynamically linked to metrics in the form of annotations. In other words, users attach comments to a metric to explain its performance, forecast the future, or outline action steps to rectify a problem.

However, static text simply takes up space. For example, some dashboard designers feel compelled to add help text to a dashboard. This is a mistake. Once users figure out how to use the dashboard, they will never need to look again at the text, which just clutters the screen. A better choice would be to create a help button that users can click if they need more information.

At a bare minimum, you need to add text to dashboards to create tabs, headings, filters, and numeric values in tables and charts. Scorecards often use text in strategy maps, gap analyses, initiative descriptions, and performance summaries.

Fonts. Selecting the right fonts for different elements is important. You should pick a font that is easy to read—such as Times New Roman, Arial, Tahoma, or Helvetica—and avoid ones that are overly fancy or unusual. Use one font throughout the dashboard, varying font size where needed. A standard font size for reading is 12 point for Times New Roman and 10 point for Arial, which work well in dashboards.

Use a bigger font size for tabs and section headings and a smaller font size for supplementary information, such as legends or footnotes. Chart and table headings should be the same size as the main text but highlighted in bold. Axis labels and row/column headings in large charts or tables also benefit from bold highlighting. If desired, use a complementary font for headings. For instance, many designers use a serif font (e.g., Times New Roman) for the main text and a sans serif font (e.g., Arial or Helvetica) for headers.

Deemphasize Design Elements

A classic mistake that developers make is to focus on the dashboard design rather than the data itself. Just because developers can create frames, borders, backgrounds, and shading doesn't mean that they should. These background graphics can compete with real data for attention.

For example, look at a vendor's demo dashboard in Exhibit 12.2. Thankfully, this is not a real dashboard because it breaks all the rules in this chapter, plus many others. The dashboard has three shades of background color: one for the dashboard, another for the tabs, and another for

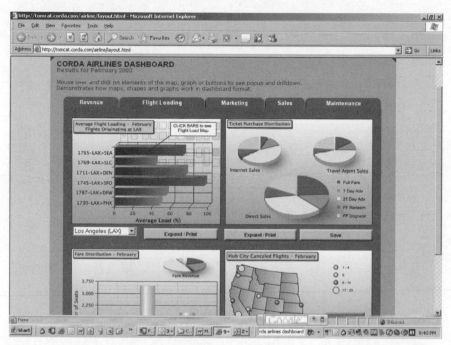

This demo dashboard breaks all basic design rules, and then some. The use of background shading to differentiate panes is unnecessary.

EXHIBIT 12.2 Poorly Designed Dashboard

the charts. The ostensible purpose of this background shading is to differentiate the four panes and charts within them.

White Space. However, a more expertly designed dashboard doesn't resort to background shading to differentiate panes or charts. (See Exhibit 12.3.) In fact, it doesn't use any shading at all, which is merely distracting. Instead, it makes clever use of white space to differentiate its three panes (i.e., "key figures," "top/worst 10," and "revenues per sales channel %"). The white space between the panes is slightly greater than the white space between individual metrics within each pane. Visually, we perceive the difference at a subconscious level, and we automatically group items based on the variation in white space that separates them.

Gestalt. The use of white space to group items is an example of the Gestalt principle of proximity. About two dozen Gestalt principles of perception describe visual characteristics that cause people to group objects together. The principles are based on psychological research conducted in Germany during the early 1900s. It would be wise to explore all the Gestalt principles before designing a dashboard. (See Exhibit 12.4.)

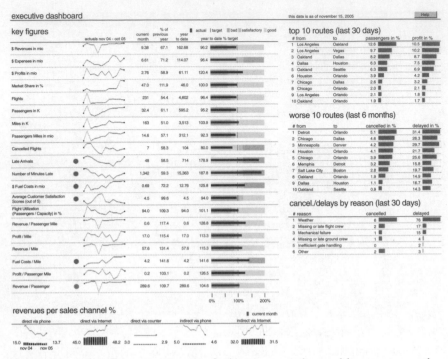

This dashboard makes exquisite use of white space and muted lines, among other things, making it possible to display almost 50 KPIs on a single page.

EXHIBIT 12.3 Well-Designed Airline Dashboard

Courtesy of Andreas Lipphardt. This dashboard was built using BonaVista MicroCharts.

Muted Lines. The well-designed airline dashboard (see Exhibit 12.3) jams almost 50 KPIs (each of which consists of multiple metrics) onto a single page. Yet it is very legible. An executive can quickly rifle through each of the KPIs without getting bogged down or visually misplacing adjacent metrics. The dashboard accomplishes this through the use of muted, dashed lines to separate each metric. You can imagine how different the user experience would be if the designer had used bold, continuous lines to separate the KPIs. It would not work nearly as well. Muted lines also work well inside charts or graphics to separate elements that would be hard to differentiate otherwise, as we'll see shortly.

Colors. In the spirit of less is more, you should avoid using color except to highlight things that viewers need to see, such as a subpar KPI. If you do use colors, Few recommends using muted earth tones rather than primary colors. To emphasize a single element, don't change the color, just

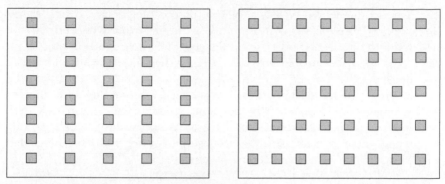

The Gestalt principle of proximity uses white space to cause viewers to see data as arranged in either vertical or horizontal sets.

EXHIBIT 12.4 Gestalt Principle of Proximity

Name		Trend	Status	Target	Actual	Variance %
🏠 **Finance**						
🔴 Decrease European Discounts		╈	✅	16.00%	15.53%	-3%
🔴 Keep APAC discounts < 17%		━	❌	17.00%	24.77%	31%
🔴 Keep N.A. discounts < 17%		━	✅	17.00%	15.66%	-9%

EXHIBIT 12.5 Color-Blind-Friendly Graphic

shift the saturation or brightness, which is enough to distinguish the object from the rest. Increase the brightness of elements that should jump out at users and decrease the brightness or eliminate color altogether for all other elements. (See Exhibit 12.8 for an example.)

It's also important to remember that 8 percent of men and 2 percent of women are color blind; thus, using color exclusively to communicate meaning will backfire for a small minority of users. To compensate, many dashboard designers complement colors with symbols or use pop-ups that display text when a user hovers a cursor over the dashboard object. (See Exhibit 12.5.)

Leverage Dashboard Themes

These guidelines are a lot to remember, and they are only the tip of the iceberg. Ideally, dashboard vendors should bake these guidelines into their products in the form of themes and templates that you can adapt to meet your company's branding and preferences.

A good theme will select a palette of complementary colors, fonts, lines, and other elements that are applied automatically when objects are inserted into the dashboard. A good template will help position objects on the screen to ensure proper flow and balance the twin demands of sparsity and density.

When evaluating dashboard products check whether they offer themes and templates and evaluate whether any resemble your company's look and feel or can be adapted to your needs. Vendors' design IQ is rapidly increasing; there is no reason that you should suffer with a product that provides minimal design guidance.

Guidelines for Designing Charts

Many of the principles described for designing a dashboard apply to designing charts or graphs. The key is to focus on the data, not the chart. Make sure the graph communicates the key message in the data and doesn't obscure it. Few writes, "Graphs give shape to numbers, and in doing so, bring to light patterns that would otherwise remain undetected."[4]

Less Is More

I create a lot of charts for research reports, and long ago, I discovered that the default chart templates in Excel are just plain ugly. They incorporate too many elements that occlude the meaning of the data I'm trying to communicate. I now use a custom template that strips most of the offending clutter from a standard Excel chart.

Exhibit 12.6 shows two Excel charts that display the same data but use different chart types and effects. The second is cleaner and easier to read. That's because I stripped out the gridlines, shading, borders, legend, and scale that appear in the first chart. I also rotated the second chart so the bars run horizontally, enabling viewers to read category text from left to right instead of diagonally from bottom to top, which is awkward.

In addition, I reordered the bars so that the longest one is at the top and the shortest at the bottom. (However, if the chart used an ordinal scale with an implicit order, such as January-February-March or highest to lowest, I would have not changed the order of the bars.) Finally, I added one element to the chart: data labels for each bar. I prefer these over a quantitative scale because many people want to know exact data values and don't want to estimate the numbers visually.

The principle depicted in the "Before" and "After" charts is simple: Less is more. Don't let the chart itself overwhelm the data it's trying to communicate. Strip out unnecessary elements; avoid graphics that look like

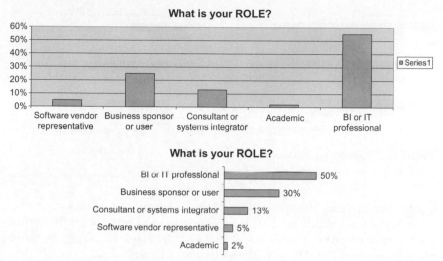

These two Excel charts depict the same data, but the second is cleaner and communicates the data more clearly.

EXHIBIT 12.6 Before and After

their real-life counterparts; and don't use three-dimensional charts. Decorating a chart takes up valuable real estate and distracts the eye.

Make Comparisons Easy

Charts make it easy for people to visually compare things, such as sales across regions or profits over time. Instead of reading numbers one by one in a table or row and calculating their differences, a chart enables us to "see" the difference visually at a glance. We can identify relationships and patterns more quickly when data are displayed graphically instead of textually.

Eyes of the Beholder. Of course, the chart designer must understand the underlying patterns in the data and what information matters most to viewers. With this knowledge, the designer can select the proper dimensions for axes in a chart or table. For example, if managers want to compare product sales by region, which of the two charts in Exhibit 12.7 best meets their need?

The charts contain the same data but are arranged to communicate different messages. The first chart is ideal for regional managers who want to see sales in their region and compare their performance to other regions. The second chart is ideal for a product manager who wants to see product sales across regions to understand which products sell best where. Designers

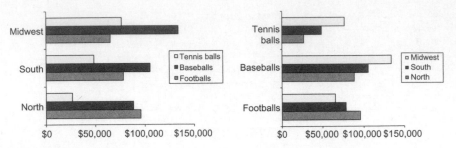

EXHIBIT 12.7 Comparing Comparisons

enable these quick comparisons by placing data in the appropriate axes (including the legend) based on what users need to see. Given the wrong chart, managers would have to work twice as hard to glean the same information even though each chart contains identical data.

Side by Side. To communicate comparisons clearly, it is best to place numbers or items side by side rather than far apart. This enables the viewer to consume the information in a single visual gulp rather than having to look back and forth across the page to make the same comparison. Charts that require less eye movement are easier to consume.

Scalar Proportions. It's also important to ensure that charts portray relationships between variables correctly. This means designers must pay attention to the quantitative scales that they use. For instance, one outlier can wreck the visual relationships in a bar chart, such as when sales for every product range between $10,000 and $25,000 but one exceeds $500,000. In this case, the chart's scale would be so big that it would obscure the relationship between all products except the outlier.

In another case, if variables have similarly high values, designers may be tempted to create a bar chart whose scale begins at an arbitrary high number so the relationships among bars is more obvious. Although is an admirable gesture, it can create a visual mismatch in which the proportional length of the bars is different from the actual numeric relationship between the items. For this reason, bar charts always should start at zero. (This does not apply to line charts, however.)

Use Preattentive Processing

Preattentive processing is visual perception that occurs below the level of consciousness. It detects specific visual attributes at rapid speed. Dashboard designers can leverage these attributes to highlight critical data values and relationships that viewers should notice when glancing at a dashboard or chart.

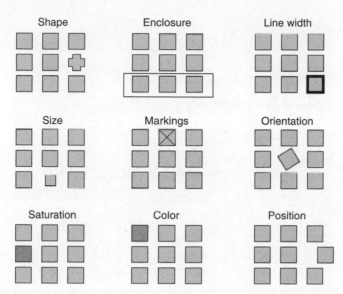

EXHIBIT 12.8 Attributes of Preattentive Processing

Exhibit 12.8 shows nine visual attributes that dashboard designers can exploit to make things jump off the dashboard page and immediately get the attention of viewers: shape, size, saturation, enclosure, markings, color, line width, orientation, and position. You can see quickly how each attribute makes a single element stand out from the rest.

For example, color is a common technique for highlighting poor performance in a KPI. Rather than creating a stoplight image, dashboard designers merely need to place a red dot next to a subpar KPI. Or they can use saturation to highlight a single bar among many in a bar chart that they want users to focus on. (See Exhibit 12.9.)

Predefine Drill Paths and Interactivity

Drill Paths. A chart should enable viewers to drill down effortlessly to see detailed data. It is best to predefine drill paths that users need and bake them into the system. Ideally, users only see drill paths that are pertinent to their role and aren't overwhelmed with too many options.

However, some users eventually will feel constrained by predefined navigation paths and request more latitude to explore data. When this happens, administrators should activate a right-click feature that exposes additional navigation options for these individuals only.

Functions. In the same way, some individuals may desire additional functionality to manipulate the output of charts and tables. Administrators

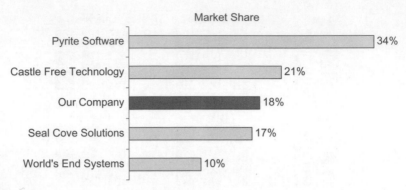

EXHIBIT 12.9 Use of Preattentive Processing

should be able to turn on chart-specific toolbars that expose new functions to these users, such as sort, calculate, annotate, export, and switch between chart types, among other things.

Be careful not to expose too much functionality too quickly to a general audience. Users can be so distracted by icons and overwhelmed by options that they stop using the tool. Think how popular Google has become by exposing a single function on its home page—keyword search—even though it has close to 100 applications to offer. Less is more.

Drill Actions. Software vendors have yet to devise a standard way to perform drill-downs, and many techniques employed today are not intuitive. Some dashboard products require users to right click to view a dialogue box—an awkward movement for most casual users. Others require viewers to click on one or more drop-down boxes to specify the parameters and then click a "go" button. Although power users like having multiple drill paths and parameters, casual users do not.

The ideal way for users to drill down is by left clicking on the actual metric name, alert, bar, or other attribute that catches their attention. They click once to view a new table or chart populated with data. They can click again to drill down even farther. Once they become familiar with the navigation metaphor and desire more interactivity, administrators can activate right-click options.

Choose the Right Graph

Graphs come in many shapes and sizes. Selecting the right graph type makes a big difference in your ability to communicate the meaning of the data. The brief descriptions on Exhibit 12.10 should help you better discern when to use which type of graph.

TEXT

Many dashboards use text to describe and encode data values. Text is used often to display numeric values in a table, particularly budget data (e.g., actuals, plans, forecast), as depicted at right. Text often is used to display data in lists or to expose hidden values when users hover their cursor over a graphical element.

	2006 Actual	2006 Plan	2006 Forecast	2005 Actual
Magazines	246,953	243,225	228,372	248,003
Reports	684,313	635,324	659,493	617,271
Web	84,023	84,280	87,313	83,335
Events	24,235	23,255	23,950	21,656
Membership	2,227	2,333	2,283	2,222

ICONS

Icons are simple images that communicate a clear and simple meaning. Symbols, such as those depicted in the first column of a crime statistics table, indicate the type of crime. Stoplights, such as shaded circles, often are used to indicate status. Symbols also are used to signify an alert or help color-blind people distinguish status levels.

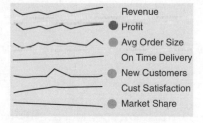

SPARKLINES

Sparklines are compact line graphs that do not have a quantitative scale. They are meant to provide a quick sense of a metric's movement or trend, usually over time. They are more expressive than arrows, which only indicate change from the prior period and do not qualify the degree of change. Sparklines are significantly more compact than normal line graphs but are precise.

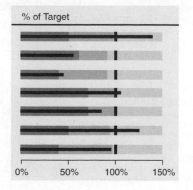

BULLET GRAPHS

Bullet graphs show the status of a metric compared to targets and thresholds. They are more compact than decorative dials, gauges, or thermometers and can be arranged vertically or horizontally, making them a flexible display object.

EXHIBIT 12.10 Graph Selections   *(Continued)*

BAR CHARTS

Bar charts compare items in one or more categories along a single measure. They instantly show the relationship among items, such as biggest to smallest. The use of a legend and color expands the number of categorical attributes that a bar chart can display from one to two or more.

Less than $100 million	28%
$100 to $500 million	17%
$500 million to $1 billion	10%
$1 to $5 billion	18%
$5 to $10 billion	6%
$10 billion+	11%
Don't know	10%

PIE CHARTS

Pie charts display the relationship of a part to the whole, such as U.S. sales to overall sales. Pie charts are not good for comparing relationships among the parts, especially if there are more two or three parts. In that case, a bar chart is preferable.

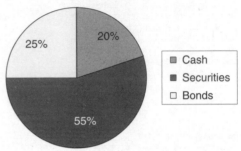

STACKED BAR CHARTS

Like pie charts, stacked bar charts also show the relationship of a part to the whole. However, unlike pie charts, the individual parts don't have to equal 100%. They are also more compact than pie charts, making it easier to display multiple stacked bar charts side by side. However, it is difficult to visually ascertain the relationships among parts in different stacked bar charts, except the first variable in each one.

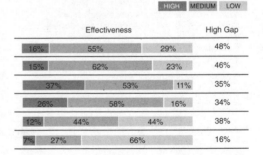

LINE CHARTS

Line charts are great for showing a continuous time series where it is important to visualize one or more trends over time versus data values for each period (although "hover" techniques let users see individual values in a line chart). The Flash chart at right includes a visual control at bottom that lets users expand or contract the time series above.

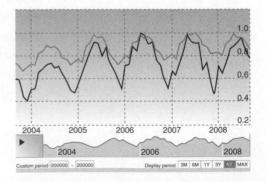

EXHIBIT 12.10 *Continued*

PARETO CHARTS

A Pareto charts is a bar and line chart that shows the 80-20 relationship among categorical items. Items represented by bars are arranged from biggest to smallest with the line representing the cumulative sum of item values. Pareto charts are one of the few bar and line charts that work effectively.

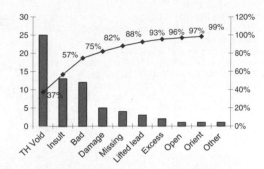

VARIANCE CHARTS

A variance chart is a bar chart that provides a great way to highlight variance between two variables, such as actuals and plan or forecast. A variance chart more clearly depicts variance than if the two variables are depicted in a time-series line chart or a table of numbers. A variance chart is a great way to complement a table of numbers.

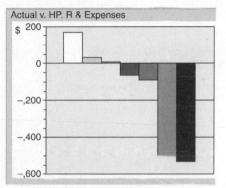

SPATIAL MAPS

Maps can be an ideal way to depict geographical trends quickly, such as the performance of rail lines serving a coal mine (see right). However, maps are often misused. They are overkill when used to depict non-geographical trends or when other displays would be more compact or meaningful to viewers.

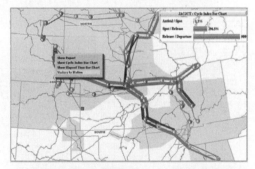

TREE MAPS

A popular newcomer to the visualization scene, tree maps display categorical data as a series of nested rectangles in which the size of the rectangle represents one attribute and color another. Heat maps are a compact way to expose hidden trends quickly. For example, the chart at right shows the performance of more than 45 metrics in a railroad company. A hover over exposes underlying metric values.

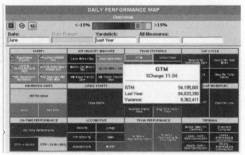

EXHIBIT 12.10 *Continued*

SCATTER PLOTS

Also known as bubble charts, scatter plots display the values of two variables as dots or bubbles on an X/Y axis. One variable determines the position on the X axis and the other the Y axis. A scatter plot makes it easy to visualize the correlation between two variables, which is usually depicted as a straight or curved trend line.

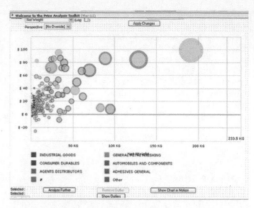

PARALLEL COORDINATE CHARTS

These graphs show how items or groups of items compare across a series of metrics represented as box plots. They are ideal for visualizing large numbers of items and how they change and compare over time or a series of metrics.

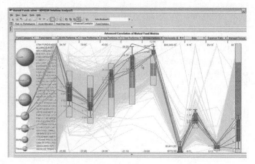

DATA CONSTELLATION

A data constellation chart shows multiple levels of a hierarchy and relationships among items in a single view. Users can examine the details of a subset of elements without losing view of the entire data set. Moving a cursor across the chart magnifies the area under the cursor while minimizing the other parts, enabling users to quickly drill into detail and view relationships.

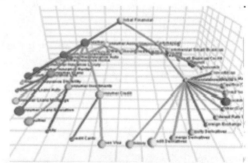

DATA BARS

Data bars visualize values in one or more columns of data, bringing visual life to a table of numbers. By sorting the columns and scrolling, users can quickly view patterns and anomalies in large volumes of data. Data bars work equally well on summarized or detailed data.

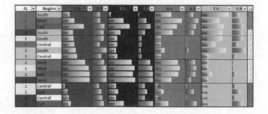

EXHIBIT 12.10 *Continued*

Summary

Dashboard design is not about making something visually pleasing or pretty; it's about communicating the meaning of the data. Too often, however, the visual design of dashboards obscures the meaning of the data in them.

Good dashboard design uses the least amount of ink to highlight key trends or relationships within the data. It leverages Gestalt principles of perception, preattentive processing, and other visual techniques to group, highlight, or sequence what's interesting in the data and minimize the rest. It selects the right graphs to monitor performance, examine relationships, or interactively explore the data.

Wise dashboard developers get training in the basics of designing visual displays of quantitative information and team up with experts to fine-tune dashboard prototypes before getting user feedback. They also leverage usability labs—whether homemade or professionally managed—to get vital clues on the effectiveness of their dashboard designs.

Notes

1. Stephen Few, *Information Dashboard Design: The Effective Visual Communication of Data* (Sebastapol, CA: O'Reilly Media, 2006), p. 36.
2. Ibid., p. 107.
3. Stephen Few, *Information Dashboard Design: The Effective Visual Communication of Data* (Sebastapol, CA: O'Reilly Media, 2006), p. 49.
4. Ibid., p. 122.

CHAPTER 13

How to Architect a Performance Dashboard

There are numerous ways to architect a performance dashboard, and the choices dictate what your performance dashboard can and cannot do. Whether you build or buy a performance dashboard, you need to understand the implications of the system's underlying architecture.

Architecture determines how fast dashboards resolve queries and respond to user inputs and how many users can access the system at once without degrading performance. It determines how easily users can navigate from summary to detail levels of dimensional information and what objects and data they are allowed to see. It also determines how easy the dashboard is to install, configure, and administer as users and requirements change over time.

This chapter focuses on a few key architectural issues that you need to consider when deploying a performance dashboard. Specifically, it examines the performance implications of various user interface technologies and illustrates a half-dozen data architectures that are most commonly used to support dashboard implementations and products.

Display Architectures

Evolution

The architecture of performance dashboards have followed the trajectory of software architectures in general, from mainframe computing to client/server computing to Web-based architectures. Today, rich Internet applications (RIAs) are gaining in popularity because they support dazzling multimedia and visual effects, boosting the appeal and usability of performance dashboards. RIAs, such as Adobe Flash, enable Web-based applications to exhibit the richness and interactivity of desktop applications.

Three Layers. The architecture of any software product involves weaving together three distinct sets or layers of functionality: (1) user interface, (2) application logic, and (3) data processing. These functions typically are processed on one or more tiers of computers. Knowing where and how these layers are processed in your performance dashboard architecture is the key to understanding whether the system will meet the unique requirements of your organization.

Back in the early days of computing, all three layers were processed by a single machine, the mainframe computer. By the 1990s, the layers were distributed across multiple machines in various types of client/server configurations. Typically, the user interface was rendered by a desktop machine; the application logic was distributed between the desktop machine and one or more application servers; and data was processed by a relational database management system.

"Thin" Clients. The advent of the Web shifted computing architectures from "fat" clients (i.e., desktop machines that handled the graphical interface and logic) to "thin" clients in which most of the client and server processing occurred on back-end servers, not desktop machines. In a thin client architecture, a Web server renders the HTML, which is displayed on the desktop machine via a Web browser, while application and data processing occurred on one or more application servers.

Thin client processing has its benefits. Since all processing occurs on the server, users don't need to purchase an expensive desktop machine to run the application or install any software on their computer. All administration is handled centrally, saving the company time and money. In addition, corporate firewalls generally don't block HTML from passing through, unlike Java applets or ActiveX controls, which are applications that can run independently on the client machine and thus pose a security threat.

However, the downside of HTML-based thin clients is lack of performance and functionality. All user inputs are sent over the network to the server, which processes the request, renders the new screen, and pushes the resulting HTML code to the browser. This round-trip processing causes an unsettling delay, especially when users want to do something simple, such as change a background color or sort a table.

Rich Internet Applications

Given the limitations of thin HTML clients, software vendors have begun to "thicken" Web clients to take advantage of the processing power of desktop computers and make Web-based applications more interactive and dynamic.

Java Applets/Active X Controls. Java applets and ActiveX controls are mini-applications that run inside a Web browser and execute within a virtual machine, or sandbox. Actions execute as fast as compiled code, making them an easy way to re-create full-featured applications on the Web. However, as mentioned earlier, they raise security concerns, and many information technology (IT) administrators prevent users from downloading such controls through corporate firewalls, limiting their pervasiveness.

DHTML and AJAX. A lighter-weight approach is to embed a scripting language inside HTML pages, such as JavaScript, that executes functions in the browser. Dynamic HTML (DHTML) uses scripting to animate a downloaded HTML page. For example, DHTML often is used to animate drop-down boxes, radio buttons, mouse-overs, and tickers as well as capture user inputs via forms. AJAX (asynchronous JavaScript and XML) takes this one step further and retrieves new content from the server in the background without interfering with the display and behavior of the page. Basically, AJAX enables users to add new data to the dashboard without having to reload the entire page. It can also be used to prefetch data, such as the next page of results.

However, DHTML and AJAX have some significant drawbacks. DHTML doesn't always work the same way with all browsers, creating a maintenance headache. And AJAX falters if users disable JavaScript in their browsers. Also, performance, reliability, and error handling can be problematic with AJAX since it uses scripts instead of a programming language, and browsers don't make good use of memory. As a result, some veteran business intelligence (BI) developers claim AJAX isn't suitable for advanced BI applications.

Multimedia Plug-ins. Another popular approach is to use multimedia development platforms, such as Adobe Flash, Java applets, Microsoft Silverlight, and Mozilla Scalar Vector Graphics (SVG), which add animation and movies to Web pages. To use these multimedia applications, users download a Web browser plug-in (e.g., Adobe Flash Player to use Adobe Flash), which remains permanently installed on their machine and serves as a runtime engine and sandbox for the applications. These multimedia platforms also offer a programming model and scripting language that enables developers to create interactive Web-based applications, much as AJAX does.

Currently, almost all browsers support the Adobe Flash plug-in, while about three-quarters support Java applets and two-thirds support Microsoft Silverlight. The next major version of HTML (HTML 5) should provide native support for SVG, reducing the need for users to download external multimedia plug-ins. Google Chrome currently supports SVG, and Microsoft has announced that Internet Explorer 9 will support HTML 5 with native SVG support. So, in the future, most Web browsers will provide native, multimedia capabilities.

Compared to Java scripting, the so-called RIA platforms provide stunning graphics and animation for displaying quantitative information, which make user interfaces very appealing to business users. For instance, 1-800 CONTACTS, profiled in Chapter 7, now uses Microsoft Silverlight to build its dashboards. (See Exhibits 7.2 and 7.3.) In addition, since these applications run in their own container (i.e., the plug-in), they don't have to be adapted to work with different browsers, making them easier to maintain. Most important, they load both visualizations and data simultaneously in a single file rather than dishing up dozens or hundreds of pages. Although this makes the initial load slower than a comparable DHTML or AJAX application, performance thereafter is exceptionally fast since data required to display all components on a page resides locally. It also means that users can run the applications when disconnected from the Internet, providing greater flexibility.

Downsides. Like any technology, RIAs have some downsides. For instance, Flash can't leverage keyboard navigation options and its animations are inaccessible to sight- or mobility-impaired customers. In addition, Flash plug-ins aren't interoperable. Users running an older version of a plug-in won't be able to view any part of the application until they upgrade the plug-in. Finally, Flash dashboard products typically offer a limited number of visualizations and can't incorporate new ones easily.

However, the biggest limitation of RIAs is scalability. When the size of the Flash file becomes too large, it takes too long to load within a Web browser, which frustrates users who don't like to wait. Ideally, Flash files should be less than 1 megabyte (MB), but files that are more than 10MB are tolerable. Obviously, these file sizes limit the size of the applications that developers can build with the technology.

Multitier Flash Applications. As RIA applications rise in popularity in the business world, developers are devising new ways to circumvent the load bottleneck. For example, some BI vendors have extended Flash from a static, browser-based, desktop application to a dynamic, multitier application that fetches data on demand as users drill into a chart or switch page views. This dynamic data retrieval reduces the amount of data that the application needs to download at start-up, improving load performance significantly.

Rules of Thumb

Mixing Elements. Dashboard architects need to consider how to mix the various Web technologies just described to deliver an attractive, interactive, and high-performance user interface.

Typically, architects use HTML for screen elements that don't change much at all, such as the dashboard frame itself. That's because refreshing

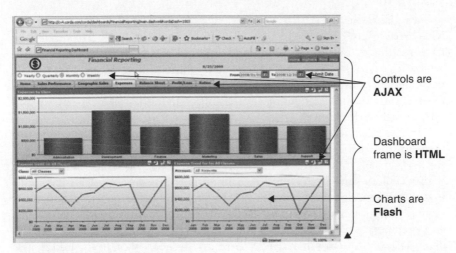

EXHIBIT 13.1 Sample Architecture

HTML generated elements requires a round trip to the server. They typically use AJAX or dynamic HTML for screen controls (e.g., radio buttons, check boxes, mouse-overs, and filters) that execute functions on the display, such as toggling between views, displaying a list of values, or exposing text. They use Flash, Java, or Silverlight for interactive graphics and animations. (See Exhibit 13.1.)

Multimedia platform vendors, such as Adobe, have enhanced their development environments for building rich Internet applications. For example, in recent years, they've added support for screen controls, scripting, asynchronous data fetching, Web services, various layout containers, drag-and-drop features, animation effects, application states, validation controls, and chart types, among other things. As a result, many dashboard developers and vendors are beginning to develop entire dashboards as a Flash or Silverlight application.

Minimize Elements. When working in a Flash environment today, developers need to adhere to a few architectural rules of thumb to ensure a successful user experience. When users first open a Flash-based dashboard, there is a delay while the application downloads the Flash animation and data. To minimize this delay, it's best if developers minimize the number of KPIs or charts per page and avoid pages that require users to scroll. The fewer the number of Flash-based elements, the quicker the screen will load. Of course, once the download is completed, response times are exceptionally fast. Going forward, the best option is to implement a multitier Flash environment that delivers aggregated data on start-up to reduce load times and dynamically fetches data as needed.

If a dashboard needs to display dozens of KPIs, it's best to allocate the KPIs to different pages, separated by tabs or radio buttons. This conforms to principles of designing dashboard displays, discussed in Chapter 12, in which less is more. This is a fortuitous alignment of technical and artistic principles. Dashboard designers and architects should strive to deliver clean, concise, and straightforward displays to both foster adoption and ensure fast performance.

In complex, layered dashboards that conform to the MAD (monitor, analyze, drill to detail) framework, Flash is perfectly suited today to the top-level monitoring layer where users can interact with charts and graphs. It may be less suited to use these technologies in lower levels of the dashboard framework where users want to perform more complex functions against large volumes of data. For instance, at the monitoring layer, queries to populate a chart may return only a dozen or so values, while at the analysis layer, queries may need to return hundreds of rows, and at the reporting layer, thousands of rows.

Where to Use Flash. Given these data volumes, dashboard designers may want to reserve Flash for the graphical monitoring environment and then switch to a custom environment for analysis and reporting. Or designers should investigate implementing Flash in a multitier environment that delivers data dynamically as users interact with the dashboard instead of all at once at start-up. (See "Multitier Flash Applications" discussed earlier.)

Data Architectures

When selecting a data architecture for your dashboard, there are three major things to consider: scalability, performance, and security. *Scalability* defines how many users can access the dashboard concurrently and how much data they can query and view. *Performance* is measured by the delay between when a user clicks on a function or button and receives a response. Generally, most users will tolerate a five-second response time but grow antsy or frustrated if they have to wait longer. Performance is affected by scalability as well as query complexity and the architecture of the underlying servers and database systems that process the requests. *Security* involves making sure users can access the dashboard easily but not view information they are not authorized to see.

Although this book won't dive into details about systems and data architectures, these issues determine whether a dashboard is scalable, performs well, and is secure. Ultimately, your developers and systems architects will need to address a host of technical issues, such as memory management, threading, authentication, application interfaces, and image rendering.

If you are planning on purchasing a dashboard product, it's important that you evaluate the underlying architecture of the product to know what you are really getting for your money.

Evaluation Criteria

At a top level, here are questions you should ask your dashboard architects or dashboard vendors about your dashboard's underlying architecture:

Data Access

- What databases and applications can the dashboard query?
- What files can the dashboard import?
- Can the dashboard query other BI tools?
- Can the dashboard access multiple sources in the same query and join the results?
- Does the dashboard access source data on demand, at predefined intervals, or on a schedule?
- Can dashboard objects query source data directly without loading it into a local database first?

Data Transformation

- Can the dashboard transform source data?
- Does it transform data on the fly or in the dashboard?
- Does it contain a transformation engine with built-in transform functions? Or does it transform data via SQL, Excel, a scripting language, or a third-party tool? Are transforms executed in memory or a database?
- Are transforms reusable in other charts and dashboards?
- Can the dashboard maintain multiple versions of metrics to support what-if analyses?

Data Management

- Where are data stored, remotely or locally?
- Does the dashboard require a database?
- Does the dashboard cache query results?
- Does the dashboard create a data mart of historical data?

Architecture

- What functions execute on the desktop, server, database?
- Does the architecture support a desktop client? Web client?

- What operating systems does it support: 32-bit or 64-bit?
- What browsers and databases does it support?
- What memory is required?
- Can the dashboard run in a public or private cloud?
- What maintenance does it require (machines, upgrades, security, etc.)?

Charting

- How efficiently does the image server render charts?
- Does it cache charts and images?
- Does it support vector or raster images?
- What chart types does it support?
- How easy is it to customize charts?
- How easy is it to apply variables to charts?

Analytics

- Does the dashboard enable users to filter, sort, rank, calculate, and visualize data in column or table?
- Can users create custom groups and apply functions to them?
- Can users view metrics by multiple dimensions?
- Can it apply a filter to multiple charts (or tables) automatically?
- Does it support regressions and other advanced analytics?

Development

- What is the development environment: Flash? Custom?
- Can it be embedded in a corporate portal?
- Does it support interfaces that enable other applications to access it?
- Does it support a semantic layer of business objects?
- Does it support gadgets (e.g., predefined report parts)?
- Can dashboard gadgets/objects interact with each other?

Security and Administration

- Does it support third-party authentication?
- Does it restrict access to dashboards and data by user, role, and group?
- Does it dynamically personalize user interface and content based on log-in credentials?
- Does it monitor usage by user, report, query, and so on?
- Does it support clustering and load balancing?
- Does it support failover and backup/restore?

- Does it migrate between development, test, and production environments?
- Does it offer impact analysis on metrics?

Design Environment

- Who is the target designer, an IT developer or power user?
- Does the dashboard come with predefined layouts and templates?
- Can users drag and drop gadgets onto a dashboard canvas?
- Is scripting required to apply filters, targets, alerts, or drills to dashboard objects?
- Does it support prompts? Hierarchical filters?

Dashboard Functionality

Does the dashboard support:

- Dimensional analysis (online analytical processing [OLAP])?
- Ad hoc reporting?
- High-fidelity printing?
- What-if modeling?
- Predictive analytics?
- Annotation?
- Collaboration?
- User-definable targets?
- User-definable alerts?
- Bread crumbs?
- Dynamically generated links to related dashboards?
- Right-click to view business metadata?
- Drill through to another system?

Deployment Options

Can you deliver an interactive dashboard via the listed channels?

- Web
- Desktop
- Mobile
- Disconnected
- Cloud
- E-mail
- PDF
- Excel
- PowerPoint

Types of Architectures

Different types of performance dashboards employ different architectures. As we've seen, operational dashboards tend to query source systems directly and apply minimal transformations, while tactical dashboards query both historical and current data from a data warehouse. Strategic dashboards often create a local data mart to cache time-series data for specific metrics. This section provides a high-level examination of various data architectures that support performance dashboards, including benefits and drawbacks.

Direct Query

In the "direct query" architecture, the performance dashboard issues SQL queries to source systems and displays the result set with minimal to moderate transformation. These tools are ideal for creating operational dashboards where users want to view current data from multiple systems in one place and don't need to perform a lot of drill-downs or analysis, or create reports. (See Exhibit 13.2.)

Direct query tools generally support interfaces to a variety of SQL and online analytical processing (OLAP) databases as well as various file types and packaged applications. Since these tools usually don't have a semantic layer, dashboard designers typically hand-code the SQL, embed it in dashboard objects (e.g., charts or tables), and define when the queries execute (e.g., on demand, at predefined intervals, according to a schedule). Data

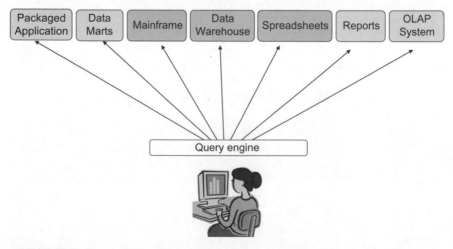

EXHIBIT 13.2 Direct Query Architecture

transformations typically are done on the fly using SQL in memory on the server using Excel or a lightweight transformation engine. The tools generally don't store data locally, although many have some sort of snapshot capability that can create a time-series data set, if needed.

The benefits of a direct query architecture is that it is fast to deploy and fairly inexpensive and offers flexible data access. Basically, it is a lightweight architecture that doesn't require a team of architects and report designers to set up and run. There is no semantic layer or elaborate security schemes to implement, no need to define facts or attributes, or to create hierarchies. The tools make it easy for developers to pull information from multiple systems and display it in one place so users don't have to hunt for the data on their own.

On the downside, the tools aren't dimensionally aware, so if you want to create hierarchies, drill paths, or summaries, you will need to write script. The queries are generally hard-wired so that if a source system changes, it will break the queries, which will have to be rewritten. Also, the dashboard issues queries to a remote database to populate metrics with data or perform a drill-down. If the queries are complex or require lots of transformation, developers will need to prerun queries and cache the results or create aggregate tables in a data mart or data warehouse (DW) to ensure adequate performance. As a result, the tools generally require an IT developer to configure and run.

BI Tools

A BI tools architecture issues queries via a semantic layer that simplifies data access by converting database schema into business-oriented dashboard objects (e.g., metrics, attributes, dimensions) that users can drag and drop onto a dashboard canvas to build dashboard pages. (See Exhibit 13.3.) Many BI tools also integrate query, OLAP, and report functionality within an integrated suite to deliver a full range of BI capabilities that enables users to switch seamlessly from one type of BI functionality to another. BI tools are great for building an enterprise BI environment on a common set of data.

BI report developers generally build dashboards using the BI tool's reporting module or a specialized dashboard module. (See the "Mashboards" section.) The reporting module enables developers to create reports in a dashboard format. Each chart in a report can link to more detailed data in the report or, if supported, link to an OLAP module that enables users to analyze the data dimensionally. Typically, BI tools run against a DW or data mart designed with a star or snowflake schema. However, in recent years, BI vendors have expanded the data access capabilities of their tools so that their semantic layers can query and join data from multiple sources.

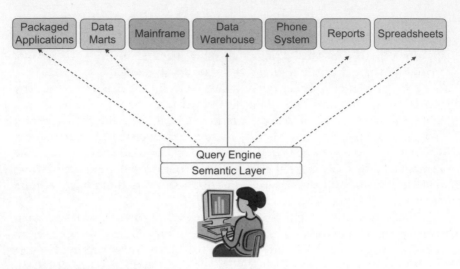

EXHIBIT 13.3 BI Tool Architecture

In some cases, the data are joined on the BI server via a transformation function while in other cases the tools support a federated query capability. (See below.)

The benefits of BI tools are that they are generally dimensionally aware, enabling full drill-down/across and slice/dice capabilities, as long as the toolset seamlessly integrates reporting and OLAP navigation capabilities. Also, if your organization has already deployed a BI platform and a DW and most of the data that dashboard users want to see already exist in the DW, it is very quick and inexpensive to build new dashboards.

On the downside, if you haven't already deployed an enterprise BI/DW environment, it will take considerable time and money before you can deploy dashboards. Like direct query tools (discussed earlier), BI tools issue queries to a remote database to populate metrics with data or perform a drill-down. If the queries are complex or require lots of transformation, developers will need to prerun queries and cache the results or create aggregate tables in a data mart or DW to ensure adequate performance. As a result, the tools generally require an IT developer to configure and run.

Mashboards

Many BI vendors have introduced specialized dashboard modules—which I call mashboards—that enable power users to drag and drop predefined content from a BI tool and external Web pages onto a dashboard canvas and "mash" them together. Mashboards are ideal for power users who want

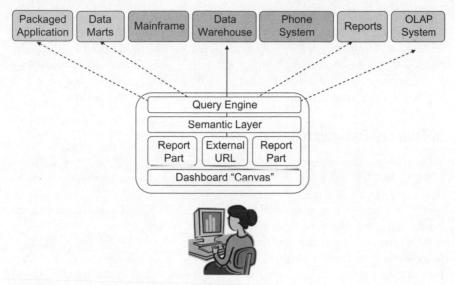

EXHIBIT 13.4 Mashboard Architecture

to create ad hoc dashboards for themselves or colleagues in their department. (See Exhibit 13.4.)

A mashboard is effectively a dashboard container for predefined BI content (e.g., charts and tables), various types of controls (e.g., radio buttons, tabs, selectors, pick lists), and external Web pages. Each mashboard object can pull data from a different source and be updated at different intervals. A mashboard leverages existing reports developed by professional report writers, which makes it easy for users with some degree of application savvy to create custom dashboards.

Mashboards don't require a DW or data mart, just a BI tool that can create reports and convert them into report "parts" or gadgets. Gadgets are mini-applications that run inside a container environment and have associated functions (e.g., a toolbar for sorting, filtering, charting, etc.) and services, such as the ability to communicate with other gadgets. For instance, gadgets may synchronize their displays automatically using a common filter without scripting.

A mashboard is the dashboard equivalent of an ad hoc reporting tool. Both let power users develop ad hoc reports or dashboards respectively without having to learn the full BI tool authoring environment. A mashboard enables users to create ad hoc dashboards without IT intervention. Some BI vendors offer mashboards at no extra cost while others charge for them.

The downside of mashboards is that you need to first implement a BI environment and write reports using professional report writers. As mentioned earlier (under "BI Tools"), this can take time and cost a significant amount of money. Also, mashboards generally limit users to using existing BI content; if they want to populate the mashboard with new metrics that haven't already been created, they are out of luck, unless they learn how to use the report writing tool. Finally, mashboards may not support all the functionality offered in the complete BI platform.

In-Memory Dashboards

In-memory dashboards have become quite popular lately because they are quick to deploy, affordable, and fast. The tools load all data into memory, providing speed-of-thought visual analysis. (See Exhibit 13.5.) Also known as visual analysis tools, in-memory tools are ideal for departmental dashboards without stringent data freshness requirements.

Originally, visual analysis tools were designed for business analysts who wanted to explore and manipulate small- to medium-size sets of data in a visual manner. The tools excel at rapidly filtering data with lots of variables and displaying results using a variety of chart and table types. The tools make it easy for analysts to explore data quickly, identify trends and outliers, create custom groups, and apply regression and other statistical functions. They also are easy to set up: Users simply load tables and link them via common keys, then they can begin their analysis. Although most data sets are loaded into memory in a batch job at night, most visual analysis tools have a query engine so users can, if they desire, add data to their data set.

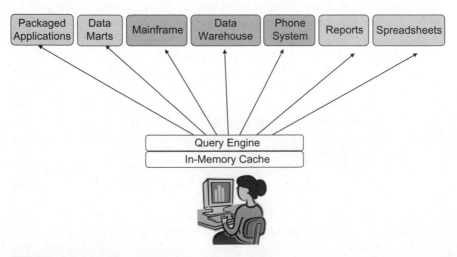

EXHIBIT 13.5 In-Memory Architecture

Today, visual analysis tools have become popular with casual users because of their highly visual, interactive interface. Typically, a business analyst creates an analysis or "dashboard" using the desktop tools and then "publishes" the view to a server where others can access and interact with the live view. Analysts generally simplify the display and turn off more advanced functions to make the tools more accessible to casual users. And visual analysis vendors have added features that make it easier to create and publish analytical output as departmental dashboards.

Because of their in-memory architecture, visual analysis tools can't easily scale beyond the amount of data that the desktop or server machine can hold in memory. Of course, as random access memory becomes more affordable and 64-bit operating systems become more pervasive, the amount of data that a typical server can store in memory is substantial. A large implementation might contain 50 million records, which is certainly a very large data mart. Users must be careful not to exceed the size of allowable in-memory storage, or they could lose data unless the tool has a mechanism to spill lightly accessed data to disk automatically. And like direct query tools, visual analysis tools aren't dimensionally aware and support light-weight transformations only. If you need to clean, transform, or integrate data derived from complex database schemas or create complex drill-downs or aggregations, you are going to do a lot of scripting.

Data Federation

Data federation uses distributed query technology and a global semantic layer to query and join data from multiple sources on the fly and display the results in one or more objects on a dashboard screen. (See Exhibit 13.6.) Data federation is ideal for creating dashboards when the data are spread across multiple systems yet users want a consolidated view of information. Many BI tools now embed data federation capabilities to provide more flexible data access.

Data federation integrates data from multiple, disparate sources inside or outside the organization on the fly. It provides business users and application developers a single, easy-to-use interface to access heterogeneous sources, making remote data appear as if it resides in a single local database. When users submit a query, data federation software behind the scenes calculates the optimal way to fetch and join the remote data and return the result. Often the tools ship data from one database to another to perform a join. The ability to shield users and application developers from the complexities of distributed SQL query calls and back-end data sources is why some vendors call this technology data virtualization software.

Data federation is ideal when you want to build a dashboard without spending the time or money to create a full-fledged data mart or DW. Many

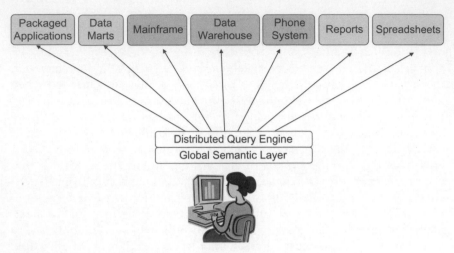

EXHIBIT 13.6 Data Federation

companies use data federation to build applications that have a short life span, such as prototypes or "emergency" applications requested by the chief executive, or to validate user requirements prior to building a data warehouse. Some federation architectures leverage XML and Web.

On the downside, data federation works only when source systems are available and have enough capacity to handle streams of ad hoc queries without bogging down transaction processing tasks. (This is also true of the direct query tools.) Generally, the tools work best with small volumes of data that are clean, consistent, and don't require much transformation. To obtain the best performance, it's best to use data federation to support short, tactical queries on current data rather than strategic queries against large volumes of historic data.

Data Marts

Data marts create a local store of data explicitly to support the performance dashboard. Data marts are designed to ensure adequate performance for dashboard metrics and ancillary applications that go beyond basic metrics monitoring. These marts include strategy maps, time-series charts, multidimensional analysis, what-if modeling, collaboration, text-based annotation, and reporting. (See Exhibit 13.7.)

Typically, designers create a logical data model or schema in a relational or multidimensional database that supports the dashboard's metrics and applications. Then developers create source-to-target transformation code that populates the data mart with the correct data, usually in a batch operation at night. The data mart then accumulates data over time to

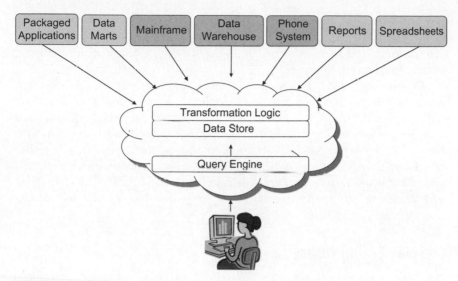

EXHIBIT 13.7 Data Mart Architecture

support time-series and other historical analyses and calculations. Some data marts may store only summarized data, but others—especially those supporting operational and tactical dashboards—may contain detailed data.

Sometimes the data mart can be a logical set of tables within the company's data warehouse. 1-800 CONTACTS, for example, used a multidimensional database to support is operational dashboards, but when the company found it difficult to update the databases with fresh data every 15 minutes, it created a set of tables in the DW to support the dashboards. (See Chapter 7.) And some direct query and in-memory tools maintain a local store of transformed data to support hierarchical drill-downs, dimensionalized queries, and what-if modeling.

Data marts often are used to support strategic dashboards (i.e., balanced scorecards) that require elaborate data models to support unique features, such as strategy maps, initiatives tracking, and text documents. A strategic dashboard model typically includes tables for objectives, metrics, people, organizational structures and hierarchies, and initiatives. For example, the Ministry of Works in the Kingdom of Bahrain uses a data mart to populate its balanced scorecards with data. (See Chapter 9.)

The main benefit of a data mart architecture is that it minimizes the risk of poor performance when data are scattered across multiple systems. Instead of trying to query remote databases on demand, as other architectures do, a data mart consolidates the data up front and stores them in a form that is conducive to fast queries. A data mart can prejoin and preaggregate data to support metrics and views in the dashboard so the query and transformation logic doesn't have to do this on the fly. A data mart is also needed to support application modules, such as strategy maps, initiative tracking, and metrics maps, among other things, that require complex joins among multiple tables.

On the downside, a data mart, like its DW big brother, assumes that you know in advance what metrics, applications, and data you are going to use in the dashboard. You can't create a good data model without such knowledge. When user requirements change, you need to revise the model, which can be tricky, since various elements in the dashboard or other downstream applications using the data mart could be affected. Also, it is harder to support near-real-time data delivery in a data mart since data transformation and query execution are separate jobs, not part of a single query stream, as in other architectures.

Complex Event Processing

Complex event processing (CEP) captures and filters real-time events and triggers actions based on predefined rules. CEP is ideal for supporting operational dashboards that are used to monitor real-time processes, such as trading systems, sensor data from pipelines, global positioning systems, or radio-frequency identification chips, or traffic data from computer networks, transportation systems, and Web sites, among other things.

Traditionally, companies have built their own CEP systems, but increasingly, software vendors provide off-the-shelf solutions. Most CEP systems contain: a data acquisition engine that captures events streaming off a messaging backbone as well as historical data from a DW or external sources; a calculation engine that aggregates events over time and holds them in memory; and a rules engine that defines targets and actions to take when an event object exceeds a predefined threshold. (See Exhibit 13.8.)

CEP is like an intelligent sensor that takes a continuous reading of activity generated by one or more interrelated business processes and detects patterns that trigger automated responses. For instance, CEP might detect when purchases of a particular item have exceeded daily forecasts by 10 percent or more for three of the past seven days and trigger an e-mail alert to the merchandising manager. Besides e-mail alerts, CEP systems can trigger dashboard alerts, initiate workflows, or update transaction databases. The systems are designed so that business users can build the rules for creating objects and triggering responses.

The main advantage of CEP is that it provides built-in support for real-time monitoring so that you don't have to rearchitect a DW to support trickle feeds or near-real-time refreshes. But CEP is not just for real-time data; it can extract historical data from a warehouse and use it to compare to current data when executing rules. Some small- and medium-size busi-

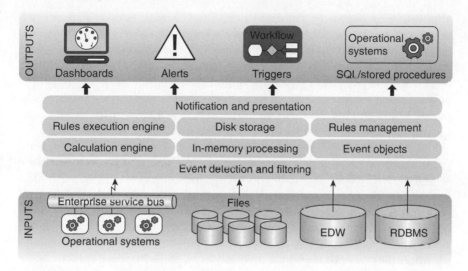

EXHIBIT 13.8 Complex Event Processing

nesses have deployed their DWs using CEP, giving them real-time capabilities from the start.

On the downside, the systems have a lot of moving parts and require technical expertise to set up and maintain. Plus, from an analytical perspective, because they cannot store large volumes of historical data, they are more appropriate for niche applications rather than a large DW. Also, users require significant training to set up and manage rules to ensure that the system doesn't spit out lots of irrelevant alerts or, conversely, fail to notify appropriate users about significant events.

Cloud

The last architecture is the newest one. Cloud-based dashboards have become popular recently because you don't need to purchase hardware or software licenses, and you don't need IT experts to set up and maintain them. Users simply upload their data to the cloud-based service, configure the tool, and quickly create and publish a dashboard. Cloud-based dashboards are ideal for small- and medium-size companies or departments at larger companies that don't have access to IT staff and don't have a lot of new information to add to a dashboard on a regular basis.

Currently, most cloud-based dashboards require you to upload data to the cloud-based service that runs on a hosted platform (i.e., database, application, server, and storage) in a third-party data center. The service works in a multitenant environment in which all customers run the same application on the same platform using different data, which often are partitioned by row or table in the underlying database. This virtualized environment provides significant economies of scale to the provider, who passes along cost savings to customers. Rather than pay an up-front license fee, customers pay a monthly subscription based on the number of users or amount of data. Customers can add or delete users and data sources easily, paying only for what they use. In addition, when a cloud provider updates the application, the revisions are available immediately to all customers.

The benefit of a cloud-based BI architecture is that it significantly simplifies the process of deploying performance dashboards. Without hardware or software to install and maintain or up-front licenses to sign, customers can quickly deploy an individual or departmental dashboard with minimal cost and planning. Companies can build and begin using an entire dashboard solution before they even pay a dime, if the cloud BI provider offers a free trial. Users don't have to estimate the number of users or data sources up front; they simply pay on a metered basis for what they use.

The downsides of cloud BI services today are data security, application flexibility, and data transfer volumes. In my opinion, data security is largely a red herring except for companies that operate under regulatory constraints that require them to maintain data on premises or be able to identify its exact location. (Most cloud services virtualize data processing across dozens or hundreds of servers so it is difficult to pinpoint where data resides at any given time.) In fact, cloud providers pay such close attention to security that your data are probably safer with a cloud provider than they are in your a corporate data center.

With a cloud-based solution, everyone uses the same application. If the application doesn't meet your needs, you are out of luck or you must contract the provider to create a custom solution for you. Finally, the cloud today isn't designed for companies that need to move large volumes of data across the Internet to a cloud-based hosting center. Such transfers take too much time and, if the hosting center is a public cloud provider, you will be charged for every kilobyte that you transfer and store. However, most cloud BI vendors maintain private clouds in their own or third-party hosting centers and don't charge for data transfer.

Hybrid Model. Because some organizations need to store data on their own computers due to security concerns or industry regulations, cloud BI providers are devising ways to let customers have their cake and eat it too. Some now enable customers to run BI software in the cloud while maintaining data in a DW on premise. The cloud BI software queries the DW without having to move the data into the cloud, eliminating the data movement bottleneck.

Cloud BI for Small Companies. Cloud-based services geared to individuals or small companies—which often provide a 30-day free trial for using the service—enable users to upload spreadsheets or files or data from common packaged applications, such as QuickBooks or Salesforce.com. Once your data are uploaded, you can view them in a standard dashboard format and share them with others whom you specify.

Cloud BI for Large Companies. Services geared to larger BI implementations create a custom data mart in the hosted environment that extracts data from various applications and systems running in a company's data center. The service provider creates a custom data model for the customer and often provides transformation services to populate the data mart with data from source systems. These services give customers greater latitude to configure the user interface to match their corporate branding, among other things. The providers will also create an entirely custom dashboard application for an extra fee and run it in a dedicated environment, if necessary. In this case, the project is simply a custom consulting project whose output is managed in the cloud.

Summary

As you can see, there are numerous ways to architect a performance dashboard. Each has its trade-offs, and many companies use multiple approaches to support their performance dashboards. The key to selecting the right architecture is understanding user requirements and the complexity of the metrics and applications the performance dashboard needs to support. The more complex an environment, the more likely you'll need to predefine data structures and models using enterprise BI tools and data warehousing techniques. The less complex an environment, the more you can use lighter-weight, less-costly approaches.

CHAPTER 14

How to Deploy and Integrate Dashboards

Where to Start and Finish?

Quest for Alignment

One common question that people ask about performance dashboards is "What's the best place to start?" And the follow-up question is "How do we integrate our existing performance dashboards?"

Most people start their performance dashboard journey with a request from the chief executive officer (CEO) or business unit head who wants an executive dashboard. But many question whether a centralized, top-down approach is politically feasible and technically practical. They wonder whether it would be better to let performance dashboards bubble up from the bottom and integrate them after the fact. Many wonder whether they should tackle an important application that is critical to the company's success or start small to minimize complexity and risk.

Multiple Starting Points. Ultimately, there is no right or wrong answer to these questions. Organizations employ both top-down and bottom-up approaches, often at the same time. For example, executives may have kicked off a balanced scorecard project that promises to cascade scorecards from the executive suite to all levels of the organization, while, at the same time, each functional group is building its own operational and tactical dashboards. There may also be an enterprise business intelligence (BI) initiative whose goal is to standardize the delivery of information across the enterprise, providing both executive and departmental reports and dashboards using an integrated BI platform and data warehousing environment.

The reality is that most organizations have a panoply of performance dashboards and initiatives. Some are spearheaded by corporate headquarters and others by business unit or functional leaders. Some are driven in a top-down manner with stringent standards for business and systems architecture, while others are implemented in a bottom-up fashion that don't adhere to any particular standards.

Alignment Is the Goal. Ultimately, no matter the starting place, the task is the same: Align multiple, heterogeneous performance management systems so everyone is working off a consistent set of information. When this happens, an organization starts to use information strategically. It can communicate strategic objectives to every group in the organization using a consistent set of objectives and metrics. And it can aggregate, or roll up, performance results from lower levels of the organization to higher levels, enabling executives to track progress and performance at any given moment. It also enables managers and staff to compare their performance to that of peers throughout the organization, increasing their motivation and productivity.

Organizations can align and link performance dashboards using either a centralized or distributed approach. The centralized approach creates a single performance management system that spawns multiple, dependent dashboards and scorecards. The distributed approach links performance dashboards that run on different BI platforms and are administered by different technical teams.

Centralized Approach. The centralized approach works best in companies with centralized or hierarchical cultures in which a CEO or business unit head can get everyone to standardize on a common set of metrics and BI platform. Organizations that have standardized their operational applications or implemented an enterprise data warehouse are likely candidates for this approach. For example, Rohm and Haas, featured in Chapter 8, implemented a single instance of SAP applications worldwide and a single enterprise data warehouse using SAP BW. Not surprisingly, it used a centralized approach when building performance dashboards. The company now has 40 highly integrated dashboards that support all departments and levels of the global organization.

Distributed Approach. In contrast, the distributed approach works best in companies with more decentralized cultures where business units, departments, and workgroups enjoy considerable autonomy and have their own information technology (IT) departments that build custom applications. For example, Cisco, featured in Chapter 9, has a decentralized organizational structure in which business units enjoy considerable autonomy. But Cisco aligns the organization by clearly articulating corporate strategies (e.g., customer satisfaction), establishing performance targets, and holding business units and managers accountable for the results. Cisco has five corporate dashboards that measure customer satisfaction and dozens of independently built departmental scorecards and dashboards that include customer satisfaction measures that align with corporate objectives.

In reality, most companies have neither a highly centralized nor a distributed organizational structure, but something in between. As a result, most use a blend of both centralized and distributed approaches to deliver a consistent set of performance management metrics.

Centralized Approach

The centralized approach builds integration into the design and project plan so all performance applications, whenever and wherever deployed, run on a common technical platform, share consistent business content (e.g., metrics, dimensions, and attributes), and are built by the same technical team.

In a centralized approach, performance dashboards are not physically distinct systems or applications; they simply are customized views of performance information generated by a single performance management system. The system dynamically generates custom views of metrics and information based on each user's role or security profile. The centralized approach makes it easy for technical teams to rapidly create multiple, customized performance dashboards for every individual and group in the organization.

Top Down

A common way to deploy performance dashboards using a centralized approach is to work from the top down, starting at the executive level and working down the organizational hierarchy in a systematic fashion. This method ensures that each dashboard adheres to corporate standards and processes for defining objectives and metrics and maintains a consistent look and feel.

However, sometimes top-down projects shipwreck on the shoals of corporate politics and scope management. Getting all business unit heads to agree on a dozen or so enterprise metrics to manage the enterprise is a tall task. As a result, many top-down projects stall before they get traction. This is especially true of strategic dashboards (i.e., balanced scorecards) that require organizations to define their strategy and objectives before defining measures. Chapters 3 and 10 discuss how to address these political challenges, emphasizing the role of strong project champions to lead the initiative.

Online Retailer. To navigate through the political minefields of a top-down approach, one online retailer hired a well-known management consulting firm to help it sort out its performance management strategy. After six months and more than $1 million, the consultancy helped the company create 24 global key performance indicators (KPIs), 18 of which were financial in nature. Each of the 24 metrics was comprised of 2 or more lower-level metrics totaling 80 metrics overall. Each member of the 100-person executive team was assigned to a metric and held accountable for its results. The company uses the dashboard metrics to focus executive meetings on top-priority issues but has no plans to cascade the metrics beyond the executive team.

Rohm and Haas. In contrast, Rohm and Haas (profiled in Chapter 8) used a much simpler approach to defining metrics. The director of BI scheduled a meeting of top executives for one hour during which they selected 10 metrics that they wanted to track across every business unit, group, and region in the company. The metrics, which are a mix of financial and nonfinancial measures, weren't new to Rohm and Haas, but the company had never monitored every business group in the same way using the same metrics, which was the intent of the executive team that commissioned the dashboard project. Today, every dashboard at Rohm and Haas enables users with access rights to drill down from an enterprise view of performance for each metric to individual group views. At the same time, Rohm and Haas has created for every major functional area dashboards that contain the global metrics plus department-specific metrics.

Architectural Standards

Architectural Standards. The centralized approach—whether working top down or bottom up—requires the technical team to create and manage all dashboards and scorecards on a standard BI platform running against a unified data warehousing environment. This approach offers greater flexibility at lower cost than developing individual performance dashboards from scratch. Technical teams quickly create new "views" (i.e., dashboards or scorecards) for individuals or groups without having to build a system or application or buy new servers and software. When users log on, the system checks their credentials and dynamically displays the appropriate dashboard or a unique set of metrics within a single dashboard. For example, the western regional sales manager might see sales only for the western region, while an eastern sales manager would see sales only for the eastern region. In this way, a single performance dashboard can support dozens or hundreds of distinct applications, which most users refer to as their dashboard or scorecard.

The centralized approach also makes it easier for companies to maintain the consistency and uniformity of metric definitions and rules because they are stored and maintained in one place by one team. (Companies call a repository of metric definitions a data dictionary, a data library, or a data glossary. Technical teams call it a metadata repository.) Another benefit of the centralized approach is that organizations can support on the BI infrastructure other analytical applications besides performance dashboards. For instance, Quicken Loans built its BI architecture primarily to drive its operational dashboards but now uses it to support other analytical applications as well.

System Standards. A development team needs to define systems standards for the performance management system. Doing this includes specifying the technologies and products it will use for Web servers, application servers, storage systems, databases, online analytical processing tools, programming languages, and reporting tools.

Although business managers often object to adhering to architectural and systems standards because they can sidetrack a thriving project or force them to forfeit a favored product (see discussion in Chapter 4), standards ensure the long-term sustainability of a project. Standards ultimately reduce the costs of development, maintenance, and training and speed delivery of applications and solutions. The business and technical teams need to work together to optimize the business value of IT, which often means making trade-offs between adhering to technical standards and delivering immediate business value. (See Chapter 5 for how to align business and technical requirements.)

Data Standards

Besides standardizing application components, the technical team needs to standardize data. This is accomplished in three ways:

1. Creating a data model that drives the performance dashboard
2. Identifying and sourcing the appropriate data in operational systems, files, and other systems, both inside and outside the organization
3. Cleaning and validating data to ensure they meet user expectations for quality and accuracy

Creating Data Models. Every application, including a performance dashboard, needs a data model. A data model represents a business process within the structure of a database. It is the brains of the application. Without it, the application cannot work.

Logically, the data model defines "things" (e.g., employee, position, manager, etc.), attributes of those things (e.g., employee can be full time, part time, current, former, etc.), relationships among things (e.g., an employee is hired by a manager), and "facts" that involve those things, such as a sales transaction or new hire. Physically, the model stores all this information in tables and columns within a relational database (or in other types of structures in specialized databases). Once deployed, the database captures events and adds rows to the "fact" tables (e.g., John Doe bought a Ford pickup truck on June 19; Mary Jane was hired as a receptionist in the finance department on October 20). Metrics represent sums or calculations various facts (i.e., rows in fact tables) for a given set of things and attributes over time.

Technical teams spend considerable time interviewing business users before creating data models. Their goal is to create models that accurately reflect the way the business works. The time required to create effective data models is directly related to the size, scope, and complexity of the project.

One advantage of commercial performance dashboard solutions is that they often contain generic data models that are tailored to various industries or functional areas. Most vendors cull the experiences of numerous customers when creating generic data models and analytic applications. While the models usually need to be tweaked for individual companies, they can accelerate project development compared to starting from scratch.

"We purchased a [vendor product] for its data model, which jump-started the project for us. It helped us understand how to roll this stuff out. The vendor product now represents only 20 percent of our entire solution, but it was worth having something to start from," says a senior manager of IT at a wireless telecommunications firm.

Identifying and Sourcing Data. IT managers responsible for populating metrics with data must identify the most reliable sources for that data. This is not always straightforward. There may be 20 places to get customer data. Which is the right source, given what the metric is designed to measure? Which sources contain valid, timely, and reliable data?

The technical team may decide to pull several fields from one source and a few from another source to populate the dashboard data model. This analysis and triage "takes weeks and months to work out with the business units," says one IT manager, "but now we have high-quality detailed data that people trust." The key is to recruit business analysts who combine a strong knowledge of the business with an acute understanding of the underlying data and systems. These individuals can make or break the data sourcing process.

Cleaning and Validating Data. The third aspect of standardizing data is the hardest: delivering high-quality data to a performance dashboard. Operational systems are often riddled with data errors—missing data, invalid values, incorrect data types and formats, invalid dependencies—that do not show up until a performance dashboard team tries to integrate data among multiple systems.

According to one IT manager who asked not to be named:

Our [performance] dashboard constantly highlights issues with the quality of data coming from source systems. We're at the end of the line and often have to deal with the garbage that others send down the pipe. We point out problems to source system administrators and ask the business owners to pressure the administrators to fix the problems, but that's all we can do. There is an institutionalized lack of rigor around maintaining high-quality information in source systems. They keep Band-Aiding the system, but we need to get it right at the source the first time.

The cost of fixing data errors increases the farther down the line they are identified. The worst-case scenario is when a data error slips into an application and can be detected by end users. When this happens, end users stop trusting and using the system, leading to the application's demise.

Obviously, the best way to achieve high-quality data is to prevent errors from occurring in the first place. Doing this usually requires source system owners to apply validation routines to check the accuracy of data entered into applications and to inform downstream application owners whenever they add or change a field in the source system. It may also require developers to rewrite outdated applications and managers to reengineer business processes so workers are rewarded for delivering high-quality data.

Most technical teams let "bad" data pass through into the performance dashboards and do not try to clean them up. The theory, which is sometimes debated, says that the business will not be motivated to fix bad data at the source unless they know that problems exist. Since bad quality data can cause users to reject a new performance management system, many project teams schedule a "beta" or trial period where users can experiment with the system and identify bugs before they officially declare it a production system. After that point, many teams rigorously analyze incoming data and don't allow users onto the system until a business owner declares that the data is valid and okay to use.

Data Governance. To obtain high-quality data, the business must view data as a critical asset, as valuable as equipment, people, or cash. To preserve this asset, companies need to create a data governance program that identifies critical data elements and assign individuals responsibility for them. *Data stewards* are senior business executives who are responsible for the meaning of the data element, *data administrators* are technical staff who ensure the integrity of those values and develop data validation and cleansing programs, and *business or data analysts* assess whether its values are in or out of range for a given report.

For example, every day, a business analyst at a Boston-based financial services firm "certifies" that data in the company's financial dashboard is clean and accurate. The analyst runs tests on the data, and when everything looks okay, the analyst pushes a button that changes the dashboard's status from "preliminary" to "final" and adds to the bottom of each screen the time and date that it was officially certified.

NetApp's Enterprise BI Environment

Like Rohm and Haas, NetApp, a storage manufacturer, designed its performance dashboards in a centralized, top-down fashion on a single, integrated BI platform. Exhibit 14.1 shows the subject areas and phases of development for its enterprise BI initiative, which it kicked off in 2008. The BI team divided the subject areas into two groups and gave each a catchy name that would resonate with sponsors and users. It dubbed the externally focused subject areas "Customer Intelligence and Analytics" (CIA) and the internally focused subject areas "Financial and Workforce BI" (FBI). Phase 1, which took about nine months to deploy, consists of subject areas shared by both groups, including booking, customer, partner, and solution. (See Exhibit 14.1.)

BI Framework. Exhibit 14.2 depicts NetApp's enterprise dashboard framework. Users enter the dashboard via one of the top three layers of the pyramid. When they log in, they see a dashboard tailored to their role but can traverse to any other dashboard they have permission to access in three clicks.

The enterprise analytics layer is geared to senior executives, the functional analytics layer is geared to departmental managers and users, and the role-based analytics layer is tailored to individual users, such as sales representatives and account managers. Below that, users can drill into subject-specific dashboards, such as cross selling, period close performance, or hourly projected bookings or 360-degree-view dashboards, which focus on customers, partners, products, or employees, among other things.

Traversing Dashboards. Each dashboard in the framework is designed using MAD (monitor, analyze, drill to detail) principles. And because the environment runs on a single platform with common metrics and dimensions, users can link seamlessly from one dashboard to another. NetApp deploys all the dashboards on tabs across the top of each screen, giving users one-click access to any dashboard in the framework. Users can also drill down or across one dashboard to reach the top of another. Exhibit 14.3 shows how a centralized, top-down deployment approach logically integrates dashboards.

Serial Development. However, one problem with the centralized approach is that one corporate BI team typically builds all dashboards, one after another. This serial approach takes considerable time to roll out. As

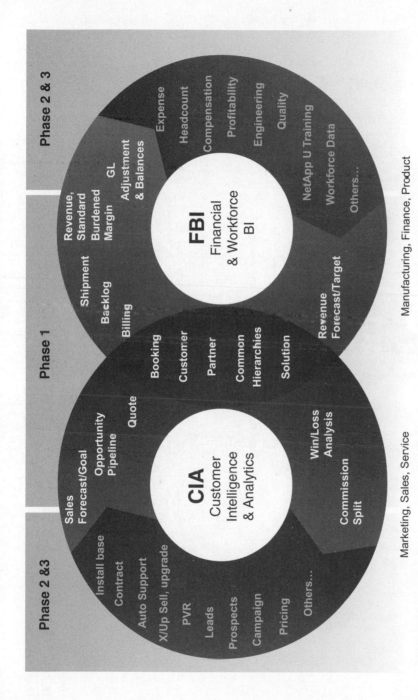

EXHIBIT 14.1 NetApp Enterprise BI Subject Areas

Courtesy of NetApp.

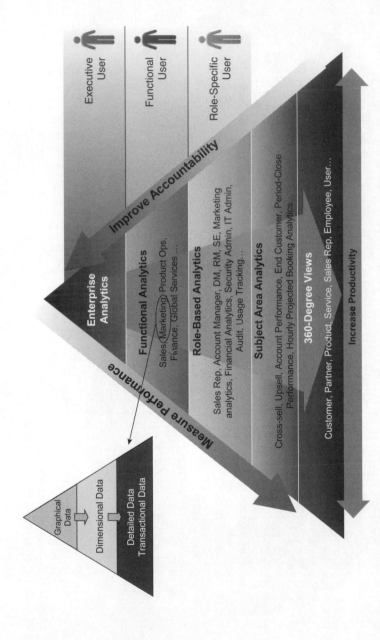

NetApp's BI framework consists of multiple layers, each consisting of sets of dashboards tailored to different roles, activities, or entities. Each dashboard is designed using MAD principles of layered delivery.

EXHIBIT 14.2 NetApp's BI Framework
Courtesy of NetApp.

In a centralized approach, all dashboards are built on a common platform by a single team using common business and systems architecture. Each dashboard is a dynamically generated, custom view of the enterprise BI and data environment based on role or subject area. Users can traverse dashboards through visual cues on the dashboard screen (e.g., tabs or links) or by drilling down and through to other dashboard views.

EXHIBIT 14.3 Traversing MAD Dashboards in a Centralized, Top-Down Environment

Courtesy of NetApp.

you can imagine, departments on the low end of the priority list often get frustrated by the slow pace of development. Often they are tempted to circumvent the centralized program and build their own performance dashboards. Doing this typically undermines information consistency and wreaks havoc on the centralized program. As described in the BI Maturity Model presented in Chapter 4, unless the central team finds a way to meet local needs more quickly, it will have a mutiny on its hands that will set back the program several years.

One solution to this problem is for executives to fund multiple development teams that can work in parallel, thus doubling or tripling their output. Or the central team can empower the local groups to build their own dashboards adhering to corporate architectural and application standards. This is how many performance dashboard initiatives shift from a centralized, top-down approach to a distributed approach, described in the next section.

Bottom Up

Grassroots Initiative. In a centralized approach, the opposite of top-down deployment is bottom-up deployment, where an initiative does not start in the executive office but in a business unit, region, or other group and spreads upward and outward from there. A large number of operational and tactical dashboards start in a business unit or department and use a bottom-up approach to expand outward to the enterprise, eventually becoming the enterprise standard.

For example, a regional group at Hewlett Packard TSG initiated a strategic dashboard project to serve its own needs, but it was so successful that it quickly spread to every region and unit in the group. The problem with the bottom-up approach is that other business units and groups are usually developing similar systems. Invariably, these groups use different metrics, sources, staffs, and methods, making their systems incompatible.

In many respects, there is not much difference between the bottom-up approach and the distributed approach discussed in the next section. The only major difference is the end result: A successful, bottom-up strategy turns into a centralized performance dashboard environment, where in a distributed approach, it does not. To be honest, few bottom-up initiatives make it this far, which means that successful bottom-up deployments are rare.

Distributed Approach

In a distributed approach, performance dashboards are built independently of each other, often by different teams using different tools and systems.

The challenge with this approach is maintaining information consistency. It is very difficult to ensure that different teams use common metrics, dimensions, and data when they are building dashboards independently of each other. The distributed approach can also be implemented in a top-down or bottom-up fashion, just as the centralized approach.

Top Down

Cascading Scorecards. In a top-down deployment, the first performance dashboard—which is typically an executive scorecard in a balanced scorecard initiative—translates the organization's strategy into objectives and KPIs that measure performance at an enterprise level. The corporate view then serves as a template for all subsequent dashboards or scorecards. Each business unit builds its own scorecard, identifying objectives and KPIs that influence the scorecard at the level above it. These displays often reuse some objectives and metrics from higher-level scorecards and create new ones that measure local objectives and processes. Once business unit scorecards are complete, the process repeats itself at the regional and district level, and so on down to the lowest level in the organization, which could be an office, a workgroup, or an individual.

Asking each business unit to figure out how to influence metrics in higher-level performance dashboards unleashes considerable creativity. Paul Niven, in *Balanced Scorecard Step by Step* (John Wiley & Sons, 2002, p. 209), writes: "One of the benefits of the cascading process is watching creativity bloom … as groups begin to contemplate how they might contribute to an organizational goal once considered well outside their sphere of influence."

Cisco. At Cisco, mentioned earlier and in Chapter 9, the Corporate Quality group built five enterprise dashboards to monitor customer satisfaction. Then each functional group built its own balanced scorecard to monitor progress toward achieving strategic objectives. Many customer satisfaction metrics from the corporate dashboards appear in the functional scorecard, especially in the Voice of the Customer perspective. (See Exhibit 9.5.)

Cisco's distributed approach is unique. Each functional group built its own scorecards but used a corporate standard tool set to do so (Oracle BI Enterprise Edition). Even though the teams all used the same BI platform to build their scorecards, each has a unique look and feel, reflecting its team and departmental origins. At other companies, a corporate development team may build dashboards for each department that meet their specific needs and requirements. In some cases, the corporate group can impose stringent standards for the look and feel and functionality of the dashboards, and in other cases, it can't.

Unfortunately, corporate development teams working on behalf of autonomous departments often are whipsawed by user demands and cannot establish technical standards that would enable them to serve customer needs better in the long run. Instead, they spend significant time re-creating the same components over and over again to meet the preferences of different groups whose needs are actually more similar than different.

Diverse Requirements. For instance, a technical team in a telecommunications company that developed a corporate scorecard complains that each department wants the same information displayed in different ways: The marketing department wants charts with a green background and special graphics; the engineering department wants the chart to display a map of the United States; and the finance group wants charts with two y axes that displays multiple metrics simultaneously. Each request requires the technical team to build or buy a new charting component. Even off-the-shelf components take them considerable time to configure and test. The senior IT manager of the technical team says, "The program office needs to go to the business and say, 'You must use these formats,' but they are reluctant to do so because they fear that business users will create their own charts and reports and not use the corporate scorecard."

This example illustrates the pitfalls of having a corporate team develop performance dashboards that span multiple business units and departments. In contrast, project teams that build performance dashboards for a single business unit or department tend to avoid many of these issues. Except for choice of tools and platforms, this is the strategy that Cisco takes. Business units can adhere to standards because there is greater homogeneity in the way people want to view and manipulate applications and data in the group.

Strong Program Office. The key to the distributed approach is making sure each group adheres to the standard definitions and rules for metrics and faithfully aligns its versions to the ones directly above them in the organizational hierarchy. Doing this usually requires the organization to create a program office that oversees and coordinates development activities. The program office, which serves as an intermediary between the business and project teams, ensures that all development efforts adhere to standards for defining and linking metrics as well as predefined technical specifications. However, the organization needs to ensure that the program office has significant clout and resources to enforce standards among various development groups and ensure the consistent usage of metrics and information among all performance dashboards.

Application Standards. The team also needs to establish development standards to ensure reliable delivery, accurate data, and consistent application performance. Development teams that establish conventions for displaying, manipulating, and navigating data can work more efficiently and rapidly. They can reuse components, such as layouts, grids, graphs, and charts, instead of creating them from scratch each time. They can also optimize these components to deliver fast response times when users navigate the performance dashboard, submit queries, or download reports.

Bottom Up

The centralized approach works well when an organization builds a performance dashboard from scratch and rolls it out across the enterprise. But, as mentioned earlier, most organizations do not start with a clean slate. They already have multiple performance dashboards, some of which overlap and compete for resources and endorsements from top executives. Given such an environment, project teams need to consider whether it makes sense to add another performance dashboard to the mix or leverage and extend what already exists.

Federation. The bottom-up, distributed approach attempts to link existing performance dashboards into a seamless whole. This federation can be accomplished in a variety of ways. It can be as easy as transferring data from one performance dashboard to another or as challenging as standardizing metric definitions in multiple dashboards so they report performance consistently. A federated approach might involve merging two performance dashboards or designating one dashboard as the master or enterprise dashboard going forward. (This is essentially the centralized, bottom-up approach described in the previous section.) Sometimes organizations pursue multiple tactics at the same time.

Inventory. To bring order to the chaos, project teams should first create an inventory of existing performance dashboards. The inventory should document a number of characteristics, such as type (i.e., operational, tactical, or strategic), business domain, sample metrics, active users, platform used, and business owner, among other things. (See Exhibit 14.4.)

Project leaders can use this information to determine whether it makes sense to create a new performance dashboard from scratch or piggyback on top of an existing one. The project leader can also use the inventory as evidence to convince a top executive that the organization has a burgeoning information management problem. The inventory can then serve as a guide to help an executive determine which performance dashboards should remain and which should be eliminated or merged and consolidated into others.

Peer-based Exchange. There are two ways to integrate existing performance dashboards: peer-based exchange and virtual mashups. With peer-based exchange, two or more performance dashboards exchange information, creating a peer relationship among them.

Peer-based exchange works best when there are no inconsistencies or overlap among the metrics and data in the performance dashboards. Here,

EXHIBIT 14.4 Dashboard Inventory

	Dashboard A	Dashboard B
Business Domain	Finance	Sales
Business Owner	John Doe	Jane Ray
Dashboard Type	Tactical	Operational
Usage Metrics	120 active users; 140 queries a day	200 active users; 400 queries a day
Platform/Tools	Excel, Essbase	Custom .NET
Data Sources	Mainframe, Excel	Sales tracking, pipeline
Updates	Monthly	Daily
Primary Metrics	AP/AR, DSOs	Orders, forecasts
Comments	Most data exists in data warehouse	Heavily used custom app with active sponsor
Evaluation	Good candidate for consolidation	Keep as is

In a federated environment, the first place to start is to inventory existing systems and evaluate whether they should be integrated, consolidated, abandoned, or kept as is.

business groups simply agree to exchange performance data or charts. For instance, the finance group might want to display charts from a human resources (HR) dashboard in its scorecard. This is a relatively straightforward process; the only question is whether the exchange is done dynamically or in batches.

For instance, the finance scorecard administrator can have the HR department send him the data via e-mail, or he can simply access the HR dashboard with permission and write down the relevant numbers. Then he can manually update the scorecard. Or the finance group might create a link from its scorecard to the HR dashboard, allowing finance users to log in and view the appropriate information directly.

Virtual Mashups. Virtual mashups are performance dashboards that access predefined content in other reporting systems and dashboards. Chapter 13 describes mashboards produced by BI vendors that enable power users to drag and drop predefined report parts and external URLs onto a dashboard canvas to create a personalized dashboard. The mashboard contains live links to those elements so users are interacting with the most up-to-date content possible. The only drawback with mashboards is that today most work only with the BI vendor's own reports and gadgets.

In the future, these mashboards will provide open access to any BI reporting elements, enabling designers to create a federated dashboard from existing content anywhere in the organization. Of course, some of this is possible today through portal technology. For instance, most BI vendors support interfaces with Microsoft SharePoint, which enables organizations to use SharePoint as a virtual mashup of dashboard content.

Cascading Metrics

Organizations that deploy performance dashboards in a top-down fashion seek to align all parts of the company behind a unified strategy represented by a shared set of objectives and metrics. Typically, top executives defined a dozen or so metrics that embody the strategy and then cascade those metrics to the rest of the organization. In some cases, the metrics are identical at each level, and in other cases, the metrics are different but related.

Scorecard Cascading. The balanced scorecard community has methodology that defines how scorecards, objectives, and metrics get cascaded from one level of an organization to the next. Each business group develops a strategy map with objectives and metrics. Each strategy map is designed to influence the objectives and metrics in the strategy map of the business group above it in the organization. Thus, in this form of cascading, strategy rolls down but data doesn't necessarily roll up. (See Exhibit 14.5.)

While strategy remains constant, each group has a different set of objectives for achieving the strategy, based on its function and level. Metrics are merely localized instantiations of those unique objectives. Thus, data rarely rolls up in a straightforward fashion, if at all. More advanced scorecard implementations, such as those at Cisco, will correlate objectives and metrics via statistical analysis. For example, Cisco knows exactly what impact a

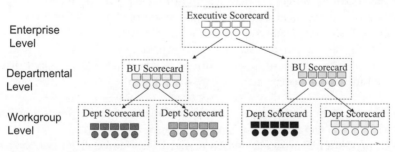

With balanced scorecards, strategy rolls down, but data doesn't roll up. Organizations can use metrics to correlate the relationship among objectives within the same scorecard and between scorecards at different levels of the organization.

EXHIBIT 14.5 Scorecard Cascading

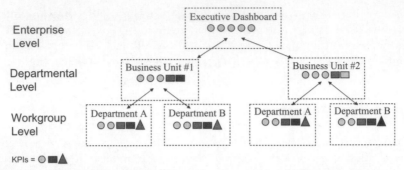

Enterprise dashboards are designed to give executives a clear line of sight to operations in all business units. In these dashboards, metrics roll down and data roll up.

EXHIBIT 14.6 Dashboard Cascading

specific process improvement will have on various customer satisfaction and experience scores and consequently revenue. (See Chapter 9.)

Dashboard Cascading. In contrast, enterprise dashboards focus more on transparency than strategy. The idea is to give executives a clear line of sight into business operations at every level of the organization and enable peer groups to benchmark their performance against each other. Compared to balanced scorecards, these types of performance dashboards tend to reuse many of the same metrics at each level of the organization. This enables executives to examine profitability, expenditures, and customer satisfaction in a consistent manner throughout the organization.

For example, executives can see the profitability of the enterprise as a whole and then drill down to view profitability of each business unit and drill further to view profits for each region, district, and functional area. The dashboard summarizes data at the appropriate level. So, in enterprise dashboards, metrics roll down and data rolls up. (See Exhibit 14.6.)

Data Roll-ups. Data roll-ups work in a variety of ways. The easiest roll-ups happen when metrics are identical at every level. This makes it easy to calculate data and speeds query performance. Data rolls up from underlying KPIs in four ways. (See Exhibit 14.7.)

1. **Direct.** The same metric exists at each level and is aggregated upward. This is the most common form of roll-up.
2. **Composite.** This occurs when a metric is created from two or more metrics. For example, sales administration expense is formed by summing sales expenses and administration expenses. A composite metric can also be a ratio in which one metric is a numerator and the other is a denominator. For example, customer loyalty might be dollar amount purchased divided by number of purchases in one year.

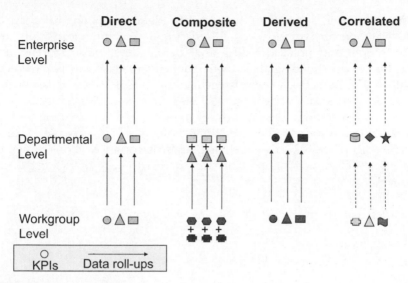

EXHIBIT 14.7 Data Roll-ups

3. **Derived.** Here, each level uses the same metric but each instance is defined differently. For instance, currency is a metric that doesn't roll up neatly if combining two different currencies. In this case, you'll need a formula to convert one metric to another or to a standard format.

4. **Correlated.** When the change in two metrics is proportional, you can calculate a mathematical formula to express their relationship. Correlation is important in strategic dashboards where you use metrics to define causal relationships among objectives.

Summary

Performance dashboards take many forms. There is no right or wrong way to deploy and integrate dashboards throughout an organization. Organizations can deploy them in a centralized or distributed fashion, from the top down or the bottom up. In reality, most organizations use a mix of approaches to deploy and then align performance dashboards. The key is recognizing which approach works best for your organization.

Today, the most common approach is to engage a corporate development team to build an executive dashboard that contains views or links to multiple departmental dashboards. But this requires the organization to establish and enforce a business and systems architecture that ensures that all dashboards share common metrics, dimensions, and attributes; access good, clean data; and use an integrated BI platform running on a shared data warehouse. Typically, centralized, top-down approaches run into scale, scope, and political issues, and, before long, business units and departments are building their own independent dashboards. However, distributed approaches in which each group builds its own dashboards undermine information consistency. Unless there is up-front consensus on metrics and development standards, each group ends up creating an analytical silo that is hard to integrate. While virtual mashups promise to create a dashboard of dashboards, much as portals do for applications, it will be some time before vendors provide open access to each other's content.

CHAPTER 15

How to Ensure Adoption and Drive Positive Change

Making It Work. You've spent a lot of time and effort creating a performance dashboard. You have sold the idea, secured funding, and created a team. You have worked diligently with the business to define metrics and targets, standardize rules, and locate data, and you have worked with the technical team to design the architecture, implement the infrastructure, and identify a roll-out strategy. Now you are ready to launch and watch the performance dashboard do its magic.

But will it?

If you have done a good job selling the performance dashboard, expectations are high. Executives see it as a powerful tool to communicate strategy and change the behaviors of individuals and groups. They want employees to work more productively and proactively, using timely information to optimize processes, control operations, and achieve objectives. They want the performance dashboard to foster better collaboration between managers and staff and improve coordination among departments. They view the system as a way to manage performance, not just measure it. To them, the performance dashboard is like a steering wheel that they can turn right and left to keep the organization headed in the right direction.

Two Tasks. To meet these expectations, you still have two tasks to accomplish; the first is obvious: Make sure people use the system! If people do not log in and view the data, the performance dashboard will not have any impact on the organization. Nothing will change except your career prospects, which will plummet along with next year's performance dashboard budget.

The second task is more formidable: Use the performance dashboard to change the culture and optimize performance. A performance dashboard is an instrument of organizational change with a hairline trigger. Aim it in the right direction and performance will skyrocket; aim it in wrong direction and results will plummet along with worker morale. Before rolling out a performance dashboard, executives and managers need to learn how to use it correctly to get the results they want. (See Spotlight 15.1.)

Spotlight 15.1 Eight Ways to Undermine Performance

Performance dashboards are powerful agents of organizational change, but they can easily backfire and cause performance to decline or stall instead of climb. These eight cardinal sins can turn a performance dashboard into a performance quagmire:

1. **Display too many metrics.** Doing this scatters people's focus and energy and makes them less efficient and effective than before.
2. **Fail to get user buy-in.** Users resent when performance dashboards are imposed on them without their approval or input, and their productivity declines.
3. **Don't assign accountability.** People will not change their habits unless they are held accountable for the results.
4. **Create metrics that are too abstract.** Users cannot improve results if they do not understand what a metric means or what steps they can take to influence the outcome.
5. **Create metrics that undermine each other.** Employees work hard, but their efforts cancel each other out, suboptimizing processes and demoralizing the staff.
6. **Use metrics to punish, not empower.** Managers who view metrics as a way to control rather than coach their staff cause morale and productivity to plummet.
7. **Attach compensation to metrics too soon.** Doing this causes workers to spend too much time debating the reliability of a metric rather than doing their jobs.
8. **Fixate on measures not management.** Managers who fixate on measures reward short-term spikes in performance, change plans too quickly, and fail to see larger trends driving performance.

Strategies to Ensure Adoption

There is truth to the adage "You can bring a horse to water, but you can't make it drink." Once you build a performance dashboard, will workers use it? Asking that question at the end of the development process is not a good sign! To ensure rapid uptake of the system, you need to develop a strategy to ensure end user adoption at the very start of the project. Several techniques to guarantee end user adoption and make the project a success are presented next.

Make the Business Drive It

The performance dashboard is a technical solution to a business imperative: the need to measure, monitor, and manage performance. To succeed, however, the technical solution must be driven by the business, not a technical team or the information technology (IT) department. The head of a business unit or department must initiate the project, secure its funding, oversee its direction, sell it to mid-level managers, evangelize its use, and assume responsibility for its outcome. Chapter 3 showed that there is a strong correlation between an actively involved and committed business sponsor and a successful project with strong end user adoption.

Too often the project team takes too much responsibility for driving a project, allowing the business to become a dispassionate observer instead of an actively involved leader. Or the IT department tries to meet the requirements of too many groups at once, which dilutes sponsorship. Without a clearly identifiable business sponsor driving the solution, the project gets mired down in bureaucracy, political infighting, and conflicting motivations. In both cases, the project gets a tepid response from target users, if it is deployed at all.

Make the Business Own It

This strategy is a corollary to the last one. It is one thing for business sponsors to drive a project and quite another for them to put their reputations and careers on the line and assume responsibility for its outcome. When this happens, they will make time to attend meetings, provide guidance, and evangelize its importance to ensure that the project succeeds. Once a sponsor is committed to the project, he or she has a vested interest in getting users to adopt the system.

Business ownership also trickles down to lower levels of the organization, where the project gains traction as a resource that end users find valuable. Here, representatives from various groups sit on governance committees that guide the project and oversee the information infrastructure. Also, subject matter experts from the business own the metrics in the performance dashboard and certify the accuracy of data on a daily basis, among other things.

Having the business involved at all levels in the design and administration of a performance dashboard creates considerable momentum for the system. Business owners will identify problems and bring them to the attention of the governance committees or technical teams rather than let the problems fester into major impediments to system usage.

Make the Business Evangelize It

Active sponsors and drivers evangelize the performance dashboard every chance they get. They discuss the system at company and departmental meetings, and they write about it in company newsletters and on the corporate intranet. This communication continually emphasizes the importance of the project to the group's strategy and plans.

Sponsors also work with the project team to establish a marketing plan to promote the performance dashboard. The plan targets the various constituencies that either will use the system or whose support is required to build it. It defines the appropriate message for each constituency and the appropriate channels and frequency with which to deliver the information. The sponsor and project team work especially hard to sell the system to mid-level managers, who can make or break end user adoption.

To promote the system, many organizations link to the performance dashboard articles that outline recent enhancements, answer frequently asked questions, and highlight testimonials of individuals who have had a major success with the system. They also provide links that enable users to provide feedback on the system, contact the help desk, request training, and search for help documents. Some organizations place this information on a corporate portal that users must go through to access the performance dashboard so it's hard to miss.

Make the Business Use It

Walk the Talk. Actions speak louder than words. Business sponsors and drivers may spend considerable time evangelizing the system, but if they do not use it, neither will anyone else. Workers pay close attention to verbal and visual cues from their managers about how much time and energy they should invest in learning a new system. When sponsors continue to rely on analysts to create reports or managers continue to use their spreadmarts, workers get the message loud and clear: Do not go out on a limb when your boss is not. However, when executives and managers start using the output of a performance dashboard (whether directly or indirectly), the trickle-down effect is powerful.

"The tip of the iceberg that got this thing going was when executives had our reports all over the boardroom table and began asking 'Where's the data to back up this decision?'" says Deb Masdea, former director of business information and analysis at The Scotts Miracle-Gro Company.

To build awareness among top executives about the power of the information now available to them, Masdea met one-on-one with many of them to demonstrate the system and get them comfortable with the output, even if they would never directly use the system.

Superusers. To ensure penetration at lower levels of the organization, Masdea established a network of superusers who create custom reports for colleagues in their department. Superusers are technically savvy business users in each department who volunteer to write ad hoc reports for their colleagues. "To get people to use [the system], we created superusers, not because IT couldn't create reports but because we needed people in the business who know how to get data and get others feeling comfortable with the system," says Masdea.

Prove the Validity of the Data

No matter how good the system looks, if users do not trust the data, they will not use them. Validating that data in a new performance dashboard are accurate is painstaking. Users tend to distrust data that they have not seen before. Even though data in the performance dashboard may be more accurate than in the reports or spreadmarts that employees currently use, they will reject the data unless you prove to them beyond a shadow of doubt that the new data can be reconciled with their own.

For example, Masdea's team also worked hard to convince executives, managers, and analysts that the data were accurate and trustworthy. "Once you automate [the delivery of information], they don't trust it. Their secretary didn't give it to them so they're suspicious. Once you get them to the point where they have looked at the data enough so they are comfortable with it, they quickly get dependent on it. Now our users can't live without logging on [to the system] in the morning!" says Masdea.

Add Personal Data to the Dashboard

Nothing gets users to employ a performance dashboard faster than displaying information that lets them calculate what their bonus or commissions will be. This process helped drive initial usage of the dashboards at 1-800 CONTACTS and others. Once users access the performance dashboard, they quickly realize that it contains other content that can help them perform their jobs more effectively, and they're hooked. In addition, allowing users to personalize the dashboard gives them added motivation to visit the site. The ability to change colors, add Web links, and select which metrics, reports, and other documents they want on the home page gives users a feeling of ownership that prompts them to return on a regular basis.

Train Users

Although dashboards should be intuitive to use, training is still critical to the successful roll-out of a performance dashboard. However, since most users do not want to attend training classes, project managers must get creative in the ways they deliver training. Organizations need to provide a mix of training options to cater to everyone's preferences and needs. Here are some of the more common methods to train workers and increase their proficiency using the performance dashboard.

One-on-one training. This option is reserved primarily for top executives and their administrative assistants. Also, superusers can provide one-on-one training to colleagues in their departments.

Classroom training. This method is important for employees who have not had any experience with the system. To encourage attendance, some organizations provide continuing education credits, keep class sizes small, and offer the course on a regular basis in a professional training center. Most courses run two to three hours in length.

Virtual classrooms. Because it is expensive and time consuming for people to travel to a training facility, many organizations provide virtual training using Web conferencing or online courseware. Web conferencing sessions or Webinars are online events that enable users to see a demonstration of the system and ask questions to the presenter via chat or telephone. Webinars can be archived for later viewing.

Online learning software. This software steps users through a series of learning objectives and uses quizzes to reinforce concepts and track users' progress. Online courseware can be delivered via the Web or CD-ROM.

Online help. Most companies provide various forms of online help that enables users to learn about different metrics, features, and functions as they go along. Online help may consist of documents and user manuals housed on the corporate intranet or dynamic links embedded in the software that present users with context-sensitive help. Some organizations let users request one-on-one help via a Web conferencing system or NetMeeting.

Release updates. Many companies are getting creative in the way they inform and train employees about the functionality contained in new releases of software. Some offer classroom training, but most inform users about the enhancements through e-mail, newsletters, online help, or intranet updates. Some build mini-online courses or animations that pop up when users log into the system, providing a painless way for users to stay current with the system if they desire.

Rotating tips. Many companies publish "Did You Know?" tips in e-newsletters and when users log in to the performance dashboard. These tips highlight high-value features, provide answers to commonly asked questions, and alert users to new content in the system. Some companies use these tips or show interesting facts other users have gleaned from the system. "These tidbits of facts and figures pique users' interest," says Dave Donkin, former group leader of Information Management at Absa Bank Ltd. in South Africa.

Help desk. Most companies also let users call the company's help desk to get answers to questions, instead of just reporting problems. Help desk personnel keep a record of the most frequently asked questions and create a link to them from the corporate intranet and the performance dashboard.

Track Usage

The best way to judge the effectiveness of a performance dashboard is to monitor its usage. Some companies closely monitor usage statistics, using them as an early warning signal of problems with the software or its training. For example, International Truck and Engine Corporation tracks usage even during the pilot phase of a new release. "If only three people out of ten are using the system, we meet with the other seven to find out the problems they have with it and make changes before we roll out the release," says Jim Rappé of International Truck and Engine.

Rappé's group has tracked usage statistics so closely that it now knows what the uptake rate should be after issuing a new release of the software. If adoption rates are lower than normal, the team jumps into action. "If usage is below the norm, we book a 30-minute presentation during a departmental meeting to provide additional education and answer questions. We try to be proactive," says Rappé.

Arizona State University (see Chapter 8) uses its dashboard technology to monitor usage of its dashboards. It can track cumulative usage by month, daily usage by month, top 10 dashboards, and top 10 users. (See Exhibit 15.1.) The usage dashboard also displays detailed data about individual usage. The dashboard displays a log of who used which dashboard at what time. The log shows name, title, department, dashboard used, time of access, and duration of use. Administrators can sort the table by any of these characteristics. To improve adoption, Rome of ASU will soon begin targeting users by title in departments where usage could be higher.

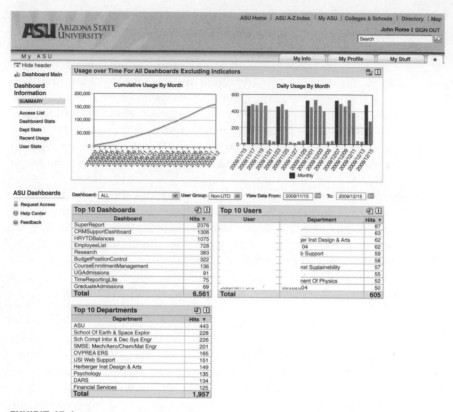

EXHIBIT 15.1 Monitoring Dashboard Usage
Courtesy of Arizona State University.

Survey Users

It is important to ask users periodically what they think of the system and to get their feedback. Doing this helps in evaluating the overall effectiveness of the system and how it can improve in future releases. Hewlett Packard TSG conducts a customer satisfaction survey every six months. International Truck and Engine issues a survey once a year that lets users express requirements for future upgrades.

Optimizing Performance through Metrics

Once user adoption is ensured, the next task is more challenging: using the performance dashboard to change organizational culture and improve performance. Dr. Bob Frost, principal of Measurements International Inc., describes the impact that measuring performance has on individuals:

There's something about performance charts. When most of us see a chart depicting our efforts, we immediately feel something—positive or negative. This feeling may be about the past or the future, but it's almost always motivational and emotional. ... If your employees know that you value metrics and track the entire organization's performance, an amazing thing happens: the culture changes. Whether mentally or on paper, employees begin to track how their own performance contributes to enterprise performance. And a "results-tracking culture" is one of the most powerful competitive advantages your enterprise can have.[1]

Managers need to learn how to use a performance dashboard to harness this emotional reaction and drive behavior in the direction that delivers the most value to the organization. This is not easy. Workers can react negatively to metrics that are improperly designed, or they can circumvent metrics for personal gain. Or performance metrics and targets can push and pull individuals and the organization in potentially different directions. Recommendations about how to use metrics and performance dashboards to drive performance in the right direction are presented next.

Test Assumptions and Drivers

Many businesspeople make decisions based on innate assumptions about how the business works. They may even set strategic objectives and targets based on those assumptions. Some assumptions may be right, and some may be dead wrong. The problem is that many executives never formally express or test their assumptions, and this can lead to disastrous consequences, if not checked. It would be unfortunate if executives launched multimillion-dollar initiatives based on false assumptions.

For instance, an executive at an online retailer believed that big-box retailers were luring away customers who worked within one square mile of their stores. Those assumptions were influencing the company's marketing campaigns and go-to-market strategies. However, a business analyst performed a statistical analysis that disproved that assumption but did show that customers with a 95 percent retention rate had placed at least four orders within the past 60 days, among other things. It turned out the classic marketing principles of frequency, recency, and monetary were more indicative of churn and retention rates than other factors by far.

A performance dashboard presents users with metrics and targets in order to achieve specific objectives. The questions that dashboard managers need to remind business executives to ask are: Are these the right metrics? Do these metrics correlate with the objectives and goals we're trying to achieve? A marketing team could succeed in improving Web site visits, but if those visits don't translate into more sales, which was the objective, then executives need to review their assumptions. If Web site visits aren't increasing sales, then what does? Maybe it's the amount of new content on the site or the background color or cross-sell items. Or perhaps certain pages on the site don't work or the shopping cart function is too cumbersome and slow or a spam attack created an artificially high number of page hits. Perhaps the company should be measuring one of these factors because it is more closely correlated (positively or negatively) to the objective.

Focus on Management, Not Measurement

The temptation with performance dashboards is to focus too much on measures and results and not enough on process and strategy. When this happens, executives fail to see the forest for the trees. They are so focused on measures that they fail to see the bigger picture of what is going on and what they need to do to move the organization in the right direction.

Whipsawing. One symptom of this problem is when executives reward or punish managers for short-term spikes in performance. When performance is evaluated every day or week, there is a tendency to overemphasize short-term fluctuations and miss emerging trends.

Says John Lochrie, senior vice president at Direct Energy Essential Home Services:

> *Just like the temperature, metrics swing significantly. You need a process to balance that. You can't throw away your plans if you don't make your numbers one week. It is very counterproductive to overfocus and overdrive specific elements. You may drive one metric up but the means you use to get there may not overall satisfy the needs of the business.*

Achieving Balance. Lochrie recommends creating a set of metrics that balance the key drivers of the business, which for Direct Energy are operational efficiency, customer satisfaction, and employee satisfaction. "You should evaluate each metric by how good it is for employees, customers, and the business. If a customer likes it, but you kill your employees in the process, then you're ultimately going to fail," he says.

Examine the Business Context. It is also important to understand what really drives the measures and continually reevaluate your assumptions. For instance, a performance decline may not mean employees are slacking off—even though this was the case in the past. Something else may be affecting performance, such as your staff is saddled with additional work or requirements that did not exist before. In fast-moving environments, metrics may be no longer valid and have to be revised.

Says Lochrie:

What I've learned is don't just tend to the numbers. Think more about what drives the numbers. Are people making the effort but just not getting there, or are people not making the effort any more because they can't overcome systemic challenges? You have to continually pause to take a breath, every 6 to 12 months, and assess the overall climate in which you operate and ask whether the current metrics are still relevant.

The important thing, he adds, is to make sure employees have the resources and training they need to be successful. This includes training their managers to provide them with assistance and guidance in the field. Ultimately, the goal is to make employees and, by extension, the organization successful.

Law of Diminishing Returns. Also, it is important to know when you become a victim of the law of diminishing returns. This is when the effort and cost to increase performance outweigh the returns. When a company first introduces a metric, performance usually increases rapidly, but then it gradually tapers off. For instance, a company that starts tracking customer satisfaction sees scores increase from 50 percent to 70 percent in one year but then can barely get the scores to nudge above 72 percent for the next three years, no matter how much effort it expends. When you have reached the point of diminishing returns, it is better to revise or replace the metric and focus users' energies elsewhere. You've maximized the benefit from measurement.

Get User Buy-in

Avoid Us versus Them. Performance management is not something you impose on workers or do to them. Such heavy-handedness always backfires. When workers see performance metrics as a stick rather than a carrot, their enthusiasm and motivation will wane. To avoid an us-versus-them mentality, it is important to get users' feedback on the validity and reasonableness of metrics and targets before applying them. This can be done in group meetings, surveys, or comment forms.

Respond to All Input. However, do not make the mistake of taking feedback and not responding to it. Every comment should be recorded and a response delivered in person or in writing. Doing this takes time, but it demonstrates to workers that you have received their input, acknowledged their ideas, and taken them under consideration. It would also be helpful to schedule open-door sessions in which workers can call, e-mail, or visit to discuss their concerns.

Expect Pushback. Workers often get nervous about the impact performance metrics will have on their jobs and compensation. So expect users to push back, but do not be alarmed; this is part of the process. "The first thing that happens when you hold people accountable for metrics is that they say the metrics don't track their performance correctly. That's a healthy feedback loop. If you are not getting that pushback, you are probably not challenging the staff enough," says Ripley Maddock of Direct Energy Essential Home Services.

Explain the Data. If a worker has a serious issue with a metric or a performance result, the first thing to do is explain how the data were collected and calculated so he or she understands the mechanics. Then work backward from individual events—a sale, a repair, a work order—to the aggregated data to see whether the system tracked the event correctly. "Too many times people will say 'I don't think that metric is right.' We try to get them down to factual examples. Let's look at this sales order and see how it was measured. If they don't think the business should measure it this way, we'll bring that back up to management for review," says Maddock. (See Spotlight 15.2.)

Spotlight 15.2 Managing Front-line Personnel with Performance Dashboards

In 1999, Direct Energy Essential Home Services, North America's largest competitive energy and home services retailer, was founded as a result of deregulation of the natural gas industry in Canada. To compete effectively in the open market, Direct Energy developed a tactical dashboard to monitor the execution of its new business strategy.

"We knew we couldn't do business like we had previously," said Ripley Maddock, director of customer management at the company. "We now had to be driven by ROI [return on investment], shareholder value, and customer needs. To make this transition, we needed a way to measure our performance against these new metrics and hold everyone in the organization—from executives to field technicians—accountable for the results."

Today, more than 400 personnel, including 300 field technicians, view their performance against budget contained in an easy-to-use Web-based dashboard that costs less than $100,000 a year to maintain.

District managers use the dashboard to compare their district's and staff's performance against other districts. They review the results with field technicians on a regular basis and showcase individuals who have exceeded targets.

In the two years after Direct Energy implemented the dashboard, the firm reduced the number of repair calls by 2.82 percent, saving the company $1.3 million while improving customer service. Most of this reduction was driven by a *repeat call* metric on the dashboard, which tracks how many times a technician visits a household to fix a problem. Direct Energy believes this metric offers a good indicator of customer satisfaction and service efficiency, among other things.

Perhaps the most important benefit of the dashboard is that it has changed the entire tenor of discussions about performance at the company. According to Larry Ryan, the group's former general manager, the dashboard is a communications vehicle designed to bring managers and staff together to discuss how to meet or exceed performance expectations and fix outstanding problems, not to dwell on excuses for underachievement.

Let Users Focus

A performance dashboard uses metrics to focus workers on high-value tasks that drive performance in the right direction. The fewer the metrics, the more focused workers can be. Thus, a critical factor in using dashboards to optimize performance is to select the right number of metrics to display on the screen for each user. Unfortunately, no one agrees on a single number. However, most believe it is counterproductive to overwhelm workers with too many metrics.

As a rule of thumb, workers managing operational processes should track fewer metrics, probably less than a handful, whereas executives responsible for setting strategic direction should view many more metrics, perhaps a dozen or more, each with multiple levels of drill-down to lower-level metrics. The more areas and activities someone manages and oversees, the more metrics that person will need to monitor. And over time, users will be capable of handling more metrics as they become familiar with the dashboard interface and their business processes.

Hold Users Accountable

It is important that there is an individual or group accountable for the outcome of each metric. This puts teeth into the measures and galvanizes the organization. It lets everyone know in a very personal way that executives are serious about using the dashboard to improve performance and change the culture.

It is best to hold individuals accountable for results. This is true even when performance is a shared responsibility among many people and groups, such as customer loyalty. However, the accountable individual must be given certain authority to allocate resources, make decisions, delegate responsibility, and reward performance to achieve the objectives.

Another way to galvanize the organization around performance metrics and reinforce accountabilities is to publicize the results broadly. Allow people to see how their performance compares with that of their peers. Doing this fosters a competitive environment in which few people want to be seen as laggards or slackers in the organization.

Empower Users

If you are going to hold people accountable, you have to empower them to act. You need to give them more leeway to make decisions and not force them to adhere to prescribed processes or procedures. You also need to make it clear how they can affect the measures. Doing this means creating measures that are easy to understand and appropriate to each level in the organization. For example, you cannot expect assembly floor managers to know how to improve net profits, but they probably have a good idea about quality problems and how to reduce scrap.

"For metrics to be motivational, people must be able to see what to do. There must be a *line of sight* between the actions employees can take and the changes that occur in the measure," writes Frost.[2]

Train Managers to Coach

The problem with individual performance reviews is that they rarely happen. Often the reason is because managers are too busy to compile the relevant information and write up the results. However, a performance dashboard collects a lot of the information for managers. It becomes an effective tool to help managers conduct performance reviews on a regular or even continuous basis as needed.

The key to using a performance dashboard for performance reviews is not to punish workers for poor performance but to help them see how they can improve. Managers need to know how to provide workers with the resources, tools, and knowledge to help their staff succeed. Doing this requires training, not just education, says Lochrie. "You can educate managers by going through the process and telling them what's good and bad, and then they go out and do their own thing. By training, you physically witness what the managers do and make sure they do the right things and behave in the right way. Then you coach and recoach them."

Reinforce with Monetary Incentives

A major way to focus workers' attention on the metrics is to pay for performance. It has been said that what gets measured gets done. However, it is also true that what gets done is what you pay people to do.

It is important not to attach compensation to metrics and targets in a dashboard until they are suitably mature. Users must understand the metrics, believe they are fair, and know how the users can impact the outcomes. The organization also needs to make sure that the metrics drive the right kind of behavior and lead to positive outcomes. It is not easy to change metrics once people's compensation is based on them. Small changes to the metrics can impact people's compensation, and they will protest vehemently if the change doesn't work in their favor. If you need to revise a metric, it's best to ensure that the change benefits a majority of staff to avoid demoralizing people or inciting a riot.

Another reason to postpone attaching pay to metrics is that it takes time to close all the loopholes that might allow staff to jury-rig the results or take unwarranted shortcuts to boost their performance scores. In a similar vein, you should not let executives design metrics and targets used to calculate their own bonus payments. If they can, they will make sure they can meet their numbers and earn a sizable bonus. Like Cisco, it's best to have several committees involved when setting metrics that affect bonus plans.

Summary

End User Adoption. A performance dashboard is a powerful agent of organizational change. However, if employees do not use the system, the dashboard will not have any impact at all. Thus, the first task of any business performance manager is to ensure that employees use the system and see it as an integral part of how they do their jobs.

Ensuring end user adoption starts at the beginning of the project when business sponsors and drivers are being recruited. Business sponsors must provide the organization with the right visual and verbal cues that the system is worth the time and effort to learn and use. Sponsors need to sell and evangelize the project, accept responsibility for its outcome, and, most important, use the system. Sponsors must also ensure that lower levels of the organization step into ownership roles, such as serving on stewardship committees and taking responsibility for defining, updating, and certifying key metrics and data elements.

Another key element to ensuring end user adoption is to get users to trust the data in the new system. Doing this requires the project team to reconcile data in the new system with data in the old systems. Other techniques to ensure a fast uptake of the performance dashboard include flexible training, usage tracking, and regular surveys of end user satisfaction.

Performance Management. A performance dashboard is a tool to help the organization achieve its strategic objectives. To do that, the performance dashboard needs to motivate individuals and groups to work on the right tasks that move the organization in the right direction. However, it is not easy to ensure that every metric has its intended effect on its target audience. In order to do this, executives must constantly fine-tune their assumptions about what is really driving performance.

Executives need to test their assumptions about how the business works and reevaluate whether they have selected the right metrics to drive behavior. They also need to beware of fixating on short-term results without considering larger trends driving performance, which may require new or revised metrics to track accurately. Most important, executives need to ensure that managers and staff have the appropriate knowledge and resources to succeed. Managers, in particular, need to be trained how to use the performance dashboard to empower staff, not punish them.

Metrics and performance dashboards naturally get users' competitive juices flowing. To sustain motivation, organizations can publicize performance results so workers can compare their performance against that of their peers. They can also attach bonus payments to performance results to turbo-charge productivity. However, before mixing pay with performance, executives need to make sure the metrics are stable, reliable, and tamperproof.

Notes

1. Dr. Bob Frost, *Measuring Performance* (Ogdensburg, NY: Measurements International Inc., 2000), p. 43.
2. Ibid.

Index

Absa Bank Ltd., 94, 95, 299
Access control, 111, 143, 146, 257–258
ActiveX controls, 252, 253
Ad hoc reporting, 13, 38, 70, 77, 78, 151, 155, 193, 194, 226, 259, 263, 297
Adobe Flash, 16, 251, 253–256, 258
Adoption, ensuring. *See* Project adoption, ensuring
Agile development techniques, 69, 71, 88, 126, 127, 130
AJAX, 253–255
Alerts
  complex event processing, 268, 269
  drill down, 244
  intelligent alerts, 31, 205
  monitoring function, 5, 10–12, 14, 17
  operational dashboards, 105–109, 132, 137
  performance dashboards, 5, 10–12, 14, 17, 31
  predictions, 128
  setting, 205
  strategic dashboards, 157, 171
  tactical dashboards, 105, 106, 149, 151, 155
Alignment of business and IT. *See* Business-IT alignment
Analytical dashboards, 111, 113
Annotation, 11, 236, 259, 266
Applications (functionality) of performance dashboards
  analysis, 10, 11, 13
  management, 10, 11, 13
  monitoring, 10–12
Architectural standards, 276, 277

Architecture of performance dashboards
  data architectures, 256–259
  display architectures, 251–256
  overview, 251, 271
  types of, 260–271
Arizona State University (ASU)
  dashboard design, 229
  dashboard usage, tracking, 299
  operational dashboards, 109
  tactical dashboards, 111, 139–147, 156
Assumptions, testing, 301, 302

Balanced Scorecard Step by Step: Maximizing Performance and Maintaining Results (Niven), 43, 285
Balanced scorecards. *See also* Strategic dashboards
  about, 5
  Balanced Scorecard Step by Step: Maximizing Performance and Maintaining Results (Niven), 43, 285
  challenges, 176
  Cisco functional balanced scorecard example, 160, 167
  cost savings, 185
  dashboards compared, 11, 12
  delay in implementation of, 53, 54
  deployment, 273, 285
  development of, 43, 184
  metrics, 118, 119, 205, 206, 212, 213, 216
  Ministry of Works (Kingdom of Bahrain). *See* Strategic dashboards
  and performance dashboards, 5
  readiness assessment, 44, 45

Barberg, Bill, 21, 53, 54, 118, 119, 213
Barr, Stacey, 200
Basel Accord, 47
Baseline Consulting, 85
Beautiful Evidence (Tufte), 227
Benchmarks
  and business intelligence, 53, 54, 73
  peer groups, 290
  and performance metrics, 118, 149,
    203, 214
  published data, 184
  and tactical dashboards, 17
BI. *See* Business intelligence (BI)
BI Competency Center (BICC), 193
BI platforms, 32, 39, 111, 112, 156,
    262, 264, 273, 274, 276, 280, 285,
    292
BI tools architecture, 261, 262
BNSF Railway, 111
Bodla, Ranga, 204
Bootstrapping, 37, 62, 187, 188
Bottom-up approach, 273, 284,
    287–289
Bread crumbs, 14, 234–236, 259
British Airways, 201, 202
Brown & Root, 21
Build versus buy, 18, 19, 104
Bullet graphs, 206, 245
Buried scores, 206
Business architecture, 18–20, 170
Business intelligence (BI)
  about, 6, 31, 32
  adolescent phase, 59
  conceptual framework, 32–34
  data integration environment, 34–36
  data warehousing environment, 36,
    37
  evolution of, 15
  governance committees, 93, 94
  infrastructure, need for, 37
  Maturity Model. *See* Maturity Model
    for BI
  and performance dashboards, 6, 22,
    39
  platforms. *See* BI platforms
  reporting and analysis environment,
    38, 39

  technical framework, 34–39
  user fitting, 39–41
Business performance management
    (BPM)
  architecture, 18–21
  background, 6
  benefits of, 26, 27
  challenges and obstacles, 25, 26
  defined, 23–25
  framework for, 28–31
  and performance dashboards, 4, 6,
    22
Business process management (BPM),
    24, 25
Business requirements
  analysts, 67, 93, 94, 183
  and business/IT alignment, 85, 86,
    93, 94
  changes in, adapting to, 71, 88
  communicating, 49, 93, 189
  forms, 215
  requirements gathering, 212–217
  responding to, 50
Business-IT alignment
  business issues, 84, 85
  business requirements, 85, 86
  communication, 93–96
  incremental delivery, 86–88
  IT issues, 83, 84
  overview, 97
  portfolio planning, 88–91
  readiness assessment, 51, 52, 55
  standardization, 91, 92
  trust, lack of, 81–83
Business-IT partnership, 21

Cascading filters, 155
Cascading scorecards, 119, 273, 285,
    286, 289, 290
Cause-effect linkages, 115–117, 172
Centers of Excellence, 71, 74–76, 94
Change agents, 197
Charts and graphs, designing, 240–249
Chasm, 58–61, 68–70, 74, 76
Cisco
  balanced scorecards, 160, 167
  distributed approach, 274, 285

governance, 170
metadata, 161, 167
operational dashboards, 109
strategic dashboards, 116, 159–172
Closed loop, 28, 146
Cloud-based dashboards, 69, 258, 259, 269–271
Collaboration, 11, 13, 16, 17, 30, 64, 92, 111, 119, 170, 174, 190, 266, 293
Compensation
aligned with strategic objectives, 30
bonuses, 170
performance metrics, 8, 294, 304, 307
Complex event processing (CEP), 108, 109, 205, 268, 269
Corda, 140, 142, 143, 201, 214
Correlation
business sponsor commitment and project success, 46, 295
metrics, 291
between variables, scatter plots, 248
Crow, Michael M., 139
Culture of measurement, 50, 51, 55

Dashboard displays
data, 225, 228
guidelines for creating, 229–240
iterative design, 229
overview, 223, 224, 249
planning, 224–229
prototypes, 225, 227, 228, 249
requirements gathering, 224, 225
resources on design techniques, 227
usability labs, use of, 228, 229, 249
user feedback, 227, 228, 249
users, 225, 226
visual designers, use of, 226, 227
Dashboards. *See also* Performance dashboards, overview
build versus buy, 18, 19, 104
cascading, 290
cloud-based, 69, 258, 259, 269–271
deployment and integration. *See* Deployment and integration
displays, designing. *See* Dashboard displays

enterprise dashboards, 111, 112, 160, 166, 189, 280, 282, 285, 287, 290
executive. *See* Executive dashboard
operational. *See* Operational dashboards
project launch. *See* Project launch
project management. *See* Project management
scorecards compared, 11, 12
strategic. *See* Strategic dashboards
tactical. *See* Tactical dashboards
themes, 117, 118, 121, 158, 173, 174, 176, 213, 239, 240
training on use of, 298, 299
usage, tracking, 299, 300
Data architectures, 256–259
Data availability and reliability, 52, 53, 55, 297
Data bars, 248
Data cleansing, 35
Data constellation, 248
Data federation, 87, 265, 266
Data governance, 93, 95, 161, 279–280
Data integration, 8, 9, 31, 32, 34–36, 43, 134, 221
Data marts, 36, 266–268
Data mining, 38–40, 95. *See also* Predictive analytics
Data modeling, 35, 277, 278
Data profiling, 35
Data quality, 110
Data roll-ups, 290, 291
Data standards, 277–280
Data stewardship, 94, 143, 215, 279
Data warehousing (DW)
data integration tools, 35, 36
operational dashboards, 109
and tactical dashboards, 111, 114
Decision making, 13
Decomposition view, 151, 152, 155
Departmental scope, 106
Deployment and integration
cascading metrics, 289–291
centralized approach, 274–284
distributed approach, 284–289, 2747
overview, 273–275, 291, 292

Detect and respond dashboard,
    107–109
Detemple, Klaus, 96
Deutsche Börse, 96
DHTML (Dynamic HTML), 253, 254
Direct Energy Essential Home Services,
    198, 217, 302, 304, 305
Direct query architecture, 260, 261,
    266, 267
Distributed approach, 284–289
Donkin, Dave, 94, 95, 299
Double MAD, 16, 17
Dow Chemical. *See* Rohm and Haas
Drill through, 259
Drill to detail, 13, 14, 111, 148, 156,
    168, 169, 256, 280. *See also* MAD
    (monitor, analyze, drill to detail)
    framework
Driver metrics, 20, 198–202
Dyche, Jill, 85

End-user query and reporting, 39
Enterprise, defined, 196
Enterprise dashboards, 111, 112, 160,
    166, 189, 280, 282, 285, 287, 290
Enterprise data warehouse, 36, 58, 68,
    93, 112, 114, 124, 142, 156, 174,
    274
Envisioning Information (Tufte),
    227
ETL tools. *See* Extraction,
    transformation, and loading (ETL)
    tools
Executive dashboard
    at 1–800-CONTACTS, 123, 127, 128,
        130
    background, 5
    controls, 130
    and dashboard cascading, 290
    deployment and integration of
        dashboards, 273, 290, 291
    display, 127, 128, 149, 150, 156
    and enterprise dashboards, 112
    at Rohm and Haas, 149, 150, 156,
        207
Executive information systems (EISs),
    5

Extraction, transformation, and loading
    (ETL) tools, 36, 69, 74, 91, 96,
    126, 127, 190

Federated approach, 287
Few, Stephen, 223, 226, 227
"Five Whys," 200, 214
Flash. *See* Adobe Flash
Flash charts, 123, 127, 128, 246
Flash visualizations, 155
Focus, 3–5, 78, 302, 303, 305
Frost, Bob, 300, 306

Goals, 45, 46, 115
Governance
    BI, 70, 71, 75, 93
    Cisco example, 170
    committees, 295, 296
    corporate, 193
    dashboard, 194
    data governance, 93, 95, 161, 279, 280
    KPI governance team, 193
    reports, 70
    and Sarbanes-Oxley Act, 26
Grassroots initiatives, 284
Gulf, 58, 60–65, 70, 74, 85

Help desk, 94, 296, 299
Hewlett Packard (HP), 44, 45, 48, 182,
    284, 300
Hill, Jim, 125–128, 130
Hsiao, David, 157, 159, 164, 171
Hub-and-spoke architecture, 36

Incent and motivate dashboards, 107,
    108, 124
Information consumers, 39–41
Information Dashboard Design (Few),
    227
Information producers, 39, 40
Information sandbox, 14
Information technology (IT), alignment
    with business. *See* Business-IT
    alignment
In-memory
    analytics, 69
    dashboards, 264, 265, 267

data, 13
processing, 269
Insightformation, Inc., 21, 53, 118, 213
International Truck and Engine Corporation, 87, 185, 186, 299, 300

Java, 96, 104, 252, 253, 255
JavaScript, 253, 254

Kaplan, Robert, 115, 116, 158, 172, 174, 184, 213
Key performance indicators (KPIs)
data collection, 220, 221
governance team, 193
and metrics, 198, 200–202
requirements, gathering, 212–217
standardizing terms, 219, 220
steering committee, 193
strategic dashboards, 116, 118
tactical dashboards, 111
targets, setting, 221
validating, 217–219
King, Lord, 201, 202
Knowledge discovery. *See* Data mining

Lagging indicators, 20, 44, 198
Law of diminishing returns, 303
Layers of functionality, 252
Layers of information, 13. *See also* MAD (monitor, analyze, drill to detail) framework
Leading indicators, 20, 199
Lochrie, John, 198, 302, 303, 306

MAD (monitor, analyze, drill to detail) framework
analyze, 13, 14
and BI platform, 111
described, 13, 14
double MAD, 16, 17
drill to detail, 13, 14, 111, 148, 156, 168, 169, 256, 280
and evolution of BI, 15
Flash, use of, 256
monitoring, 13, 14

and NetApp dashboard design, 280, 281, 283
and three-tier delivery framework of Rohm and Haas, 148
Management scorecards, 115, 116, 158
Marketing, and project sustainment, 192
Masciandaro, Michael, 147–149, 154, 155
Masdea, Deb, 296–297
Mashboards, 111–113, 262–264, 288
Mashups, 111, 140, 287–289, 292
Maturity Model for BI
Adult stage, 58, 70–72, 75–79
business value, 77, 78
Chasm sticking point, 58–61, 68–70, 74, 76
Child stage, 58, 65, 66, 75–79
Gulf sticking point, 58, 60–65, 70, 74, 85
insights to action, 78, 79
maturity dynamics, 74–79
overview, 57, 58, 80
Prenatal/Infant stage, 58, 61–65, 75–79
return on investment (ROI), 78
Sage stage, 58, 72–79
stages, 58
stages, regressing, 60
stages, skipping, 60
sticking points, 58, 60, 61
Teenager stage, 58, 66, 67, 75–77, 79
users and usage, 76, 77
Metadata
and application development, 87
and BI tools, 39
Cisco example, 161, 167
management, 96
properties of, viewing on dashboard, 141, 210, 259
repository, 277
updating, 69
Metrics
accuracy, 210, 211
actionable, 199, 210
activity metrics, 200
attributes, 202–205

Metrics (*Continued*)
  balancing, 208, 209
  benchmarks, 203
  calculating, 221, 222
  cause-effect relationships, 201
  characteristics of effective metrics,
    209–212
  creating, 197–222
  data collection, 220, 221
  described, 20
  designing, 212–218
  displaying, 205–208
  driver metrics, 20, 198–202
  ecosystems, 208, 209
  effectiveness, 197, 209–212
  goals, 45, 46
  graphical view of data, 14
  indicators compared, 198
  key performance indicators (KPIs),
    200–202. *See also* Key performance
    indicators (KPIs)
  number of, 206–208
  objectives, 45, 46
  operational dashboards, 109
  outcome, 20, 44, 198, 199, 202
  overview, 197–198, 222
  ownership, 210
  performance dashboards, 103
  and performance management
    architecture, 20
  predictive, 199
  ranges, 203, 204
  relevance, 212
  requirements gathering, 212–217. *See
    also* Business requirements
  revising, 192, 193
  risk indicators, 200
  standardization, 211
  stoplights, 204. *See also* Stoplights
  strategic, 209
  strategic dashboards, 116, 118
  tactical dashboards, 115
  targets, 203–205, 221
  terms, standardizing, 219, 220
  time frame, 202, 203, 210
  types of, 198–202
  understandable, 209, 210

  validating, 217, 219
  value, 202, 203
Mid-level management support, 47, 48,
    55
Ministry of Works (Kingdom of
    Bahrain), strategic dashboards,
    158, 172–178
Mission, 45, 115
Mobile use of dashboards, 137, 155,
    259
Monitor, analyze, drill to detail
    framework. *See* MAD (monitor,
    analyze, drill to detail) framework
Mouse-overs, 126, 154, 253, 255
Mozilla Scalar Vector Graphics (SVG),
    253

NetApp, 280–284
Niven, Paul, 43, 48, 285
Norton, David, 115, 158, 172, 174
Now You See It (Few), 227

Objectives, 45, 46, 115
Office of Strategy Management, 119
1–800-CONTACTS
  executive dashboard, 123, 127, 128,
    130
  operational dashboards, 107, 123,
    124–131, 137
  personal data on dashboards,
    297
Online analytical processing (OLAP), 1,
    13, 38–40, 77, 111, 113, 259–262
Open source products, 69, 124, 126,
    155
Operational dashboards
  1–800-CONTACTS example, 107,
    123, 124–131, 137
  action oriented, 107
  alerts, 105–109
  appearance, 105
  Arizona State University example,
    109
  Cisco example, 109
  data quality, 110
  detect-and-respond dashboards,
    107–109

incent-and-motivate dashboards, 107, 108
information, 109
metrics, 109
overview, 17, 101, 107, 123, 124
prevalence of, 102
real time versus right time, 107, 109, 110
refresh rates, 109, 110
Richmond Police Department example, 106, 107, 124, 131–137
tactical and strategic dashboards compared, 105, 106
updating, 107
use of, 103
users of, 107
Oracle, 142, 159, 160, 285
Organizational change, 5–8
Organizational culture, 50, 51, 55, 300
Organizational readiness. *See* Readiness assessment
Organizational restructuring, 47
Outcome metrics, 20, 44, 198, 199, 202
Ownership, 210, 295, 296

Parallel coordinate charts, 248
Pareto charts, 168, 169, 247
Pareto drill-downs, 160
Parmenter, David, 200, 201
Performance dashboards, overview
applications, 10–13, 22
architecture, 251–271
balanced scorecards, 5. *See also* Balanced scorecards
benefits of, 6–8
build versus buy, 18, 19, 104
and business intelligence (BI), 6, 22, 39
characteristics of, 105, 106
composition of, 10–18
dashboard displays. *See* Dashboard displays
defined, 10
described, 4, 5
historical background, 5
integrating, 18
as layered delivery system, 10

layers, 10, 13–17, 22
metrics, 103
and organizational change, 5
overview, 22
and performance management, 4, 6, 10, 22. *See also* Business performance management (BPM)
performance management architecture, 18–21
prevalence of, 6
project failures, reasons for, 9, 10
scorecards compared, 11, 12
success factors, 10, 21, 22
three threes, 5, 10–18, 22
types of, 10, 17, 18, 22, 101, 121. *See also* Operational dashboards; Strategic dashboards; Tactical dashboards
users of, 103
Performance management. *See* Business performance management (BPM)
Performance management system, 10
Performance metrics. *See* Metrics
Performance reviews, 306, 307
Preattentive processing, 242–249
Predictive analytics, 13, 38, 72, 113, 259. *See also* Data mining
Principle of proximity, 237, 239
Project adoption, ensuring
failure, reasons for, 294
overview, 293, 294, 307, 308
performance optimization, 293, 294, 300–308
strategies for, 294–299
success factors, 192–195
Project launch
funding, 187, 188
mid-level management support, 185, 186
overview, 181, 195
sponsorship, 182–185
staff buy-in, 186, 187
Project management
dashboard development, 191, 192
KPI team, 189, 190
overview, 195

Project management (*Continued*)
  project champion, 189
  starting point, 188
  steering committee, 189
  sustainment, 192–195. *See also*
    Project adoption, ensuring
  teams, creation of, 189–191
  technical team, 190, 191
Prototypes
  creating, 227, 228
  data federation, use of, 266
  and KPI design, 214
  metrics, 170, 171
  performance dashboard, 184, 225,
    227–229, 249
  testing, 229, 249
  use of, 184, 185
Purple people, 96

Ranges, 203, 204
Rappé, Jim, 87, 186, 299
Readiness assessment
  balanced scorecards, 44, 45
  business and IT alignment, 51, 52,
    55
  criteria for, 43, 55
  culture of measurement, 50, 51, 55
  data availability and reliability, 52,
    53, 55
  mid-level management support, 47,
    48, 55
  need, 46, 47, 55
  overview, 54, 55
  scale and scope, 48, 55
  sponsorship, 46, 55
  strategy, 44–46, 55
  team and resources, 49, 50, 55
  technical infrastructure, 52–55
  technical readiness, 57–80
Real-time
  and complex event processing, 268,
    269
  and data marts, 268
  and detect-and-respond dashboards,
    108
  and forecasting, 107, 136
  intraday updates, 72

material events, 27
near-real-time, 72, 108–110, 125, 126,
    129, 130, 137, 268
operational dashboards, 109, 110,
    124, 126, 129–131, 136, 137
and readiness assessment, 72, 73, 79
right time compared, 107, 109, 110
strategic dashboards, 164
Refresh rates, operational dashboards,
    109, 110
Regulatory compliance, 26, 27, 47
Reporting
  ad hoc, 13, 38, 70, 77, 78, 151, 155,
    193, 194, 226, 259, 263, 297
  tools, 32, 38, 73, 78, 185, 226, 263,
    277
Rich Internet applications (RIAs),
    251–255
Richmond Police Department,
    operational dashboards, 106, 107,
    124, 131–137
"Right time" data, 8, 11, 12, 63, 67, 72,
    109, 110, 131
Risk indicators, 200
Risk metrics, 175
Road maps, 60, 67, 71, 74, 88–89, 155
Rohm and Haas
  centralized approach, 274, 276
  executive dashboard, 149, 150, 156,
    207
  tactical dashboards, 106, 111, 140,
    147–156
  three-tier delivery framework, 148
Rome, John, 141, 143, 146, 229, 299

SAP, 147, 148, 151, 154–156, 204, 274
Sarbanes-Oxley Act of 2002, 26, 27, 47
Scale and scope of project, 48, 55
Scatter plots (bubble charts), 113, 248
Scorecards
  cascading, 119, 273, 285, 286, 289,
    290
  dashboards compared, 11, 12
  strategic dashboards, 115. *See also*
    Strategic dashboards
Self-service BI, 8, 13, 32, 59, 70, 131,
    136, 140

Semantics, 19, 20, 58, 63, 68, 69, 74, 193, 222, 260–266
Service-oriented architecture, 126
Show Me the Numbers (Few), 227
Silverlight, 124, 126, 128, 253–255
Sparklines, 206, 245
Spatial maps, 247
Speed of thought, 38, 113, 124, 264
Sponsorship
  readiness assessment, 46, 55
  role of sponsors, 296
Stewardship, 58, 94, 143, 161, 162, 171, 215, 279, 308
Stoplights, 14, 112, 116, 118, 119, 149, 204, 205, 231, 232, 243, 245
Strategic dashboards
  alignment, 119
  appearance, 105
  balanced scorecards, 18, 115–117, 158. *See also* Balanced scorecards
  cause-effect linkages, 115, 116, 172
  Cisco example, 116, 159–172
  collaboration, 119
  corporate scorecard example, 120
  key performance indicators (KPIs), 116, 118
  management scorecards, 115, 116, 158
  metrics, 116, 118
  Ministry of Works example (Kingdom of Bahrain), 158, 172–178
  navigation, 118, 119
  operational and tactical dashboards compared, 105, 106
  overview, 18, 101, 115, 157, 158
  prevalence of, 102
  strategic expenditures, 119, 121
  strategic reviews, 119
  strategy, 115
  strategy management, 116–118
  targets, 118
  types of, 115, 116
  updating, 106
  use of, 102, 103
Strategy, readiness assessment, 44–46, 55

Strategy management, 116–118, 158, 172, 176, 178
Strategy management office, 158, 178, 194
Strategy maps, 29, 30, 116–119, 158, 172–176, 213, 228, 236, 266–268, 289
Summerhayes, Martin, 48, 182, 185, 187, 188, 191
Superusers, 39, 40, 193, 194, 297, 298
Surveys of users, 300

Tactical dashboards. *See also* Enterprise dashboards; Mashboards
  access control, 111
  alerts, 105, 106, 155
  analytical dashboards, 111, 113
  appearance, 105, 111
  Arizona State University example, 111, 139–147, 156
  BI platform, 111
  BNSF Railway, 111
  data, 114
  enterprise dashboards, 111, 112
  key performance indicators (KPIs), 111
  mashboards, 111–113, 262–264, 288
  metrics, 115
  operational and strategic dashboards compared, 105, 106
  overview, 17, 101, 110, 111, 139, 140
  portal based, 111
  prevalence of, 102
  refreshing, 114
  Rohm and Haas example, 106, 111, 140, 147–156
  types of, 111, 112
  updating, 114
  use of, 102, 103, 110, 111
  visual analysis tools, 113, 114
Targets, 118, 203, 204
Technical architecture, 20
Technical readiness assessment, 52–55, 57–80
Templates, 217, 218, 232–234, 239–241, 259, 285

Testing
  and agile development, 88
  dashboard development, 191, 192
  dashboard display, 228, 229
  data, 280
  and incremental delivery, 87
  metrics, 211, 213
  off-the-shelf components, 286
  test assumptions, 301, 302
Visual Display of Quantitative Information (Tufte), 227
Themes, 117, 118, 121, 158, 173, 174, 176, 213, 239, 240
Thermometers, 232, 245
Thin clients, 252
Three threes, 5, 10–18, 22
Top 10 lists, 36, 108, 141, 155, 200, 236, 299
Top-down approach, 273, 275, 276, 285–287
Training, 298, 299, 306, 307
Tree maps, 247
Tufte, Edward R., 227

Updating
  operational dashboards, 107
  strategic dashboards, 106
  tactical dashboards, 114

Usability labs, 228, 229, 249
Usage monitoring, 11, 13, 147, 192
User mantra, 15, 40, 41
Users
  accountability, 305, 306
  buy-in, 303–305
  empowering, 306
  end-user adoption, 307, 308
  focus, 305
  operational dashboards, 107

Values, 45, 115
Variance charts, 206, 247
Virtual mashups, 287–289, 292
Vision, 45, 115
Visual analysis, 113, 114, 124, 264
Visual Explanations (Tufte), 227

What-if modeling
  BI environment, 64
  dashboard functionality, 137, 257, 259
  data marts, 266, 267
  and MAD framework, 15, 16
  performance dashboard applications, 11
Whipsawing, 286, 302
Williams, Neal, 201, 214